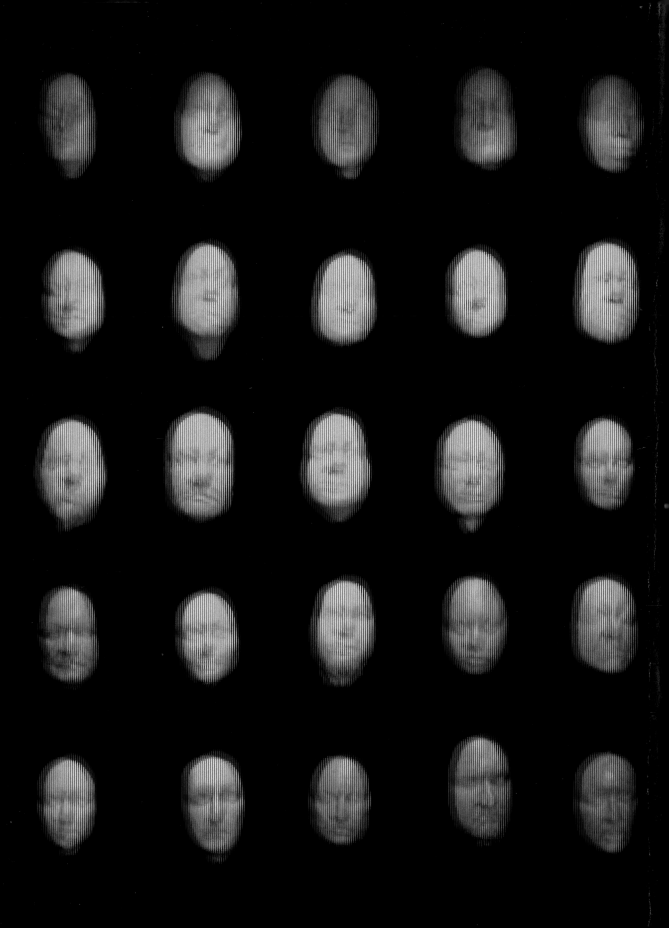

CHARLIE BROOKER & ANNABEL JONES

WITH JASON ARNOPP

INSIDE
BLACK MIRROR

EBURY
PRESS

Foreword
Charlie Brooker, executive producer

Doubt. I've been writing for years, but even now, sitting down in front of a blank page still floods me with crippling doubt. Which is probably why I put off writing this foreword until the publishers wept.

Writing a script involves constantly ignoring a whiny little voice in your head telling you to stop, and attempting to encourage a more cheerful voice urging you to press on. For me the trick is to try to picture the finished film in my head, and describe what I'm seeing and hearing. It's a bit like wishing a world into reality. What follows is an oddly magical process in which that imaginary world gradually becomes real, via a series of waypoints – the first design sketches, the first read-through, the first day of shooting, the first rough cut. Every one of these events still shocks me a little. Something that only existed in your head now exists in the world, like an imaginary friend suddenly ringing your doorbell.

But then imagination becoming reality seems to be a recurrent theme at the moment. It never fails to surprise me that *Black Mirror* (or, as Americans call it, *Black Meer*) has been around for almost a decade now. We started working on it way back in 2010 – which, in technological terms, was virtually a different epoch.

In the current era of 24-hour online screaming and Russian disrupt-o-bots, it's hard to remember – but way back then, in 2010, the general view of technology was still a rosy one. The worst thing anyone said about Twitter was that it was full of people wasting their lunch breaks. Apple launching a new iPhone model still seemed like an exciting proposition, and the Arab Spring was just around the corner, something social media platforms seemed only too happy to take the credit for. Fast-forward to now and suddenly smartphones are twice as addictive and harmful as cigarettes and your timeline's full of fascist memes and photographed atrocities.

It's all gone sour. It's all gone a bit '*Black Mirror*', in fact. Which is bad for human civilization, but good publicity for our little TV show. Every cloud, eh? I sometimes wonder if I'm well equipped to cope with our terrifying dystopian present because having worked on the show for all this time, I've already repeatedly experienced what it's like when *Black Mirror* stories slowly manifest themselves in the real world. Not sure that's going to be much comfort when I'm being chased across an irradiated landscape by an autonomous robot bum-on-legs with the Facebook logo etched on its perineum and a Make America Great Again hat perched up top, but you can't have everything.

Anyway. This is the story of how we created and continue to puke out *Black Mirror*, how the scripts were written, the costumes stitched, the footage filmed. Like any production, *Black Mirror* is a huge team effort.

Never trust anyone who mentions auteur theory or discusses a film or TV show as though it's the work of one individual. Each *Black Mirror* film (and we insist on pretentiously considering them 'films') is the product of months of heavy lifting by literally hundreds of people. In this book you'll get to hear from just a few of them. A heartfelt thanks to every single person who's worked on the show, to my co-showrunner Annabel Jones who is too modest (not to mention illiterate) to write a foreword herself, and also to Jason for weaving this book together.

Now, please. Stop reading this bit of the book and start reading the other bits. Go on. Get the fuck off my page.

SERIES ONE

<u>In Conversation</u>

Charlie Brooker – executive producer
Annabel Jones – executive producer
Shane Allen – then Channel 4 Head of Comedy
Barney Reisz – producer

Charlie Brooker: So, how did Annabel and I meet? This is like the scene in *When Harry Met Sally,* when they interview those couples.

Annabel Jones: Yes. Old people who wish they'd never met.

Charlie Brooker: My first memory of Annabel is her mocking me. I was in the [TV production Company] Endemol building on Bedford Square in London, playing the video game *Counter-Strike* with three other comedy writers, when Annabel came up and took the piss out of us all, for being grown men pretending to be counter-terrorists.

Annabel Jones: At Endemol, my job was to look after its smaller companies, including the comedy label Zeppotron. Sharing a love for counter-terrorism, we all got on and I became managing director. We were making it all up as we went along of course, and then Charlie and I started working together on the *Wipe* shows that he presented for the BBC.

Charlie Brooker: While working on Channel 4's *The 11 O'Clock Show,* I met Shane Allen, who would eventually commission *Black Mirror.*

Shane Allen (then Channel 4 Head of Comedy): Charlie was one of *The 11 O'Clock Show*'s topical writers and I was a producer on the topical footage team, so we'd cross paths. He was chosen for his work on the website *TV Go Home* which enjoyed an early following. I got to know Annabel around this time as part of the same social group. Charlie and I worked together on Chris Morris's 2001 *Brass Eye* special again after that and kept crossing paths. I got the job as Channel 4's comedy commissioner in 2004.

Charlie Brooker: I wrote a 2005 Channel 4 sitcom called *Nathan Barley* with Chris Morris, which had a really long gestation period. It would also inspire a *Black Mirror* episode, but we'll cover that later ...

Charlie and Annabel's transition from comedy to drama began with 2008's Dead Set, *which saw a fictional* Big Brother *house invaded by zombies.*

Charlie Brooker: Conceptually, *Dead Set* sounded like a comedy, with its preposterous conceit. But despite that, we were keen to impress on people that we were going to play it straight.

Annabel Jones: We wanted it to be an uncompromising and credible TV horror show. *Big Brother* was Endemol's biggest show and, being part of Endemol, we hoped we could make *Dead Set* in an authentic way, with access to the presenter Davina McCall, the *Big Brother* house, the branding ...

Shane Allen: In about 2006, Charlie and Annabel had pitched *Dead Set* to Channel 4 drama, who ultimately passed. So Charlie and Annabel brought it to my attention with a first episode script and series treatment. It was instantly gripping: the core concept was brilliantly irreverent in taking this huge Channel 4 pop culture brand and rooting a genre thriller at the heart of it. Beyond that, the writing was pin-sharp in how it set up the world, nailed the characters and rattled through a page-turning narrative.

I connected with it immediately and was beguiled with the notion of it as a smart contemporary satire on reality TV, as well as a zombie thriller in its own right. Charlie and Annabel had such a clear vision and went to great pains to explain that it wasn't a comedy and it wouldn't be funny. It had to work as a piece of credible and rooted real-life drama and they set me homework to get a sense of tone. I had to watch the 2004 *Dawn of the Dead* remake, read Cormac McCarthy's novel *The Road* and see [photographer] Gregory Crewdson's profound stills. To this day *The Road* remains the most affecting and haunting book I've read – thanks for fucking up my world view so fundamentally.

Dead Set *became a piece of event television, stripped across a week on Channel 4's younger-skewing offshoot E4.*

Annabel Jones: Shane said, "Okay, what next?" because it had gone down really well and was BAFTA-nominated. It was a real surprise hit for Channel 4.

Charlie Brooker: I'd been writing TV criticism for quite a while, and was still doing it then. So I'd see lots of shows that maybe otherwise I wouldn't have watched, such as the *Battlestar Galactica* reboot. But that show was actually really good and I wondered why we weren't doing things like that here in Britain. I miss all those silly US shows like *Manimal*, *Automan* and *Knight Rider*. At the time, everything on British TV was a detective drama or a costume drama, and it felt like there wasn't much in between. But *Doctor Who* was huge, having come back and been an enormous hit, so you knew there was an appetite for something else.

Annabel Jones: Charlie wanted to do an anthology show. He was familiar with *The Twilight Zone* and I was familiar with *Tales of the Unexpected*, and that all felt something that was really missing in the TV landscape at the time. There were no ideas-driven single dramas.

Charlie Brooker: I didn't like the idea of doing something where it's the same thing all the time, partly because I find it hard to work out how that would stay interesting over weeks and weeks and weeks. I also don't tend to have ideas that last beyond an hour.

Shane Allen: Enter Charlie and Annabel's *Black Mirror* pitch, about doing modern parable stories around the theme of social media, technology and AI advances. By this point I'd been made head of comedy, so was drunk on ego and power.

Annabel Jones: We pitched *Black Mirror* as the fears of the day. Things that hadn't been dramatised. Things that people didn't quite realise were unsettling them.

Shane Allen: Charlie and Annabel were incredibly animated about telling one-off tales about a world that could be just around the corner. They had an entirety of vision about what a modern *Twilight Zone*-esque anthology series could tackle. They would identify a social media trend or piece of technology and do a "What if?" extreme cautionary tale with it. At the time, anthologies were seen as prohibitively expensive and each week you'd be resetting the audience connection button. It was also seen as a commercial dead end, as you'd never be able to sell it abroad, because one-offs didn't travel.
　　This time, my homework was a box set of the original *Twilight Zone*.

Charlie Brooker: The pitch became more finessed. One pitch document literally said, "Just as *The Twilight Zone* would talk about McCarthyism, we're going to talk about Apple." It got more and more targeted, at a time when the really happy shiny adverts for Apple were appearing. Everyone was walking around going, "This shit's great, look at my iPhone, it's brilliant." Twitter and all this stuff was in its early days.
　　Being a paranoid person, as soon as I see any advert where everyone's happy and smiley I immediately think it's a bit like a sinister advert in a dystopian movie. It should pan down to me watching it in a pod, while crying and eating Soylent Green [the dubious wafer from the 1973 sci-fi film of the same name]. The fact that it looked so happy meant it couldn't last, so I was immediately unsettled by that.

Shane Allen: There's a culturally different approach in drama, compared to comedy, which is probably why Charlie and Annabel stuck with me with what is essentially a drama-shaped piece. In comedy, the writer is king or queen and is usually the creative centre of gravity. In drama, that focus shifts more towards the director. Charlie and Annabel have always been showrunners in the US sense rather than the UK series-producer sense, in that they are the key creative influence on the show. I was able to help them retain the creative whip hand on the series, because we had a good understanding of how they worked by this point.

Charlie Brooker: The original idea was that *Black Mirror* was going to be eight half hours, all by different writers including me. Technology wasn't the sole focus. It was mentioned in the early pitch documents, but so were terrorism and generally contemporary things. In the same way that you wouldn't say *The Twilight Zone* was about UFOs, technology was definitely mentioned but it wasn't a focus to quite the same degree.

Annabel Jones: There's a huge discipline to the short film form. We're slightly more trained now, but at the beginning we spent a long time questioning every single element of the world and addressing every detail in the script, in an attempt to make the film feel comprehensive, cohesive and authentic. But we couldn't do it all justice in a short film, so we had to streamline the stories. We found ourselves telling more fruitful and satisfying stories by keeping the worlds slightly smaller.

Charlie Brooker: When you focus on the smaller story, it often actually becomes more relatable.

Annabel Jones: I think one of the successes of the show is that people like it because it feels very relevant, or it resonates with them. There is a human element, and by virtue of being a smaller show, we have always held onto that.

Charlie Brooker: A lot of shows you watch are not relevant to your life, basically. Except maybe if you see the TV detective at home and he bangs his knee on the table, and you go, "When I bang *my* knee that really hurts too!" That's not a good example! Well, you know …

Annabel Jones: I can't remember whether Charlie wrote the first *Black Mirror* script and then we thought, "Actually, this should be more like 60 minutes" or whether we, from a prosaic, budgetary point of view realised we could get more bankroll with 60 minutes.

Charlie Brooker: I can't remember either, but I think it was a bit of both. That's why the first script, *Fifteen Million Merits*, came out at about 45 minutes. So I think we delivered the first script, which Shane liked. And then Jay Hunt, Channel 4's Chief Creative Officer, asked for a second script to get a sense of what the series could be.

Barney Reisz (producer): Annabel and Charlie came to me with the script for *Fifteen Million Merits* and a commission for three hour-long episodes. They had no idea what the other two episodes would be, but they wanted to get on with it. We met in Cafe Boheme in Soho, had a chat and we all got on, so I signed on to produce. I liked that Charlie was writing really wonderful character detail, but with a background of futuristic stuff. He puts human situations first and technology second.

Charlie and Annabel are incredibly un-starry. They're not demanding in the way that incredibly talented people can be, which is very refreshing. The truth is, Shane Allen created that great, creative atmosphere for them because Charlie's so talented. Shane knew that if he made it as easy as possible, great things would happen.

The other channels were not in the slightest bit interested in anthologies. They thought *Black Mirror* was a mad idea, because you needed lead actors across a series who audiences would get to know and love. And of course, nowadays, everyone's trying to do anthologies, but nowhere near as good as *Black Mirror*.

Annabel Jones: The original second script, called *Inbound*, involved war. We were already in production for the first series and had gone as far as getting a director on board for *Inbound*. We were all ready to go, and then Jay read the *Inbound* script and didn't like it. She had some very valid concerns, I think.

Charlie Brooker: Probably the fact that people were speaking Danish for half of it was one thing. There was an idea that surfaced later in *Men Against Fire*, of people speaking Danish, and you were meant to think they were aliens.

Annabel Jones: Jay felt it was a bit heavy handed. Which it was. Jay absolutely wanted and believed in the series, but she just wanted another idea as her second episode. So Charlie then went and pitched her a new idea.

Charlie Brooker: We all knew that I was going to pitch the idea of the British Prime Minister being forced to fuck a pig on live TV. So it wasn't like I blurted it out. But I can't remember why that seemed a sane thing to do. It was certainly an idea that sticks in your head. An elevator pitch. A strong flavour to come out with, so to speak.

Annabel Jones: Jay went for it. She said, "Write a script, and we'll do it." No-one else in the world would have commissioned this series apart from Channel 4. I absolutely believe that, so we are very grateful to Shane and Jay for taking that risk. No American network would have done it at that time.

Charlie Brooker: As we entered production, there was no time to be nervous. Once you've got a deadline, you can worry about it, but ultimately you either do it or you jump off the roof. Or both.

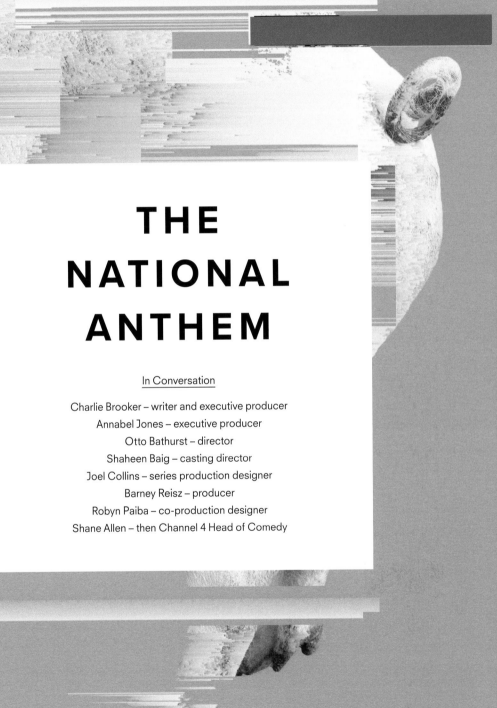

THE NATIONAL ANTHEM

In Conversation

Charlie Brooker – writer and executive producer
Annabel Jones – executive producer
Otto Bathurst – director
Shaheen Baig – casting director
Joel Collins – series production designer
Barney Reisz – producer
Robyn Paiba – co-production designer
Shane Allen – then Channel 4 Head of Comedy

The British Prime Minister Michael Callow is woken by a phone call, unaware that this will be the worst day of his life. Princess Susannah has been kidnapped, and will be killed unless he has "full unsimulated sexual intercourse with a pig". As the pressure mounts from social media, news channels and Callow's own advisors, he is forced to grasp this dilemma by the trotters.

Charlie Brooker: The fact that we start *Black Mirror* with *The National Anthem* does throw quite a lot of people, perhaps because it makes them feel quite sick, in a horrible, doomy way. There's a queasy inevitability about it. I know it makes it difficult for some people to recommend the show! Some people just do not get that one, but I see it as darkly funny. People say it's ridiculous, and of course we know it's ridiculous, but we play it straight. It's supposed to be ridiculous to start with and then it's not. I'd had the idea before that it would be a very funny episode of *24* if Jack Bauer was presented with a dilemma of having to fuck a pig. And then I thought that if you played that totally straight it would be hilarious. But while working out the beats of the actual story, you realise that it wouldn't be very funny. And having done *Dead Set*, I was more confident that you could take something preposterous but make the tone very straight.

Charlie had also been inspired by the British jungle-based reality show I'm A Celebrity ... Get Me Out Of Here!, *in which various celebrities are forced to do terrible things, often live on ITV as presenters Ant and Dec look on.*

Charlie Brooker: I was watching somebody like Peter Andre – I can't remember who – but they were absolutely terrified, almost in tears, shaking, crying, sweating. They had to do something like eat an arsehole with an eyeball pushed into it, that's been rolled in dog shit while a spider crawled over the roof of their mouth. They were gagging, and there was something about seeing it live. I thought, "I'm not enjoying this, what the fuck, this is awful!" At one point it cut to Ant and Dec and I thought Dec looked infinitely sad, like he had gazed into the abyss.

Annabel Jones: *The National Anthem* was about humiliation and the public's appetite for humiliation. The public will celebrate anyone if they are prepared to humiliate themselves for the public's entertainment. Celebrities had begun to realise this: some were going on *I'm A Celebrity ...* for redemption, and others to try and extend their careers. But it wasn't just celebrities – when *Dead Set* was on air, Brian Paddick was in the jungle. The previous year he'd been Deputy Assistant Commissioner in the Metropolitan Police Service and standing to be the Mayor of London! How nuts is that?

Otto Bathurst (director): I'd had a job cancelled, literally at the last minute. My agent then sent me the script for *The National Anthem*, which I read on Friday and then we were in production on Monday. Boom!

Annabel Jones: Otto agreed with us about playing it all straight, and he tonally held the line. In the casting and the production design, this had to be as real as it could be. So we were blessed to have Rory Kinnear as the Prime Minister Michael Callow. I'm very anti casting any comedy actors in *Black Mirror*. At the very beginning, this approach felt crucial, because we needed this to not feel like comedy. Charlie's history, and the perception of him in the UK, was as a comedy writer, so it could have tipped too far that way.

Charlie Brooker: There were probably more jokes in the original script. In one scene, the porn star Rod Senseless has a conversation with the

Prime Minister, but its weird comedic tone felt misplaced. At that point in the story, the milk had already curdled and the tone had already gone all disturbing and heavy. And then suddenly, Rod Senseless pops up to give the Prime Minister advice on how to fuck a pig.

Otto Bathurst: Actors fundamentally want to do interesting stuff and there's little interesting stuff around, so actually it was very, very easy to cast. We got our first choice for every single role, because everybody thought, "Okay ... I've no idea what's going to happen here, but let's give it a shot!" At this point, nobody knew what *Black Mirror* was. The budget was tiny, so it felt like a mini experiment that no one was paying too much attention to.

Shaheen Baig (casting director): I loved that there was no pressure whatsoever to have stars, which was really rare. Charlie's concept and script were the stars, so it was just about finding the best person for the part.

Otto Bathurst: The stroke of genius was getting Rory. He's one of the greatest actors of his generation, completely phenomenal. I actually can't think of anybody who could've carried off that tonal balance. He was a pretty despicable character, but there was a vulnerability and a tragedy to him, so by the end you felt rather sorry for the guy. If you have any compassion, you can feel sorry for these leaders sometimes, because they are boxed into such horrendous corners by people pulling their strings. Yes, of course the Prime Minister doesn't fuck pigs, but metaphorically he's having to do that kind of stuff every day. That's politics. To maintain power, you have to do appalling, awful, compromising things every day. Rory nailed that absolutely beautifully.

Charlie Brooker: The story is mainly about Callow, but it does ping around all over the place, which was useful for me while writing. Sometimes we just jump away from Downing Street because I'd have no idea what they would say. So you can just skip to the people in the hospital commenting on what's on the news, or you can have the news as an fucking exposition delivery system. So it does allow you to do all kinds of shorthand things, but that was one story with a lot of spinning plates.

Joel Collins (series production designer): I ran the visual effects on *The Hitchhiker's Guide to the Galaxy* movie for a year, having started in puppets and Muppets at Jim Henson's company. With an anthology, you get to put your hand in a bag of sweets. There's nothing better than trying a different flavour each week, for someone who really enjoys moving around complex genres and technical issues. Our team made the *Black Mirror* logo with the cracks: it was very exciting to do all that.

Barney Reisz (producer): Joel has a great eye, is incredibly inventive and is as mad as Charlie, in a different way. He had his company Painting Practice, with brilliant people like Justin Hutchinson-Chatburn and Dan May around him doing VFX [visual effects], pre-visualisation and all sorts. So they were perfect for us, because they were very technically savvy, having come from a features background. They embraced *Black Mirror* as a fun experiment.

'Well I'm not fucking a pig. Page one, that's not happening'
– Michael

Above: The cast putting their feet up between takes: from left to right, Lindsay Duncan, Rory Kinnear, Tom Goodman-Hill and Patrick Kennedy.

Joel Collins: With *The National Anthem*, I just tried to keep it grounded. You're trying to take something fucking absurd so seriously. But the awful thing about it is, no matter how much you want to laugh, you know it's just an awkward laugh. So it was about making it feel real and subtly straight. Robyn Paiba helped run that one with me. I remember her laughing about how *Black Mirror* conversations can go from the complexity of rigging televisions to how a pig might have sex with a human, and whether they have normal or coiled penises.

Robyn Paiba (co-production designer): Pig Fuck, as we called it, was of its time. Whilst we were shooting, the London riots were happening, which were enabled by early social media and messaging services that had not had to be monitored on this level before … and we were shooting a story that was all about an inability to control the internet-based media form.

Shane Allen (then Channel 4's Head of Comedy): I do remember a debate about why it had to be a pig. Charlie considered a duck too small and absurd. A horse or donkey seemed too cinematically cumbersome.

Barney Reisz: At one point there was talk of doing it as a chicken, rather than a pig. In the end, Charlie stood his ground. We were quite far in by that point, so we had to shoot something.

One memorable scene sees Callow lose his temper and physically attack the home secretary Alex Cairns (Lindsay Duncan) in his office.

Charlie Brooker: It's quite shocking when Michael literally launches himself at her. In the script, it just says he loses it. He finds out she's been trying to find something to get him off the hook, but now she's put everything in jeopardy. I didn't really know how a Prime Minister would react, so I thought I'd just have him go bananas.

Otto Bathurst: It was meant to be a visceral scene. Lindsay's performance is fantastic: she's *happy*, and it's really, really evil. What I find so shocking is that she barely bats an eyelid. That kind of abuse is accepted within the job. In theory, he should be kicked out of politics, kicked out of anything, but the pressure and the abuse inherent in that job, means that she just steps away and smooths down her skirt. Another day in the office …

Charlie Brooker: I assumed that Callow implicitly trusts Alex. So when he discovers she's gone behind his back, he's furious, in an odd way that he possibly wouldn't be with someone he doesn't know as well. He's not just angry, he's betrayed. I think it was actually scripted that they end up on the floor: he tries to launch himself at her and then he falls and it was all a bit ridiculous. But what *would* someone do if they were put in that position where they might have to fuck a pig on television? And it makes it more real, all of a sudden, because you certainly don't expect Callow to lose his fucking mind for a moment. *And* it's a woman, which makes it even more shocking.

Rory does so well at humanising the Prime Minister. It's a really clever performance. He's a little bit prickly, he's not particularly nice to people around him because he's so worried. He seems like he's quite a decent guy but he can be a little selfish and explosive and lose his rag. He's so good at being someone who's just dropped into this nightmare early on. It's weird, as if suddenly the Prime Minister becomes the underdog in the whole episode as he gets all of his powers stripped away from him. And then there's that moment where Alex turns on him and says there's no way out.

Annabel Jones: A lot of times in drama there's a tendency to have political caricatures, and it just gets a bit wearisome. It would have been very easy for us to have a Tory Prime Minister that everyone hates, so that we can enjoy heaping this public humiliation upon him. But I wanted the focus to be on the public's appetite for public humiliation. So if we could set up that Tory PM, but then show the ramifications for his family, to his wife – that seems more interesting than "Let's hate the Tory".

Charlie Brooker: It's a weirdly sympathetic portrayal of a Prime Minister. We deliberately don't ever say what party he is, although he is seen wearing a blue tie at one point, which implies he's a Tory. He does seem like he's probably a Tory PM but we don't ever say. He's actually one of the most sympathetic characters in it. My sister-in-law is an Ealing MP, and you see how hard she works. Callow's set up to be someone with a whiff of public school about him. You'd normally go, "Fuck that guy", so this felt like quite a nice reversal. There's a key moment about halfway through when his wife comes in and faces off with him, really upset. That's when you see the personal impact it's having.

Annabel Jones: Callow's wife Jane plays a key role in placing it in the personal. When he says, "But it won't happen," and she says, "That doesn't matter, they're thinking it already, so it might as well have happened."

Charlie Brooker: I don't know how some viewers can be angry with Jane for telling Michael how she feels. That feels like a misreading of what's going on there, because it's not meant to be that she betrays him in any way. It's more that she's communicating how upset she is. She's worried and, you know, they've got a fucking baby. What's going on has irrevocably changed something in their relationship and she can't deal with that.

Otto Bathurst: Actors often draw on personal experience. So if they're in a tragic scene, they'll think of what it'd be like if a loved one died. But when you're pulling your trousers down in front of a pig, it's quite hard to know what to draw on. That scene where Callow's walking down the corridor, approaching the pig – that look of absolute horror on his face. In lesser hands, it could've become farcical. If we'd got it wrong, you'd have laughed.

Robyn Paiba: I had to avoid scaring off the animal handlers, while gently talking them through the basic storyline about a Prime Minister having to perform a sex act on their lovely pig. Practical considerations about the height of the pig, etc., really highlighted the ludicrous nature of my job sometimes!

Otto Bathurst: I think we did two takes with the pig and that was it. The pig then got a bit wise to it all and started wandering off. We were never, ever going to show anything more graphic than what we got. But Rory went right up to it, pretty close. We shot more than what the film eventually showed, but he never dropped his boxers in front of the pig, that's for sure.

Charlie Brooker: The pig was called Madge. Me, Annabel, Otto, my wife Konnie Huq and Barney Reisz were all hiding in a cupboard that day, staring at a monitor, in the room where the pig scene was being filmed. No one shouted cut for quite a long time on the first take of Rory approaching the pig. He sort of went up to it and had to pull his trousers down … and then he moved up … and said, "That's as far as I'm going, everyone!"

Annabel Jones: I have to say, it was very brave of Rory to take that role on, in terms of what he was being asked to do – especially with *Black Mirror* being unknown and never having gone out before. It was a very risky move on his part, so I'm grateful.

Otto Bathurst: Everyone on set was more concerned about the pig than Rory! I absolutely assure you that the trauma would have stayed with Rory a lot longer than it would've stayed with the pig. The pig was fine: it had its face in a bowl of food, with no idea what was going on.

Charlie Brooker: During that live broadcast of Callow and the pig, there was a scene we cut out. We'd shown lots of people in a hospital throughout and now they're watching the news as work grinds to a halt. The journalist Malaika had been shot in the leg, but at the end there was a punchline where she gets taken to this hospital and she's just left on a gurney when the Prime Minister starts fucking the pig. So no one helps her because they're all glued to the TV, and they've left her at an angle where she can't quite see the screen. So that was a little joke that didn't make it in, but I can't remember if we filmed it or not. And so it's never explained why these people are in a hospital, but there's enough going on that you don't really notice.

With The National Anthem *locked and loaded, the team approached the London press screening with no small degree of trepidation.*

Charlie Brooker: We had no idea how that would go. Fucking nerve-wracking.

Otto Bathurst: Everybody came in, and because it was Charlie Brooker everybody thought it would be funny.

Charlie Brooker: When the ransom demand was made, everyone just laughed, which was the reaction we wanted. Oh, it's a black comedy! And then gradually they got more and more worried and felt more and more sick …

Otto Bathurst: The very pivotal moment was with the onscreen people in the pub, watching the live broadcast. It suddenly becomes very clear that actually humanity, society and media and all of us are responsible for this. The tone in the screening room was absolutely thrilling. Everybody was completely silent.

'It's already happening in their heads. In their heads, that's what you're doing, what my husband's doing'
– Jane

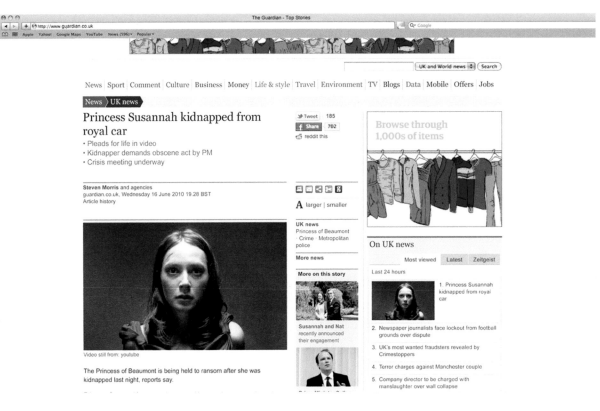

The Guardian - Top Stories

Princess Susannah kidnapped from royal car
· Pleads for life in video
· Kidnapper demands obscene act by PM
· Crisis meeting underway

Steven Morris and agencies
guardian.co.uk, Wednesday 16 June 2010 19.28 BST
Article history

Video still from: youtube

The Princess of Beaumont is being held to ransom after she was kidnapped last night, reports say.

Above: The *Guardian* newspaper reporting the kidnap of Princess Susannah, provided by the *Guardian* with help from the art department.

Opposite: A selection of tweets using the hashtag #PMpig in response to the kidnapper's demands upon PM Michael Callow, created by the art department.

Annabel Jones: When the journalists in the press room did exactly what the people in the pub were doing onscreen, that's when we knew we'd got the tone of the series.

Charlie Brooker: They went from incredulity and amusement to disgust and sadness. You're meant to be left with sadness at the end of that. It's sad and it's pathetic and everyone is cheapened by it.

Otto Bathurst: The roundtable press discussions afterwards were amazing. People were very affected by it. I think that's because of Rory and the way he plays it. When he's broken down and slumped in the toilet at the end, you feel real empathy for these guys. And that's what I like about it: it's complicated. It's all too easy to throw trite comments around about how politicians are destroying the country, but I wanted to show how it's more complex than that. These people are really flawed human beings.

Charlie Brooker: *The National Anthem* was named after both the national anthem that we sing, like patriots, and there's also a Radiohead song called *The National Anthem*. Often I'll name things after songs, but that one just came up on Spotify and I thought it was a good title. I probably can't articulate why, but ... everyone's singing the same song. There's patriotism in it, there's a royal connection, there's a sort of chorus of people throughout the whole episode and there's something about doing your duty. So it felt like the title summed it up somehow, like a statement in some way.

Twitter / Search - #PMpig

http://twitter.com/#!/search/%23PMpig

twitter #PMpig ⌕   Have an account? **Sign in**

Results for #PMpig

Tweets Top ▾   Refine results »

54 new tweets

MrJoelene Joel Collingsway ⇄ by mrarrongeorge
So what if **Callow** screws a pig? He's already screwed the
Country. #kidnap #trottergate #PMpigt
1 minute ago
Retweeted 6 times

SimoneAbrox_official Simone Abroxley ✔
I think it's snoutrageous #PMpig
1 minute ago

hubertmole Elle Shank
What's got six legs and makes you laugh? Michael **Callow**
fucking a **pig**.
2 minutes ago

AmieDG31 Amie Desengeorge
Hope we get a money shot where he cums on its snout
#pigfuckercallow #PMpig
3 minutes ago

Follow "#PMpig" and more on Twitter

Twitter delivers instant updates on what's
happening around the world. Sign up today
and follow your interests!

Sign up »

People results for **#PMpig** · view all
PM_PostHouse Polly Media Post House · Follow

Trends
#PMpig
#trottergate
#snoutrage
Princess Susannah
#kidnap
PIG
#pigfuckercallow
#snoutrage
Prime Minister Callow
WhoCares
#bestshowever
#bilderberg
PM Callow

WAKE UP SHEEPLE THIS IS FALSE FLAG OPERATION - GET
SYMPATHY FOR **PM** THEN BOMB YEMEN #PMpig #kidnap
#trottergate #bilderberg
4 minutes ago

RobP3000 Roberta Pinn
OINK OINK **CALLOW** :-D #PMpig #kidnap
5 minutes ago

MrDanielXandyr Daniel Xandyr
Callow gonna get pig AIDS LOL #PMpig #kidnap
#pigfuckercallow
5 minutes ago

jasonlorriver Jason Lorriver ⇄ by patrickvallorby
I see Jane **Callow**'s going to be spending the next few months
sucking bacon juice off her husband's cock #PMpig #kidnap
7 minutes ago

PeterClacy23 Peter Clacy
Apparently if you have sex with a **pig** you get a nasty rasher
#kidnap #PMpig
8 minutes ago

jasonlorriver Jason Lorriver ⇄ by patrickvallorby
I see Jane **Callow**'s going to be spending the next few months
sucking bacon juice off her husband's cock #PMpig #kidnap
8 minutes ago

PeterClacy23 Peter Clacy
Apparently if you have sex with a **pig** you get a nasty rasher
#kidnap #PMpig
8 minutes ago

SHEL_MCV Shelby McVentor
Who's going to play the **pig** in the film adaptation? Shame
Brando's dead #trottergate #PMpig
9 minutes ago

ConClor Conrad Cloresse
If I was **Callow** Id practice 1st by sticking my cock in a
bacon sandwich #PMpig #kidnap
9 minutes ago

ericamcewan Erica McEwan
Obv 'false flag' - Mid East will EXPLODE if Callow does it -
talking WWIII people #kidnap #PMpig
10 minutes ago

Otto Bathurst: You feel culpable for what's happened to Callow. You kinda go, "Oh shit, this is awful – look what I've done!" We all buy the papers and get on the Twitter feeds. If that story broke now, the speed at which it would go viral is horrendous. Everybody says we're powerless, but we've actually never been *more* powerful. For once, we actually do have power and the opportunity to change things. Thirty years ago we didn't, because news was fabricated by the barons of Fleet Street and we couldn't get our hands on it. You couldn't get your opinion out there and now you can, incredibly easily. We're in a position of real power. We also have real responsibility, and we're not taking it.

Charlie Brooker: Starting *Black Mirror* with a big, noisy film certainly didn't hurt, but I had no idea of how that was going to go down. We consciously didn't allude to what was going on in it, in any of the pre-publicity. There was a whole trailer campaign for *The National Anthem* that deliberately made it look like a much straighter story where a princess has been kidnapped and the Prime Minister had a terrible dilemma to face. Channel 4 also did weird things, like run a trail for it on ITV and a couple in cinemas. So a lot of people did tune in thinking it was going to be a political thriller, and then when that bomb drops in the first five minutes or so ... At that point you either going to go, "I'm in", or, "Nah". So we knew it was divisive.

In September 2015, four years after The National Anthem *was broadcast, allegations emerged that the British Prime Minister David Cameron had placed a 'private part' into the mouth of a dead pig as a student initiation rite. Cameron denied that this ever happened.*

Charlie Brooker: Oh God, that was weird. That was so odd. Especially because our art department created onscreen tweets for the film, which included the hashtag #snoutrage. Which then ended up being the hashtag for the Cameron scandal in real life. So that's really quite mental.

Annabel Jones: Lots of people asked, "So did you know?" I mean, imagine Cameron when that episode went out! He must have thought, "They fucking know! They're coming for me!" I think they did watch it – or that's what I heard.

Charlie Brooker: When that actually happened, I had a moment of weird vertigo. For a moment I genuinely worried that everything in the universe is a figment of my imagination.

Annabel Jones: I love how that was Charlie's 'go to' theory! Rather than "Maybe someone had told me", he goes straight to, "I'm living in a parallel reality"!

Charlie Brooker: It was just such a weird coincidence and I knew no one had told me! So for a moment I thought, "What if all of my life is a dream?"

Annabel Jones: The Cameron story ruined a good line that we always used to say in interviews. Whenever someone said how we seemed able to predict the future, we'd say, "Well, except for *The National Anthem*". And then that was stolen from us.

Charlie Brooker: For fuck's sake. It's so weird that *The National Anthem* was the most prophetic one we did!

Otto Bathurst: I'm proud of *The National Anthem* because it's so close to being awful and ridiculous, but we walked that tonal tightrope. For the scale of what it was, we made a pretty big footprint. When I'm talking to people, it's constantly referred to. *Black Mirror* is way, way bigger in the States than it is in the UK – especially *The National Anthem*. The idea of Obama or Trump being put in front of a pig ... in America they'd never be allowed to make a show like that! Whereas in the UK, we're used to very heavy satire, so it wasn't quite as shocking. It was such fun to do. I've done movies that took two years to make and *Black Mirror* took three months. There was a lot of fun in this new territory we were discovering.

Charlie Brooker: It's a bit annoying that people do refer to *The National Anthem* as the one where the Prime Minister fucks a pig, because that spoils it in a way. When people first encountered the episode, they probably thought, "Well, that can't happen because they won't be able to show it." Normally the day is saved, but here the day was not saved and that's slightly unusual. So, the fact that people feel the need to warn others about what happens kind of pre-emptively spoils it. But what can you do?

FIFTEEN MILLION MERITS

In Conversation

Charlie Brooker – co-writer and executive producer
Konnie Huq – co-writer
Euros Lyn – director
Annabel Jones – executive producer
Barney Reisz – producer
Joel Collins – series production designer
Shaheen Baig – casting director
Stephen McKeon – composer

In a society wallpapered with endless video screens, Bing and his fellow citizens earn 'merits' by riding stationary exercise bikes. When Bing falls for gifted singer Abi, he decides to use his enormous stash of merits to buy her a place on the popular talent show Hot Shot. *Horrified by the results, vengeful Bing sets out to rage against the machine.*

Charlie Brooker: *Fifteen Million Merits* was inspired by a lot of different things, but it mainly happened because my wife Konnie took the piss out of me. I was sitting on the sofa with an iPad and a laptop, and probably a phone, and a television, and she said something along the lines of "Literally, you'd be happy if you were in a box and the walls were all screens." And I thought, "Yes, that's quite an arresting image." Also, I probably would.

Konnie Huq (co-writer): Charlie was quite into Twitter at the time and so was often swiping away at his phone. We had just got a new huge TV in what was not that big a living room. I commented that, in the future, walls would just be one giant TV screen, and then people could just swipe away at the walls. Light switches, lights, TV, internet: all electrics could just be incorporated within the giant touch-screen walls.

Back then, I was presenting [*The X Factor*'s ITV2 sister show] *The Xtra Factor*, and these panel-judging shows were at their peak in popularity. And when I was presenting [BBC children's show] *Blue Peter* and asked kids what job they'd like to do, they often said they wanted to be famous, but they didn't know what for! In *Fifteen Million Merits*, the people on screens are the famous ones that have made it in life. The 'worker' society are not allowed possessions or any luxuries. In a longer cut, Abi originally made things and did origami out of waste packaging, so as to have possessions.

Charlie Brooker: There was something that appealed to me about the idea of an incredibly reductive piss-taking version of capitalism, with the whole of society peddling desperately on fucking bikes for some coins to spend.

Konnie Huq: I had often thought gyms should be powered by the exercise equipment in them, so they could be totally self-sufficient. In the same way that TVs could be powered by the people watching them as they exercised.

Charlie Brooker: I was playing a lot of Xbox 360 games, and they'd just updated their system so you saw these little cartoon avatars of yourself. The Nintendo Wii had also come along with little cartoon avatars of everyone, and you could spend a lot of money, buying these things that didn't exist. I'd been reading about people being beaten to death over objects they'd bought in online games that weren't real.

At the same time, Konnie and I had watched Nigel Kneale's one-off play *The Year of the Sex Olympics*, set in a dystopian society where everyone is fed entertainment all day long. They basically invent reality television to keep the masses entertained. So that was a really strong influence. In-flight entertainment systems were yet another inspiration. They're something you cling to in an uncomfortable place. A teat you suckle to distract you from being on a plane.

So all these things came together. But the idea was an Apple store version of Hell. With these screens on the walls, a room was a prison cell but looked sort of chirpy. The Xbox Kinect had just come out with hand gestures and movements like that, so we put a lot of that into it as well.

Euros Lyn (director): Charlie had seen my episodes of *Doctor Who*, and liked them, then written something about how my name was worthy of sci fi, because it was so peculiar. This really made me laugh.

Charlie Brooker: Hang on; I gave his episodes a good review! But yeah, Euros' name looked like something out of *Star Trek*.

Euros Lyn: I'd always loved reading Charlie's articles in *The Guardian* and I loved *Nathan Barley*. So when he sent me the script, I knew I really wanted to direct. It was all a bit scary, because what was *Black Mirror* going to be? What was its tone? It felt utterly original. We knew we had a huge ambition, but that the cash was pathetic. At times, it felt like we were a bunch of students making a short film. Especially as the location for this one was the campus of an old college in Buckinghamshire.

Annabel Jones: Suddenly you have to build a whole new world, to suggest that everyone's living in this massive tower block of conformity. How do you do that on a Channel 4 budget? We reused sets. Everything seen is in

that one set that we've redressed for the bedroom, or the bathroom, or the lift. They're modular sets being reused and reused.

Barney Reisz (producer): Because everything had to be designed from scratch, we needed a whole lot of prep time. We were low-budget, but it wasn't no-budget. We certainly made the money stretch.

Euros Lyn: Joel Collins is such a talent, and a nice guy, which really helps. So I was working with him and his co-designer Dan May, to figure out the modular idea. Our set was built in a gym, so it had to fit in a certain space. We also knew we didn't want the CG to feel "look at me". We didn't want to expose ourselves, in terms of not having enough cash, so we were really disciplined in exactly when we showed the audience that this set was one room on multiple floors of thousands and thousands of cycling chambers.

Joel Collins (series production designer): The whole thing was shot almost entirely live. When Bing makes a hand gesture, all that stuff is on the screen for real. It was quite a feat, but if we didn't do it, we wouldn't have the time or money in VFX for post production. Ultimately, it was a shitload of screens, with people behind those screens pressing buttons to trigger animations we'd created in our office. Thousands of avatars all doing different things. It was mental.

Annabel Jones: We had to fill all the screens in the cycling chamber. I remember one particularly uncomfortable day when we filmed *Botherguts*, a fictional gameshow that humiliated overweight people. Our 'contestants' had these water hoses and they had to try and knock down the people who couldn't continue cycling, and were considered to have 'gone lemon'. We couldn't afford to film lots of different fictional programmes, so Endemol let us use two of their gameshows! If you look carefully you can spot *Don't Scare the Hare* and *The Whole 19 Yards*. Endemol haven't got *Botherguts* commissioned yet …

Euros Lyn: Thanks to all this live content, the whole thing became almost like a theatre piece, which was also much better for the actors, who could see it there in front of them, so that their performance was in the moment. Because, as much as the technical stuff was important in telling the story, I really, really wanted to make the audience care about Bing and Abi, so that there was a love story at the heart of this epic nightmarish future.

   We saw lots of really good actors for Bing, but from Daniel Kaluuya's first audition there was no question about who would play him. He wasn't particularly known: he'd done *Skins* and *The Fades* and he was a face people recognised, but he wasn't a name. The scene we asked him to do was Bing's onstage mental breakdown, which was really unfair! But he blew me away.

Shaheen Baig (casting director): Daniel's audition was extraordinary. That kind of performance means there's only one person for that part.

Euros Lyn: In rehearsals, Daniel and I worked a lot on his back story. Bing mentions his brother who died, and so we talked about their relationship, and this terrible sadness and grief he carried with him. So all that stuff isn't explored in talky dialogue scenes, but it's all there and he's feeling it all the time. That, in part, is why Daniel's performance is so fantastic. And his timing is brilliant. He does this thing where a thought drops in his mind, and he does the slightest twitch of his eye. It's so witty and warm and revealing of what's going on inside.

   Jessica Brown Findlay was utterly charming and brought the part of Abi to life. At the time, she'd just come out of [ITV's period drama] *Downton Abbey*.

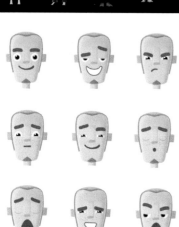

Charlie Brooker: Bing's room was shockingly small when you actually saw it. When Daniel was smashing up the room, he put his foot through the screen at one point, by accident, and I think cut his foot quite badly. We left it in.

Annabel Jones: While Bing's room is a cell and it should feel like one, you want it to be a cell you would love to live in. The design is all about

Above and opposite: The development work for the onscreen avatars, the virtual representations of each citizen, created by Painting Practice under the direction of series production designer Joel Collins and co-designer Dan May.

seduction and beauty. Dan and Joel really did a good job of that. From the simplicity of brushing your teeth, to the exact measurement of the toothpaste, it was all highly designed.

Rupert Everett, Julia Davis and Ashley Thomas were cast as Hot Shot's *Judge Hope, Judge Charity and Judge Wraith respectively.*

Shaheen Baig: Rupert's not afraid to have fun. At the time, he was just really game and wanted to work with interesting stuff. He played up the vanity of his character beautifully.

Euros Lyn: When I talked to Rupert about how to characterise Judge Hope, our touchstone was some of the larger-than-life 70s Radio 1 DJs from my youth. At one point, he wanted to wear a jumpsuit with a pilot's hat! So we weren't trying to impersonate Simon Cowell, we just used that as a starting point.

Annabel Jones: We were honoured to get Rupert. No one knew what the show was and Charlie wasn't well known as a drama writer, but Rupert just engaged with the script and loved it. He came onto set and remained in character for the few days he was with us.

Euros Lyn: Rupert and Julia [Davis, Judge Charity] had a bit of a tussle over who got to use the Australian accent! Julia told me, "Oh, I've had a brilliant idea and I'd really like to play her with an Australian accent." It was around the time that Dannii Minogue was a judge on all those talent shows. But then Rupert Everett came on set and said, "I've had this brilliant idea!" It was like, oh God, who gets to use it?

Annabel Jones: We weren't expecting any accents, because we had gone to great lengths not to define where the world was, what year it was in, or what country it was in. It was all irrelevant, so we didn't want to feature it or even address it. So then we thought, "Fuck, does this accent destabilise the world?" Maybe we over-think things, but Euros went down to talk to Rupert about it and Rupert was saying, "Hmmm, no, I've already developed this accent and this is who I think my character is."

Charlie Brooker: I thought, "I'm going to talk to Rupert next," so I went down there, and he said the same thing and I went … oh. What I'm only realising now, weirdly, is that I suppose it does help distance him from Simon Cowell. It's actually not a bad thing to do.

Annabel Jones: Our next worry was that people might think Rupert looked like George Michael, because he wore those glasses! So we sent someone down to explain our worry that Rupert might look like George Michael. And Rupert, as calmly as you want, just said, "We've all got to look like someone." And that is the classiest line I've ever heard.

Barney Reisz: In the end, Rupert agreed to take the glasses off after the beginning of his first scene. Perfect compromise.

Charlie Brooker: And no one has ever said to me, "Is he meant to be George Michael?"

Annabel Jones: But our job is to over-worry. Our job is to question and challenge everything.

Stephen McKeon (composer): Euros and I agreed that the score had to sound natural and be recorded with live musicians to contrast with the artificial world the characters inhabited. I also took a huge stylistic chance by giving Bing a distinctly 60's western/cowboy theme. I did this for two reasons: he lived in a cell with a western theme projected onto the walls, which presumably he chose, and that dovetailed nicely into the traditional representation of the hero in westerns; it also sets us up emotionally for the huge fall Bing takes when he fails to save Abi and in fact helps her towards her doom.

Composing the music for the porn channel *WraithBabes* caused embarrassment at home. My daughter Tara Lee, who was 16 at the time and a singer, agreed to provide the voices for the Wraith tracks. If anyone can come up with a way to direct your 16-year-old daughter in voicing music for a futuristic porn channel, please keep that information to yourself.

My favourite part of the score was the sequence where Bing attempts to achieve 15 million merits on the exercise bike. It was a challenge

Opposite: The development work for each of the sets, including the individual 'cells' to the exercise bike area, designed by Joel Collins and Dan May with live playback motion graphics created by Painting Practice.

because it's a five-and-a-half minute cue and had to build throughout. No joke, I actually sampled an exercise bike and used it as part of the rhythm in the track. It sounds like panting, so that was an added bonus.

I had no hand, act or part in the selection of the very wonderful song *Anyone Who Knows What Love Is*.

Euros Lyn: That song was in the script from the first moment I read it, chosen by Charlie and Konnie. So I don't know if it's one of their favourite songs! It's certainly one of my favourites now.

Charlie Brooker: I was looking for a piece of music that was very earnest and beautiful and poignant, and didn't sound like it belonged in this dystopian hell.

Annabel Jones: It's evocative of a time gone by. A hand-me-down in a world where everything is intangible.

Charlie Brooker: It's got the tone of a song that sounds like you should know it. The original sounds like an old track, it's got an old '60s feel and it's immediately catchy. You feel like, "Why isn't this a really famous song?"

At the film's emotional climax, Bing enters the Hot Shot *competition and performs a dance routine, then delivers a searing diatribe with a shard of glass held to his own throat.*

Euros Lyn: You'd never know it from that intense performance, but Daniel sleeps a lot on set. You'd be asking if anyone had seen Daniel, and he'd be under a table, having found a little corner of the set where nobody was working. He's so focused in life and what he chooses to do with his talent and career, and the same is true on set. He thinks very peacefully, and then when it's time to do the work he switches it on.

I'd arranged for a choreographer to work with Daniel on what the dance was going to be. I briefed them both on how I wanted it to make me feel and how Bing might express himself through dance. So they went off and didn't show me what they'd done. Daniel and I decided that we wouldn't do any camera rehearsals and we would shoot first time. The only time I'd seen him do the speech was in his audition, and so it was one of those moments where you set the fuse alight and let the explosion come. We knew it was one of those things where you'd only get one chance at it.

Charlie Brooker: I typed that speech out in a real rush, to mirror Bing's delivery. The speech doesn't entirely make sense. Occasionally people have transcribed it or quoted it, and they often get things wrong. There's also a few lines in it that are a bit more 'written' than they should be. He says something like, "You're sitting there slowly knitting things worse." which is a weird thing. But people just hear it as "making" anyway.

Euros Lyn: We did do two takes, but ran three cameras on Daniel, because we knew the speech demanded 100 per cent. I'll always go for a second take, because something could happen to the exposed film stock, and digital material can get corrupted. The first take was fantastic, but maybe a line of dialogue had gone awry in the first, so we did the second take

Above: Co-writers Charlie Brooker and Konnie Huq behind the camera on set and in conversation with director Euros Lyn.

'The song's good.
It's old. My mum
used to sing it.
And she learned
it from her mum.
A hand-me-down'

– Abi

with it back in. There's a little bit of switching between takes in what you see, but invariably a first take will have something you'll never, ever get again.

I'd say the speech is 99 per cent how it was written. There's this sort of existential rage at this meaningless world and the way it's imprisoned its citizens. And then there's an emotional rage at the way the woman he loves has been taken from him and corrupted. So Daniel had to keep hold of those two peaks of fury, and deliver this cleverly structured polemic. And on top of that, he had to do a really peculiar dance immediately before it!

Annabel Jones: We didn't want to deliver a massive message here to the audience. I think Charlie has an innate fear of people thinking that he's trying to be clever. He doesn't want to force opinions or thoughts or observations down people's throat, because he doesn't have that conviction in his opinion or thoughts. But what Charlie does so well, is getting that balance where it feels guttural and instinctive. Daniel is so believable and so engaging that you just feel for him. The combination of Daniel's acting and Charlie's writing just made that a really powerful scene.

Charlie Brooker: We're really fortunate Daniel was cast. I don't think the speech really changed from the first cut we saw, because he's just phenomenal. Jordan Peele cast him in [the smash-hit 2017 horror film] *Get Out*, because he'd seen that. Jordan and Daniel confirmed it was specifically that speech.

Annabel Jones: Even in the dance, you can see that sort of anger channelling through every limb. Gosh, it's a beautifully charged performance.

Euros Lyn: For the early *WraithBabes* ads, we had two real porn stars. It seemed best to cast real porn stars, who knew what to do and would have fewer hang-ups. So we tracked down two women, and one of them asked a guy to come in, but he'd never done it before – he was just one of their boyfriends! Suddenly, we were watching this scenario play out, with this guy snogging two women and getting it on. They were getting really carried away, and I was going, "Stop! Stop!" If I hadn't shouted 'cut', they would've been literally doing it. So that was probably the most embarrassed I've ever been on set.

On a hard drive somewhere, there's an even worse version of the *WraithBabes* video featuring Abi, because I shot something that was far too horrible to show. Oh God, I remember this awful phone call one Saturday morning. Charlie and Konnie had watched the scene and been utterly speechless! So we recut it.

Charlie Brooker: You don't want to feel like you're trying to titillate people in the wrong way. So we went with him putting his thumb in Abi's mouth, which is a weird violation and says it, without having to show anything further than that.

Annabel Jones: Jessica's dead eyes just spoke so much, anyway.

The bleak ending of Fifteen Million Merits *reveals that Bing has sold out to the system, having been co-opted into streamcasting pre-packaged rants to an eager audience.*

Euros Lyn: There's an inevitability to that. Because we have to eat and survive within a system, there are certain things we tolerate and accept, in return for the nice apartment, food on our table or clothes on our kids' backs. I don't judge Bing harshly for what he ends up doing. Sometimes an individual cannot overturn an injustice. The world is full of injustice and that's the truth, so it has validity.

Annabel Jones: It's an uncompromising, unhappy ending, but one that feels like it probably would have *been* the ending. There's an authenticity to it. You could also call it highly autobiographical for Charlie!

Charlie Brooker: Konnie and I did jokingly call it the *Screenwipe* Story, because I was doing this BBC Four show *Screenwipe* in which I sort of rant about stuff. And Bing ends up effectively doing a show where he rants and raves and there's no point to it.

Annabel Jones: Bing has a better set than Charlie, too.

Charlie Brooker: In one quickly discarded draft, Bing and Abi were living together in the end, but they were both really unhappy. Abi had been given loads of plastic surgery and she was addicted to this compliance drink, so it was awful. There was originally another slightly different ending, too, with Bing still living alone in this big, plush place. After his rant, he's anxiously looking at the ratings for his stream, worried about the numbers he's getting for his show. So you realise he's just swapped one treadmill for another. That ending just wasn't quite as nice or ambiguous.

Annabel Jones: I recall another ending where it pulls back to reveal that the bikes aren't connected to anything. But you sort of think that anyway, as a viewer.

Charlie Brooker: It's implied that they're doing it to power something, to keep society running, but the idea was that it's basically just powering the in-flight entertainment system!

Fifteen Million Merits *was first broadcast on Channel 4 on 11 December 2011. This was the same night as the final of ITV's* The X Factor, *the talent show with which it shared distinct parallels.*

Charlie Brooker: That wasn't stunt scheduling! Channel 4 didn't realise that was going to happen, but I looked at the schedule and saw it was even scheduled at the same time. So I sent quite a worried email to Channel 4 and they moved it back by 40 minutes or something. We knew we'd lose viewers in a later slot, but that was the trade-off. Then quite cannily, Channel 4's trailers literally said, "It's on Channel 4, after *The X Factor* final." They even advertised it within *The X Factor* on ITV!

Our *Hot Shot* show wasn't meant to directly be *The X Factor*. Talent shows are not the same thing in our society as they are in that society, where they seem to be part of the state, so that you either sit in a cell or you go on that show. It's incredibly reductive in that respect and it's more about entertaining ourselves to death: the focus on trivia and having no control over it. This unrelenting focus on consuming and also consuming things that are utterly pointless. In that society everything was stripped back, so the only entertainment available to you was pretty much mindless. I always like to think it's a sarcastic vision of the future. It's more sarcastic than accurate.

Joel Collins: We were nominated for a BAFTA [for Best Production Design], which was brilliant, because it was understood to be as complicated as it was. People wondered how reflections of screens were really in Bing's eyes, and of course the answer was that everything was real.

Konnie Huq: Shortly after we made *Fifteen Million Merits*, a weird coincidence happened when Charlie and I went on holiday to Australia. We went to a hotel on Kangaroo Island, where there was a huge glass-windowed wall overlooking a vast expanse of greenery exactly like in the closing sequence of *Fifteen Million Merits*. They even gave us each a freshly squeezed orange juice to drink as we looked out …

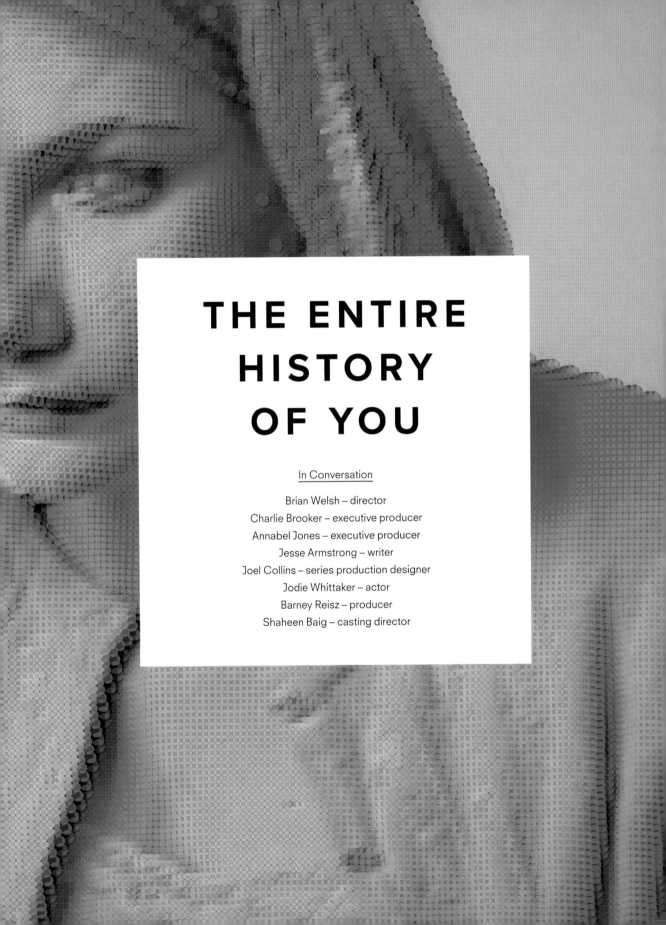

THE ENTIRE HISTORY OF YOU

In Conversation

Brian Welsh – director
Charlie Brooker – executive producer
Annabel Jones – executive producer
Jesse Armstrong – writer
Joel Collins – series production designer
Jodie Whittaker – actor
Barney Reisz – producer
Shaheen Baig – casting director

Young lawyer Liam becomes preoccupied by the idea that his wife Ffion slept with her friend Jonas, during a period when she and Liam were separated. As Liam interrogates Ffion, his suspicions become a dangerous obsession thanks to the Grain – a widespread technological device that allows the user to store and replay their audiovisual experiences.

Brian Welsh (director): On Day One of the shoot, I got a phone call from an old friend who was in floods of tears. She'd just found out, through Facebook, that her husband was cheating on her. So I could see there was something in what we were doing with this film.

Charlie Brooker: It had always been our intention to get someone else to write a script for Season One, because it seemed madness not to.

Annabel Jones: We were out talking to writers who we thought were like-minded. People who could be satirical and entertaining, but still have meat within their stories. Jesse Armstrong's name was obviously going to be on that list.

Primarily a sitcom writer, Armstrong had co-created Channel 4's POV-[point-of-view-] based Peep Show, *as well as working on the likes of* Four Lions *(2010) and* The Thick of It *(2005–2012).*

Jesse Armstrong (writer): I'd met Charlie a few times via various projects and meetings. At that stage, *Black Mirror* was quite a vague concept, because they hadn't made the show yet! I keep a notebook and I did have one suitable idea in there, which I might never had done anything with, otherwise.

I'd been thinking about the exponential growth of the capacity of computers to store memory. As your iPhone got more and more powerful, soon you'd be able to keep a passive memory of everything that ever happened to you. So I started thinking about the importance of being able to remember things. But also, in relationships and elsewhere, the importance of being able to forget things. So that was the germ of the idea I pitched and they were receptive.

Annabel Jones: The concept of being able to replay what you'd seen was such a clear, engaging, brilliant idea, that it didn't even require any explanation.

Jesse Armstrong: I had the idea of this really small memory chip that records everything for your convenience. I called it the Grain early on, because it was the size of a grain of rice. Joel Collins and his design guys realised it brilliantly in such a compelling way.

Joel Collins (series production designer): One of the key flavours was to give everything a texture. If you look at most shots, you'll see stone, with wood, with metal, with organic material, to take everything away from science fiction. I wanted the Grain app to look as if your life was stored in the rings of a tree. As it grew, and you got older, your rings increased.

I found houses that were tonally unusual for Britain. The technology of *The Entire History of You* was slightly beyond our reach, so we set it in 2050. Then I made it feel like 1950, with a subtle mid-century feel in the clothes, the tone. By journeying backwards to bring it forwards, the audience always feels comfortable. The episode is extraordinarily organically designed, in order to make them feel really settled.

Charlie Brooker: With *Black Mirror*, it's really useful to sit and ping-pong comedy ideas about. Especially with someone like Jesse who is a comedy writer, so quite quickly there was a funny conversation about all the

ramifications of the Grain. We had a long conversation about copyright law: what happens when you go to the cinema? Do you just record a film while you watch it? We then had an idea I quite like, about people going to cinemas to have clandestine conversations or affairs, because the recording technology is automatically disabled on copyright grounds. So people go and have sex in cinemas, because then their other half won't know.

Jesse Armstrong: Charlie came up with all these baroque things, like how kids at school would get changed under white shrouds as a protection against paedophiles. He's really good at thinking of spooky, weird corollaries, and then it was fun to put them all in. But it resulted in a sprawling, movie-length first draft.

Charlie Brooker: We spent a lot of time working out the story and tone, but as soon as we tried to go bigger than the world of one couple's life, we were in trouble. You either have to go full *Blade Runner* and the logical ramifications go through the roof, or you keep it very contained within a domestic bubble.

Annabel Jones: What really felt rich from the very beginning was the ability to crucify yourself with your own footage. The ability to replay every faux pas you've made. Every poor job interview. Every insensitive thing ever said …

Charlie Brooker: … which would take Annabel a long time.

Annabel Jones: Oh yes, I remember that joke. Every time! Any technology that we have in the films has to be something that people would embrace, and want and welcome in their lives. Because if they don't, it feels like you are forcing something on someone that they won't want to engage with, or that we won't believe.

Charlie Brooker: "Why am I walking around with this testicle-punching machine?"

Annabel Jones: Yes, but maybe even more satisfying than that would be the ability to record your child's birthday party, to be in the moment, without holding up a camera between you and them.

Dead Man's Shoes *star Toby Kebbell was cast as Liam, while future Doctor Who Jodie Whittaker became Ffion.*

Jodie Whittaker (actor): *Black Mirror* is its own genre. When someone gets sent a *Black Mirror* script now, they already know *Black Mirror*'s amazing, but back then *The Entire History of You* was unlike anything I'd ever read before. I knew it was extraordinary. We'd seen those kind of POV shots on *Peep Show*, but when it's your own memory being used against you, that's so dark and fascinating.

Barney Reisz (producer): After Jodie auditioned and left the room, Brian Welsh and I chased her downstairs, saying, "Will you do it?"

Jodie Whittaker: That never, ever happens! You usually have to wait. I remember getting my raincoat on as I headed for the tube, when they caught up with me!

Shaheen Baig (casting director): I'm a big Toby fan. He's got a huge emotional landscape as an actor, funny and very sympathetic. He and Jodie are very similar actors, in a way: very emotionally open and easy to read, but subtle and complex. They could be the couple living next door.

Barney Reisz: Brian Welsh had been at film school and then done an amazing film called *In Our Name*. I was very keen to get him on board. He was so inexperienced, that instead of saying "Cut!" at the end of a take, he would say, "Okay, stop now!"

Brian Welsh: I didn't even know what a jib or a dolly were! I'd been a massive fan of *Nathan Barley*, and suddenly I was working with Charlie Brooker. You could say I was overwhelmed. But in many ways, I think my naivety helped, because I became very focused on Toby's brilliance, and his capacity for tapping into something very real and pure.

I could identify with the exploration of jealousy within the story, because it was really universal. So I knew I could push the right buttons and go somewhere quite dark and painful, coupled with Jesse's comedy. I made the set a real play-space. I remember the chaos being a little too much for Charlie at times, as we tried different intonations, or even improvisations.

Jodie Whittaker: The dinner party scene was epic. That whole scene had to set up and explain the time we were living in and the opinions of that time. It had so many key cast members around the table, with added elements like

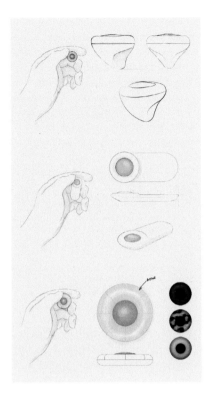

Above: The development work for the pebble device, developed by Painting Practice under the direction of series production designer Joel Collins and co-designer Robyn Paiba.

the eye contact between different characters that Liam would later try to pick up on. That was also a tough scene because we were eating the whole way through, and I made a terrible food choice – a quesadilla or something!

Brian was the perfect director for that piece. My favourite scene to shoot was when Liam and Ffion got back from the dinner party and we were looking at the nanny-cam footage. That's when the kernel of mistrust really grew. Before one take, Brian told me, "Liam is a grenade that could go off at any point. Treat him with care," and then on the next take he'd go, "Just don't give a fuck. You can't be arsed, you're tired." So that was really fun. I loved that Toby and I didn't know which note we were being privately given! It made it really interesting to not know how the other person was going to play it.

Between takes, Toby often tended to concentrate and stay focused, whereas I'm someone who has to get up, walk around and have a chat! Every actor brings a different approach, which is completely normal – and in this case I think it added to the sense of separation and mistrust between our characters, which is great.

Brian Welsh: Toby and Jodie are very, very funny people, and I think that comes across, especially early on in the film when Liam and Ffion are enjoying each other. Toby smashed one of the fake sugar-glass vodka bottles over my head, which kind of sums up his personality! Particularly as he did it towards the end of the day when everybody was really fucking stressed. I think I was talking to Barney about whether we were gonna complete that day or not.

I'm embarrassed that we went ridiculously far with the footage we shot of the Grain-memory sex scene between Liam and Ffion. In order to make Jodie comfortable, I had to play her part for a bit, because it was all shot as POV. None of it really made the cut, but somewhere in among the rushes, there's probably me being fucked by the cameraman.

Jodie Whittaker: Ha, yeah. That's probably a moment where they'd lined all the shots up, then I came on set and said, "Nah, I'm not doing that!" Poor Brian!

Charlie Brooker: Originally in the script, all the memories were played back on TV screens. So for instance, when Liam and Ffion have sex, they were scripted to be simultaneously watching footage of one of their earlier sexual encounters on their bedroom TV, like a couple watching porn. But it became apparent during pre-production that compositing all the POV footage onto screens would be a logistical nightmare – we'd either have to shoot it all in advance and play it in live, or paint it all in in post at great cost. So at some point I said, "Hang on, if they're recording this footage with their pupils, can't they play it back in their pupils too?" It made it far easier, because we could just intercut full-frame footage of the memories with shots of the actors with their pupils 'milked out'. But most importantly, it made everything feel much more intimate and invasive and eerie. The sex scene is a great example – because now rather than both watching a screen, they're both watching something in their heads. It made a scene that might've been amusing and a bit sad into something downright haunting.

The jump from screens to 'in-eye' tech also meant we had to focus a lot on the interface and the little remote control device they use – we

Above: More development work for the pebble device, developed by Painting Practice under the direction of series production designer Joel Collins and co-designer Robyn Paiba.

Opposite: The user interface for viewing a 're-do' via the Grain device, developed and animated at Painting Practice.

called it the 'pebble'. It had a circular pad on it, which corresponded to the in-eye display. Joel's idea of making the interface reminiscent of the wood-grain of a tree, a physical embodiment of passing time, was a nice thematic touch. It was such an intuitive-looking device. In fact, we really ought to patent and market them. And make billions. And use the money to construct a death-ray inside a dormant volcano full of uniformed henchmen. That's my dream.

Liam's growing obsession with investigating Ffion leads him to assault Jonas and threaten him with a broken vodka bottle.

Jodie Whittaker: Your sympathy for Liam wanes when he can't control his actions, or when he's hurting somebody. You understand it, but can you side with it? I don't know.

Charlie Brooker: Some people have a really reductive take on the story and go, "Wow, poor Liam. He found out that his wife was a bitch." I really don't think that's what the story is.

Annabel Jones: Liam's an obviously obsessive guy from the beginning, driving Ffion away. They had a break, during which she has a different relationship.

Jesse Armstrong: The story's about someone whose natural tendencies are enabled by a piece of tech, so I think Liam already had that jealousy in him. But in a reductive way, it's a cautionary tale about someone getting tech that allows the latent bad parts of their character to come out.

Charlie Brooker: Liam's the benchmark for a lot of *Black Mirror* characters, in that he's a weak, frightened, flawed person. He's a bit of a bully to Ffion, and not that pleasant. But I hope you see that it stemmed from his insecurity. This tech has effectively granted him the superpower to go back in time and obsess over this footage, so it's a very *Black Mirror* story where somebody slowly destroys themselves with a gadget.

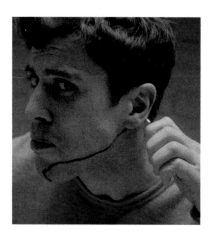

Jesse Armstrong: I'm quite promiscuous in my ability to empathise, even with quite shitty characters who do bad things. Certainly, Toby brought a tragic depth and darkness to that character. But how much sympathy does Liam deserve? I don't know ... as a human being, I find it very easy to imagine being tortured by incidents from the past. Liam's not a *nice* person and doesn't act with as much charity as a really good person, but he's also been driven a bit mad by this piece of technology.

Brian Welsh: Sometimes people get too hung up on sympathy. But what I will say, to contradict myself, is it was quite a hard film to get right in the edit. When you put certain, interesting takes together, you found that Liam was unlikeable and it was hard to stay with him. The turning point came when we pushed more towards the material where he was funnier.

Charlie Brooker: For me, the most horrible moment is when Liam asks Ffion to prove she used protection with Jonas. So he watches his worst nightmare unfold, and he knows there's no way back from that. There can be no, "We said a few things last night that none of us meant, so let's just have our breakfast, and I love you darling." He's fucking burnt the relationship to the ground.

Jodie Whittaker: The hardest scene to do was the emotional climax, with the full bedroom argument. You have to go from crying your eyes out, covered in snot and tears, to resetting the scene and shooting another take!

Annabel Jones: Maybe there's a slight redemption for Liam, in that he realises what has happened and he rips the Grain out. It's such a wonderful ending, because in doing so he knows he's losing all memories of his family.

Charlie Brooker: It's very powerful. Sometimes people think Liam's killed Ffion, but the reality is she's simply moved out. Or they think that he's not the dad. But Liam *is* the father of the child, so he's ruined his life. The moral, if there is one, is he shouldn't have gone looking for something that was only going to upset him. His wife loved him and there were secrets in the past, but he should have let them lie.

'It's like I've had a bad tooth for years and finally I'm getting to dig my tongue in there and just root around in all the rotten shit'

– Liam

When we had the BFI screening, a lot of comedy people came along – but it goes a bit Ingmar Bergman! It goes a bit fucking *Scenes from a Marriage* or something. It's pretty raw.

Brian Welsh: At that screening, you could feel the audience tensing and cringing and laughing. We've all experienced jealous moments in our lives and it's just that fucking car crash.

Jesse Armstrong: I'm not really a sci-fi person, but I felt very fortunate to be in a position where Charlie asked me. It was a happy accident and *The Entire History of You* is quite an outlier on my CV, but I'm very proud of it.

Charlie Brooker: I think the week after the episode went out, Facebook launched some new form of timeline: something we take for granted today, the ever-flowing roll of photos and memories. Very 'Grain-like'. The timing felt downright spooky.

Jodie Whittaker: I met someone in LA, who stopped me in Whole Foods Market and asked if I was that girl from *Black Mirror*. I said, "Oh yeah, that Grain thing was terrifying, wasn't it," and he said, "I thought it was an amazing idea!" He worked at a massive tech company. I was like, "Wow, how can he not see this is not the way we should go …"

SERIES TWO

In Conversation

Shane Allen – then Head of Comedy, Channel 4
Charlie Brooker – executive producer
Annabel Jones – executive producer
Joel Collins – series production designer

Shane Allen (then Head of Comedy, Channel 4): There was now a huge buzz around *Black Mirror*. It felt like the quintessential C4 show which would have been swerved or mangled elsewhere. Season One had that air of talked-about event television, because *The National Anthem*'s concept was so audacious. That film met with a lot of coverage and opinion pieces, so it was terrific to then have two very distinctive and tonally very different pieces coming down the tracks for the rest of that first series, so that people could appreciate the range and ambition of Charlie and Annabel's vision.

Charlie Brooker: We couldn't believe we got away with the first series. And the way my brain works, I always think, "Oh we did all right there, so now I'm fucked because this will be the one where I totally cock up and everything goes wrong." And then every time you don't cock up, the stakes get raised. So it's like rolling a six, five times in a row. Eventually it's going to come up one!

Annabel Jones: Charlie's always disappointed when we deliver a good season: "Why did we *do* that?"

Charlie Brooker: Not disappointed ... it's just that the sense of ominous terror grows. It's like climbing further up the side of a building, going, "This is going well, now I'm clinging to the 20th floor!" And at any moment, someone could just open a window and go, "Wait a minute, what's he doing on the side of the building, the fucking fool?"

Annabel Jones: Season One did throw up one of the disadvantages of being an anthology series: our viewing figures dipped across the series. You get a massive PR and marketing push for the first episode, and then the show has to survive by itself. When you don't have any story or cast continuity, what are you going to pull people back with? And you can't set up too much of what the next story is because of spoilers, so it cripples you. The show was being very well received, though, and had high production values, so everyone seemed happy.

Charlie Brooker: Channel 4's marketing team had been very good. It was very hard to promote each individual episode without spoiling it, so they made these great promos for the series as a whole. And I think it was the second season where they came up with the image of the cracked woman's face thing, which weirded people out on tube platforms. There were also some complaints when it went up on billboards opposite a school.

Joel Collins (series production designer): Underground people thought the show was edgy and cool, so you think about what to do next. In some ways, when we moved to Season Two, we could've done with the cash injection we later got from Netflix. We needed to take it up a notch, but it's very hard when your constraints are identical and you've moved on creatively a year or two later.

Annabel Jones: *Black Mirror* was an expensive show for Channel 4 to make, because there's no economies of scale across the episodes. You're not reusing sets or using the same actors. But they still went ahead and commissioned a second series because it had been well received. I don't think we needed any extra money. We were trying to make very intimate, interesting, engaging films. We didn't want to be a high-octane sci-fi show.

Shane Allen: On top of the UK buzz, the international appeal was clear to see from the off, with that first series winning Best TV Movie/Miniseries at the 2012 International Emmy Awards and Best Comedy at the 2012 Rose d'Or Awards. A second series was pretty swiftly ordered and the cycle began again with everyone really buoyed up by what an impact the show was having.

Charlie Brooker: The second series feels more epic in scale, but more intimate in scope. That's a real cunty phrase I just came out with, but there is a slight difference between Seasons One and Two. *Fifteen Million Merits* had been so high-concept in its look: there was a lot to invent there, whereas Season Two is all a little more understated. We were deliberately hiding technology, so there's not big flashy gadgets around all over the place. It's not in a hyper-idealised world. But that wasn't in any way a budgetary consideration. That was just the way the stories came out.

There's also a weird symmetry, where the first two seasons mirror each other. *The National Anthem* starts out like warped political satire; *Fifteen Million Merits* is a dystopian hellscape with somebody who's trapped in a sort of prison; and then you've got a relationship torn apart by technology. But during the second season, those things come in reverse order.

BE
RIGHT
BACK

In Conversation

Charlie Brooker – writer and executive producer
Annabel Jones – executive producer
Hayley Atwell – actor
Owen Harris – director
Joel Collins – series production designer
Robyn Paiba – co-production designer
Barney Reisz – producer

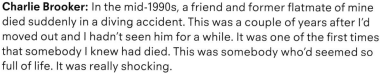

When pregnant Martha's partner Ash dies unexpectedly, she's plunged into grief. In an attempt to ease her pain, she reluctantly tries an AI program that allows her to communicate with a virtual simulation of Ash via text. She progresses to speaking with Virtual Ash on the phone, then finally orders his unnervingly accurate android replica. While Martha comes to realise that this android can only ever simulate the real Ash, she also struggles to let go.

Charlie Brooker: In the mid-1990s, a friend and former flatmate of mine died suddenly in a diving accident. This was a couple of years after I'd moved out and I hadn't seen him for a while. It was one of the first times that somebody I knew had died. This was somebody who'd seemed so full of life. It was really shocking.

And then about a year later, in the days when you still had limited numbers you could store in a phone, sometimes you'd have to delete things. So I was going through the list, and there was this guy's name and number. I thought I should delete that, but suddenly I couldn't. To do that would've felt disrespectful, callous and wrong. It was a memento, so I should keep it and find someone else's number to delete. It was a very *'Black Mirror'* moment.

A lot of *Be Right Back* stemmed from that: the notion of a souvenir that you know is not real, but which reminds you enough of somebody that it's painful.

Annabel Jones: It's a story about love and grief in the 21st century. How do you mourn in the modern world, where everyone is digitally present? We're no longer living in a world where there'd be a shoe box of old photos in the attic. Your dead husband's image and videos are still playing on Facebook and you can carry them and him around with you all the time. How do you let go in that scenario? If you're heartbroken, I totally understand the impulse to hide away and lose yourself in that. But Charlie's stories are so rich, it's not just about that. It's also about the disparity of our real selves and our 'online' selves.

Charlie Brooker: This script felt like a bit of risk, as it's a relatively small story about two people. It's mainly about Martha's emotional reaction to Ash's death, although there's still this high concept of the robot based on his online presence. She's lucky that he's not some maniac: if you did that now, based on someone's Twitter presence, you'd get a total monster living with you, constantly taking photos of himself.

I wrote that just after Konnie and I had our first kid. I wrote it in shifts while Konnie would sleep, and then I would look after him while she slept. This discipline actually meant I got the script written really quickly. I knew it was going well when I was annoyed to be interrupted, because it meant I'd got into the flow. Time and space disappeared, until I saw what I'd written. When you have a baby you go fucking haywire for a bit, so I definitely allowed myself to be more soppy and emotional than I might have been comfortable doing before.

I was aware that the first series had all had male protagonists, and so it was deliberate for *Be Right Back* and *White Bear* to have female protagonists, just as a balance. Also, *Be Right Back* would feel weirdly sleazy with a guy ordering this female sex doll. I don't know why.

Annabel Jones: My first inclination for the character of Martha was Hayley Atwell. We were taken aback that she had seen the first season and loved it.

Hayley Atwell (actor): Those first three episodes were inventive, chilling and smart. I reached out to Annabel and Charlie to let them know what a huge fan I was, and to ask if they would consider me for future episodes. When I read *Be Right Back*, the hairs on my arms stood up. I found it

Above left: An early design for the online chat on Martha's laptop, initially designed in the art department by Erica McEwan and animated for visual effects by Painting Practice.

disturbing and moving – a study of grief in the technological age. It felt surreal and bizarre, but plausible and humane. I thought it would be a hard shoot emotionally, but I felt confident we'd make something quite beautiful and haunting.

Owen Harris (director): The script made me feel I had the opportunity to create an emotionally compelling story. The episode came along just when we were all starting to feel a little unnerved by the amount of technology in our day-to-day lives. What drew me to the episode most, though, was the fact that it also explored these grander themes of love and death and loss, but in a human, intimate and typically *Black Mirror* way.

I especially enjoyed working with Hayley, because she wanted to create a grounded character. I wanted Martha to feel like the girl next door. No huge dreams or ambitions. Just someone who wanted to build a simple life with her partner, only to have that snatched away. It was something we can all relate to, and her portrayal was heartfelt and honest.

Hayley Atwell: I wanted to bring naturalism to every moment. To make Martha's grief feel real. That helps the slightly futuristic and sci-fi elements seem plausible. I've never lost someone like that, thankfully, but I wanted to play it as truthfully and sensitively as I could. I was tired by the end of each day, but I loved the story and the team, and that just kept me going.

Before the shoot, I had a giggle with Domhnall Gleeson, who played Ash. We went to Dans le Noir restaurant in Farringdon, a restaurant where you're served a meal in the dark. That certainly broke the ice. Domhnall and I wanted the audience to get a sense that this couple had a loving, playful relationship, so all the little montage clips of our time before his

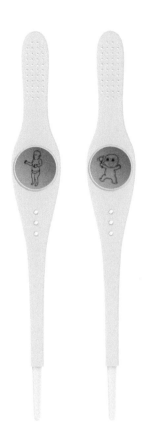

character's accident are full of humour and warmth. I suppose it serves to make the loss greater.

Joel Collins (series production designer): The story is so upsetting and complex emotionally. Technology-wise, all it needed was that nudge to the next day, rather than the future. We needed to establish that this stuff could be real. So we made laptops and phones that are almost real now, because we made them so long ago. At the time, they seemed fantastical. For me, the future is detail. Unless there's a catastrophe and the world gets rebuilt, the rest of the future is in the details around us, such as the roads being emptier because we're all inside on computers all the time. Those details are more relevant than a wide shot.

Owen Harris: I wanted the technology to be something that you might see if you walked into the Apple store tomorrow. You wouldn't be totally blown away to find them trialling digital paper like Martha's drawing board. It needed to feel practical and tactile, so that it sat comfortably within the story, rather than sticking out, screaming for attention. The return of Ash as a cyborg starts to stretch the 'near present' sense of future, but by then I hoped you'd be accompanying Martha on her journey and indulging her steps towards the horrifying arrival of her manufactured 'ex' in a box.

Above left: The pregnancy test and dancing baby were designed in the art department and later animated by Painting Practice.

Above right: The development work for Martha's digital drawing board, designed by Joel Collins with motion graphics created by Painting Practice.

Joel Collins: That was the beginning of us setting the tone for subtlety in vehicles. The petrol station at the beginning has these micro cars. If the future is electric, it might mean small cars. It's a subtle beat in *Be Right Back*, but it's the beginnings of those ideologies and that thinking. Maybe the future's simple, small, eco-friendly and all that stuff.

Robyn Paiba (co-production designer): We found an amazing farmhouse which was quite rundown and needed work, but fitted cinematically. The farm had an elderly owner and an even older dog who managed to defecate in one room during the tech recce whilst we were all standing there. Tonally we went for a warm, but pared-back colour palette.

Joel Collins: The shoot involved incessant journeying. One day on the M25, someone drove past me in a van and could see Domhnall Gleeson's fake body in the boot, wrapped in plastic.

Owen Harris: I really wanted to film Ash's accident. I wanted the shock of the accident to affect the viewer as well as Martha. So we set about choreographing the stunt, finding the locations, scheduling the days … and then I got a tap on the shoulder and a reality check.

Charlie Brooker: The accident wasn't in the script. I think Owen had an idea for quite a startling image, of a van spinning through the frame in slow motion. But we just felt we didn't need that. It's more powerful that Ash just goes off and you don't know what's become of him. And so, when it's confirmed to Martha that something has happened, it's confirmed to us as well.

Barney Reisz (producer): I'd made a mistake, because our budgets were a little bit higher for Season Two. So when I was trying to persuade Owen to do *Be Right Back*, I'd told him he could do whatever he liked. That's the sort of things producers say to directors!

Owen Harris: So after a brief wave of disappointment, you regroup and look at what tools you have to portray that sudden sense of shock and loss. And in the end, the answer came from the house Martha lived in. The isolation that Martha and Ash had longed for as a couple suddenly became empty. And over a few brief beats, we created this sense of waiting that would make the solitude feel suddenly quite overwhelming. So instead of the drama of the accident, we had the quiet emptiness of being terribly alone.

Charlie Brooker: Martha shutting the door in the police's faces was probably inspired by the scene in *Saving Private Ryan* when a woman's washing up and a jeep arrives. The minute she sees it's an army guy and a chaplain, her knees buckle. It's really upsetting and tells you everything you need to know without any dialogue.

Ash is called Ash quite pointedly, because he fucking dies, almost straight away.

There was a lot of debate about his robot body that arrives in the box. Sometimes I get very insistent about things, which I refer to as getting 'Taliban' about them. The idea was: the body arrives blank. You put it in the bath, it somehow connects to the cloud and downloads his characteristics, then morphs its shape and textures. So I was adamant that this thing should have no features, no hair, nothing … and then we ended up shooting this thing with ginger hair. We finally altered the shot using CGI to put more foam chips in the box and cover the hair up.

'You're just a few ripples of you. There's no history to you. You're just a performance of stuff that he performed without thinking and it's not enough'

– Martha

Annabel Jones: Charlie's always good at getting away with things that are slightly implausible, or that require a bit of a leap. He often undercuts it himself or gets the characters to undercut it, so here the robot Ash says, "It's a bit creepy," and you just embrace it. Whereas if you try and present something as being ultra-sophisticated and straight, it's a harder sell.

Charlie Brooker: The episode is odd, because it's quite comic in places. It's also heartbreaking, but Martha and Ash have a nice little rapport, and there are some slightly absurd moments. And then it's weirdly like a supernatural story. You can see a Hammer Horror version of that story where you have to go to Ash's grave and spread a particular fluid on it. *'I Piss On Your Grave'*: the romantic horror of the century.

Domhnall had a really hard job to do. He effectively had to be the C3PO version of himself, a slightly naive, blanker version of himself, and he pulls it off really skillfully. One thing I was very keen not to have happen was for Ash to start feeling emotions and suddenly fall in love. There was no need for him to do that, because he's all surface.

Annabel Jones: Martha and Robot Ash's interactions mirror the stages of online dating. First they text. Then they ring each other. And then they meet. Felt very fitting.

Robot Ash was based on real Ash's online persona, so a lot of Robot Ash's limitations and annoyances stemmed from that. So when Robot Ash struggled to read Martha's moods, he carries on wisecracking. When Robot Ash shares the photo of himself as a young boy at the safari park, he's making light of something tragic. Although there was some upside: as we tend to only upload our best photos it meant Robot Ash came back slightly more handsome!

Owen Harris: Domhnall and I talked about how much to play Cyborg Ash like the real Ash, and he was generous enough to allow me to play it both ways. I might suggest a little more Ash, or a little more cyborg, depending on which way the scene needed bending. This allowed me to fine-tune just how Ash-like the cyborg was, because in the end you want to care about him, and it's a great accolade to Domhnall that you do.

Charlie Brooker: Martha's whole predicament is having a version of Ash that isn't him, but it's enough like him that she can't just throw him away. And she can't teach him to be him, so she's stuck and there's no solution to the problem. For a while, I became obsessed with psychics who profess to communicate with someone's dead relative. Because surely the relative, on some level, knows it isn't really happening, but it's like comfort eating. I can understand why you'd do it, but surely it can't be helping.

Hayley Atwell: I still don't know how I feel about the idea of this resurrected android fiancé. It would be both horrendous and comforting, perhaps. It's an impossible situation and that's what makes it compelling. Martha's grief pushes her into taking actions I doubt she would ever have anticipated. At first she resists this 'grieving tool' and thinks it's sick and disrespectful. Then, alone in that house and in total despair, she becomes desperate for some sort of balm. Some contact with the dead to lessen her pain.

Owen Harris: I find the idea of bringing a loved one back as a cyborg totally horrifying. But for the story to work we had to infuse it with a sombre romance. Martha needs this so much, and she's being given the opportunity to have Ash back. But you're always going to be faced with something that is so much more cyborg than it can ever be human. And then the horror comes from the notion of having to 'delete' him.

Annabel Jones: The scene where Martha finally accepts that she can't live with robot Ash anymore, on the cliff edge, is one of the most emotional and poignant things Charlie has ever written. Just heart-wrenching.

Owen Harris: We went round the houses a few times on the ending, but I think we pretty much ended up where we'd started. A big part of the success of *Black Mirror* is the logic Charlie applies to his outlandish ideas. He's happy to examine the narrative, as long as it doesn't affect the logic. That's not to say that we always 100 per cent agree on the logic that's being applied, but on the whole it's good to have something solid to push up against.

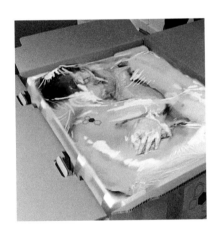

Above and opposite: The model of android Ash, shrinkwrapped and boxed as well as in the bath, before being activated.

Owen Harris: The ending, I never found optimistic. It always disturbed me a bit. But I liked the way it was unresolved, for Martha especially. She just couldn't hit delete. Nor could she live with him. It was also a bit spooky how Ash had now become a part-time dad, or a part-time toy, in the attic. I would often console myself with the idea that a whole bunch of people out there might rather like the idea of a manufactured version of their partner, with only the best bits – and utterly malleable to their every whim and desire!

Annabel Jones: I think Owen wanted them to have a family dinner downstairs. We preferred the idea that Martha's compromise was allowing her daughter to interact with her dead father once a week, as a special treat at the weekends.

Charlie Brooker: When Martha's standing at the bottom of the ladder, having a thousand yard stare moment, she's thinking, "What the fuck has my life become?" Because she's sort of trapped.

Hayley Atwell: She's numb. I'd even suggest she's been medicated. Her grief has been replaced with having to manage this thing which is not him, but enough of him to keep in the house. It's a very pessimistic ending, but *Be Right Back* is moving and smart and deeply disturbing. I'm very happy to have been a part of it.

Charlie Brooker: Ash in the attic was one of the most expensive shots in this whole series! Domhnall was about to shoot something else, and at that point in the schedule he had a beard that contractually we couldn't shave off.

There was some debate about whether an android would grow a beard, and whether it could be useful in conveying that he's been up there for a while. But ultimately we had to CGI out the beard. So the bottom half of his face is a fucking CGI reconstruction. It's a nightmare, because he's talking and he's walking through shadows and light. We were really worried for quite a while, because we saw early versions and thought it just wasn't going to work.

No-one's ever gone, "That's weird, what's up with his face?" But if you're looking for it, you can see something a bit weird's going on.

I'm really fortunate, because very rarely have I had to go through the grieving process. So I was particularly nervous about writing *Be Right Back*. But sometimes people who are grieving find it too painful to watch. Either that, or they find it cathartic.

WHITE BEAR

In Conversation

Charlie Brooker – writer and executive producer
Annabel Jones – executive producer
Carl Tibbetts – director
Barney Reisz – producer
Joel Collins – series production designer
Shaheen Baig – casting director
Jon Opstad – composer

Victoria wakes up in a suburban bedroom, with no idea of who she is or how she got here. A strange television signal is turning members of the public into impassive voyeurs who film her with their phones. With only a survivalist named Gem to tell her what has happened to the world, Victoria must flee a roaming group of psychotic hunters while trying to remember the truth of her own identity.

Charlie Brooker: I can absolutely trace back to where *White Bear* came from. We were shooting a scene in *Dead Set*, where our actor Riz Ahmed was running up the road being chased by zombies. Some local kids turned up, just to watch what was going on. They got their phones out and started taking photos rather than video, this being 2008. So Riz runs past and they don't help him because they're taking photos. I was struck by that as an image: everyone just casually standing around. Not even enjoying it, apparently, but bored as they film your discomfort. I thought, "God, there's something more frightening about that than what we're filming."

So I wanted to write a story which used that as a central image. And I thought the way to do that was a high-tech zombie movie, so I wrote a script where literally it was that. The story started in a newsroom. A signal was making this symbol appear on screens around the world. When people saw this symbol, 90 per cent of them turned into dumb voyeurs who were filming things, and the remaining percentage just went mad and started attacking the others. It was never explained where this had been coming from, but it was a bit of a rip-off of the end of [Hammer Film Productions' 1967 sci-fi horror movie] *Quatermass and the Pit*. Anyway, it didn't really make sense and would've been incredibly expensive.

Annabel Jones: Maybe because we'd done *Dead Set*, we didn't want *White Bear* to be the generic zombie story. There was also the sense that society was changing a little, when you'd hear of various crimes or assaults and people would be taking their phones out to film them. There was that awful story about the group of kids on the South Bank in London, who kicked some guy to death and filmed it. So our story had become more about voyeurism.

The imagery and themes of *White Bear* felt very prescient at the time – phone cameras up, people rubbernecking, the idea we're all citizen journalists now so can absolve ourselves of any responsibility or emotional engagement.

Charlie Brooker: The next version of the script had an opening I really liked, with someone describing to their psychiatrist how they've been getting violent impulses and vivid dreams. The psychiatrist asks them to draw a symbol they keep seeing in their sleep, and they draw this glyph, the symbol that we would ultimately use in *White Bear*. The patient goes away, then of course the psychiatrist goes across the room, opens a drawer ... and there are these identical sketches by loads of other patients. The psychiatrist shuts the drawer with a very worried look on her face and I thought it was a great opening.

I was trying to concoct a story about this weird conspiracy, and this strange signal that's been buried somewhere in TV broadcasts since the changeover from SD to HD. As a result, society's gradually becoming more selfish. This second version went a bit more [the 1973 film] *The Wicker Man*, with people filming real public crucifixions and executions. Some of the characters that ended up in *White Bear* were in it, such as Michael Smiley's character Baxter. It was still a bit like a zombie thriller, and that was what we were going to film. We'd spoken to the director Carl Tibbetts and outlined the idea. I was going to redraft the script so it made more sense and Carl liked how chilling the central image was, of someone being pursued while everyone just watches and enjoys it. And then we started to scout for locations, and everything changed.

Carl Tibbetts (director): *Black Mirror* came to me because *White Bear* was going to be a contained thriller, much like a film I'd co-written and directed called *Retreat*. I seem to remember Charlie being influenced by that footage of Colonel Gaddafi being dragged through the streets and how quickly that had gone viral. So I got the job on that script, but then the second meeting I had, they were like, "Forget that! We're doing this."

Barney Reisz (producer): *White Bear* was built from the bottom up, out of necessity. We'd spent so long getting *The Waldo Moment* ready and *Be Right Back* wasn't cheap, so we had little money left. So I told Charlie we had to shoot all of *White Bear* within our base, which was these military barracks at RAF Daws Hill. That was incredibly liberating. Charlie's brilliant when he's under pressure. Put him under pressure and he'll always deliver.

Charlie Brooker: This former US airbase had an abandoned housing estate on it. So we had all these houses we could film in, things that looked like shops, and a thing that looked like a garage. But then, as the location manager showed us around, a giant chicken-wire fence around the whole place got me thinking. For weeks, I'd known there was something not quite right with the script, but I couldn't quite see how to fix the thing. It's like being a chiropractor, when you know if you just crack it in the right place ...

Suddenly I thought, "Hang on a minute, what if there is a fence around the place because it's all *not really happening*? That's even better!" I suddenly got really excited and it gave me a much better idea.

The story became that Victoria, the person we're following, thinks this is really happening. I'd already had the elements of the weird conspiracy story they were going to tell her, but now I had both sides. The conversation very quickly turned to why somebody might be in a camp like this. I said that if they brought Jimmy Savile back to life, people would willingly go and watch this happen to him. Or Myra Hindley; someone who's done a terrible, terrible thing. And then you turn it into a business, which gives me the *Wicker Man* story that I wanted to do about the person whose discomfort is being enjoyed by the population as a whole.

White Bear is a good example of how sometimes a limitation or a problem actually provides you with a solution. But also I find it somewhat terrifying, because I quite often like to suddenly change the entire premise at the last minute, if the new premise is better. It's quite Darwinian, but it can be a bit destabilising.

I had to write the new script in a frenzy, because we were already in pre-production. Luckily, I was excited. And as soon as you know what the ending is, and you've got enough answers for the awkward questions that are going to pop up along the way, you're eager to get there.

Joel Collins (series production designer): Within a week or so, the *White Bear* script came through. Somebody asked how he'd managed to find every single location so perfectly, but Charlie had triangulated the entire idea over everything we'd seen. It was one of the cleverest bits of writing I've ever experienced.

Charlie Brooker: At first, I made Victoria innocent, but that was too complicated because we were trying to tell you two different things at once. It seemed much more powerful to have her be guilty without realising. Lenora Crichlow had already been cast as Victoria and read the previous script, so that's quite a thing to hit someone with: "Oh, so now you're a child murderer. Sorry about that."

To Carl's credit, when he heard the new story, he embraced it and had lots of ideas about how the *White Bear* people should guide Victoria through the theme park. He suggested details, like the shoes, that I would not have thought of. And that gave me things to do in the final scenes, when they're resetting all these little visual cues. They're putting the shoes down, they're pulling the patio doors open slightly. They're putting the trail of bread crumbs back down, which is chilling.

Carl Tibbetts: Even at that stage, *Black Mirror* wasn't hard to cast. People like Michael Smiley loved being in the show. They knew they were only making a short commitment to something. Even if the script wasn't all there yet, there was a great concept to get people involved and interested. Michael plays his role brilliantly. There are occasions where all the casting pieces fall together and that was one of them.

Shaheen Baig (casting director): The *White Bear* auditions were distressing, because the content was so intense. What I mainly remember from the sessions is actors screaming!

Carl Tibbetts: Lenora said it was one of the strangest jobs she's ever had. She wanders around in her tracksuit, not looking her best, as beautiful as

'Oh my God, what's wrong with those people? Why aren't they helping us? They're just watching'

– Victoria

she is, and screaming a lot! We were careful to pace it: we knew which scenes were coming up, and when to let the terror go, otherwise it was going to get exhausting for her. The episode does have some moments of calm, where she can take her foot off the gas a bit.

Joel Collins: It was like making an action movie: something like *28 Days Later*. You're never going to invent that entire world, because the tone has to feel apocalyptic. So you use reality to create a feeling. With something like the petrol station, you smash windows and you do what you'd do on an action movie. Then you build a set for the finale, when the wall splits in half – a theatrical reveal which makes the illusion more shocking. And suddenly you've got an audience. So throughout the film, you build your way up to making it feel more controlled.

Carl Tibbetts: When Charlie designed the balaclava symbol, that felt like a crucial turning point. He's very big on those things: graphics, ticker-tape, the way the news appears, anything like that. I've seen people dressed at Comic Con as Michael Smiley's character, with that balaclava and symbol, so these things take on a life and identity of their own.

Charlie Brooker: I think I drew that logo in the script. I chose it as just an ominous but simple symbol, after experimenting with lots of different things. It's a bit like an upside-down Y, or a road sign for two lanes that are going to merge into one. I've started seeing those symbols everywhere – not as a hallucination, but because people often tweet me pictures of paving stones where they're laid out like that.

Annabel Jones: The sequence in the woods, I find particularly horrifying. Obviously we wanted it to be nasty – I think we actually toned down the language and cut some of the action from this scene in the edit as it was so off-putting – but when Victoria is pleading with the onlookers to intervene and everyone carries on filming and no-one is helping, it's just horrifying.

Carl Tibbetts: Our big reveal, obviously, is that the whole thing's been an illusion.

Charlie Brooker: I suppose *White Bear* was our first one with a really big twist. We carefully balanced the flashbacks to what Victoria had done, as we were quite worried we'd give too much away. Very few people see that twist coming. I'm sure a few did but not many.

Carl Tibbetts: When Victoria puts her shoes on and steps outside for the first time, the actual white bear's hidden in the garden. She doesn't notice, but it's visible at some point by the fence. Mostly, for me, it was all about those first five or ten minutes when we're with Victoria as she wakes up and looks around. It was about sticking with her as much as possible. Even when we're inside the petrol station with her, we never go outside the glass. What helps make it more frightening, is you're constantly with her throughout the experience until the very end. As we experienced the park with her the first time around, we very much shot on handheld cameras, close to her, very intense and personal, one on one, making you feel you were her.

Above: The Manhunt video game provided inspiration for the costumes in *White Bear*.

We never came out of that point of view until the end reveal that it's been one long, deliberate trick, one big show being put on for Victoria – and we *are* her, so that show is being put on for us. During the end credits stuff, where we reveal the theme park side of things, I wanted to shoot that very much still and static as an observer. The viewer mightn't be cognisant of that change, but it has an effect.

The Perspex van that Victoria's in towards the end, we called that the Wicker Van! *The Wicker Man* was a big touchstone for me in *White Bear*. Edward Woodward's investigation was never going to go anywhere, because it was all a performance put on for him.

Annabel Jones: At the time, there had been protests with people calling for Jimmy Savile's body to be dug up, so our Wicker Van in the theme park didn't feel that exaggerated.

Charlie Brooker: In the original cut, Victoria's van journey went on even longer! Half the crowd is digitally inserted in, but there were quite a few people there, and they were encouraged to scream and shout. Some of them were given phones and you see footage from some of these phones within the climax.

Annabel Jones: The showbiz ending is fabulously eerie and then I love the fact that the 'Day Two' reveal is just so throwaway, intercut into the end credits. Just snatched glimpses of another day at the theme park. That

felt quite bold. Cutting these last few scenes down like this was an idea Charlie had in the edit. It made *White Bear* one of the shortest episodes we'd ever done. A normal Channel 4 hour was 45 to 48 minutes but *White Bear* was about 41 minutes. Channel 4 were happy to support it, though.

Jon Opstad (composer): My biggest challenge musically was how to characterise the ending when everything resets and we're back in the same room with Victoria waking up. We're seeing the same events as at the beginning, but in a completely different light. So the music at this point needed to somehow have a different character that helped emphasise this shift, while not feeling like it came from a different score entirely.

Up to that point the score has been very electronic, so I decided that introducing some contrasting acoustic elements could help with the shift in perspective. Going entirely acoustic didn't fit the world that we're in, though, so I finally landed on the pizzicato cellos motif that the final cue was built from, then built some spidery atonal lines over this to maintain the sense of discomfort.

Charlie Brooker: I'm always quite interested in the reasons why people don't like a particular episode. Sometimes people don't like *White Bear* because they can't conceive this would happen and it's not financially viable to build this whole theme park around one criminal. Which is true. It makes a sort of dream-nightmare logical sense at the end. It makes enough sense that I think it's okay. It should leave you feeling a bit sick and not quite sure how you feel about what you've just watched. You feel sympathetic towards this person but also repulsed by what they did. It's a nice sense of queasy vertigo.

Carl Tibbetts: I don't know what the answer to *White Bear* is, but whatever Victoria did, does not mean that we should take pleasure in torturing somebody. I don't think she knows what she did, and it's not really about whether she's right or wrong. The piece is about not torturing people, whether they've killed children or not. For me, the question of Victoria's guilt or innocence is slightly irrelevant.

Annabel Jones: The focus is very much on how we bring people to justice and what outrages we can do if we feel we're morally justified. It's pretty clear in the film that Victoria's an accomplice. She aids and abets and goes along with it. I think you need to know she's guilty, because otherwise it looks like wrongful persecution. And I always take from it that Victoria's incredibly remorseful about what she's done. Being constantly shown the evil things she's done to that little girl, it's obviously destroying her, and there's real remorse there.

Charlie Brooker: My take on this is slightly different. Because Victoria can't remember what she did, she's woken up and everything that happens in that episode is like a nightmare. It's almost got nightmare logic to it, including the pull out to reveal this nightmare society. So if you had a nightmare in which society tells you you're a child killer, and everyone thinks you're a child killer, you would be terrified. And then at the end, when she's strapped to the chair, she's having to watch the torture and murder of a child, and the thing on her head looks fucking painful as well. So I don't think she's got remorse for what went on. I'm sure you'd feel really guilty, but I think it's more confusion and animal fear above anything else.

One of the many things I like about this episode is the slight *Hammer House of Horror* vibe. That old anthology show had this nasty British feel, because they just filmed it all around Amersham on a budget. Because they were just filming it in 1979 or something, outside a Tesco, that made it much more creepy, sinister and threatening than the Dracula movies.

I was really pleased with the contrast of *Be Right Back* and *White Bear*, back to back. I quite like the fact that we went from a more emotive one into one that's so fucking horrible. *White Bear* is one of my favourites, although I have favourites for different reasons, so it really varies. But *White Bear* is one I'll sometimes use as verbal shorthand. Like, "I'm looking for a *White Bear* moment."

Carl Tibbetts: *White Bear* is one of my high points, career-wise. In terms of concept and execution, it pretty much nailed everything I wanted it to do.

Charlie Brooker: There's a sequel idea that we've discussed for ages. What if the memory-wipe thing stops working? What if Victoria does start to get déjà vu? There was an idea where she does try to break out of the prison. I would never rule out a *Return to White Bear*. That's the title! I know the title and two things that happen in it. I've always wanted to do a 'Return to' story. *Return to San Junipero*! Or it's *Crocodile* again, but backwards, like *Memento*. *Crocodile Two: Back in Business*!

'Last but not least,
enjoy yourself'
– Baxter

THE WALDO
MOMENT

<u>In Conversation</u>

Charlie Brooker – writer and executive producer
Annabel Jones – executive producer
Bryn Higgins – director
Byron Broadbent – co-production designer
Russell McLean – then animation producer, Passion Pictures
Joel Collins – series production designer
Justin Hutchinson-Chatburn – VFX supervisor
Barney Reisz – producer
Jodie Foster – director, Arkangel

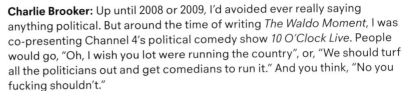

Failed comedian Jamie Salter catches a break when he becomes the voice and puppeteer of Waldo, an irreverent digital bear who interviews authority figures. When Waldo goes viral and runs for Parliament, Jamie uses the character to derail the career of Labour candidate MP Gwendolyn Harris, who he feels spurned him after a fling. When the US government shows interest in Waldo, Jamie has to decide how much further he's willing to go.

Charlie Brooker: Up until 2008 or 2009, I'd avoided ever really saying anything political. But around the time of writing *The Waldo Moment*, I was co-presenting Channel 4's political comedy show *10 O'Clock Live*. People would go, "Oh, I wish you lot were running the country", or, "We should turf all the politicians out and get comedians to run it." And you think, "No you fucking shouldn't."

The Waldo Moment is about satire, in a way, asking what satire's about. Sometimes Jamie just says things that are straight out of my gob, like when he says that going on [the BBC's political debate show] *Question Time* would be his worst fucking nightmare.

It's very easy for me to sit there and say Ed Miliband's fucking ineffectual, or this person's a prick, and actually that's what I had to do week in, week out on *10 O'Clock Live*. You're trying to be entertaining and make knob jokes, often in front of an audience. And so there's literally a bit where Gwendolyn Harris asks Jamie what he's for. At least the Tory candidate MP Liam Monroe stands for something, whereas Jamie's just saying 'bollocks' to stuff.

This whole episode was really tricky to write. In retrospect, *The Waldo Moment* should have been a mini-series, or a two-parter, or a movie. Having faffed around so much rewriting *White Bear*, I ran out of time, so couldn't really think it through. I had to just do it, and then afterwards you think about all the things you might have done differently with all the time in the world.

It's probably trying to do too many things in one episode. The idea of an avatar that you create, that becomes a lightning rod for dissatisfaction with politicians, that concept makes absolute sense, but it's slightly underdeveloped. There are a few moving parts there that I wasn't sure about. I didn't have time to do as much research as I wanted, although I do remember speaking to my [MP] sister-in-law, who told me things like how Tory voters' houses are really far apart.

Annabel Jones: Charlie didn't think that our main character Jamie's stakes were high enough, that he didn't have enough jeopardy.

Charlie Brooker: Comparatively speaking, that's true. Because it's life or death in the other two episodes that season. Maybe we didn't have time to set up quite what the stakes are? Jamie's depressed about his career and he's quite miserable. He's reticent about taking part in the campaign for a sort of ideological reason, but it's like he's complaining about something abstract.

Afterwards, of course, I realised what I should have done. Jamie has this fling with the Labour candidate Gwendolyn Harris, and while writing that, I wondered if they should be exes, but decided that was too big a coincidence. But actually, I think you'd have swallowed the coincidence. That would have been fine, and would have explained why Jamie didn't want to campaign in that area, because he didn't want to bump into the girl whose heart he broke or who broke his heart.

Immediately, you'd have had a bit more emotion brought up. You'd have been more invested in these people and what was going on. Things like that bug me after the fact, and I think, "Argh! Why didn't I just … "

The basic concept of The Waldo Moment *was born during the development process of 2005's Channel 4 sitcom* Nathan Barley, *which Charlie wrote with* Brass Eye *creator Chris Morris.*

Charlie Brooker: The Nathan Barley process was really pleasant, but tortuously long. Literally, we were talking about Nathan Barley pre-9/11. One of our many ideas was the launch of an animated candidate MP, along the lines of the band Gorillaz. That struck us as an annoyingly plausible thing to happen. And then there was the notion that you could then roll that out around the world and just have competing avatars that you vote for and nothing would ever change. Then we wondered how the fuck we'd do that as a *Nathan Barley* episode and it never happened.

Annabel Jones: *The Waldo Moment* was then also influenced by the rise of the Mayor of London, Boris Johnson.

Charlie Brooker: It was that whole notion of cartoon Boris. He goes on some TV panel show like *Have I Got News for You* and everyone thinks he's a legend.

Annabel Jones: And it doesn't matter what Boris says, as long as he's entertaining. We'll forgive you anything if you make us laugh.

Above: The visual development work for the Waldo character by Painting Practice. The team at Passion Pictures then went on to live animate Waldo.

Opposite: The virtual cat, Ratz, from BBC1's flagship Saturday morning children's programme *Live & Kicking*, who provided inspiration for Waldo. On screen here with John Barrowman.

Bryn Higgins (director): Not too far in the future, there probably will be cartoons in actual political campaigns. The whole thing has become so stage-managed. In terms of the tone, this episode's comedy was always implicit, so it was never a case of wanting to ramp that up, or you'd over-play your hand. So we tried to shoot it as a fairly slick modern thriller.

Charlie Brooker: We were keen for this one to not feel like sci-fi, so Jamie puppeteering the digital Waldo is not massively beyond what's possible. I'd remembered the first series of the BBC's Saturday morning kids' show *Live & Kicking*, in which the disembodied head of a cat hovered on a screen and spoke in real time: "Hello Boyzone, how are you today?" or whatever. So I incorporated that idea too.

Byron Broadbent (co-production designer): Early on, we knew that we wanted Waldo to be puppeteered live on set, so as to have the character naturally reacting live with the actors, instead of inserting him in post production. There was a lot of work in prep to design Waldo at [the design studio] Painting Practice, which had to be signed off months before the shoot began.

Russell McLean (then animation producer, Passion Pictures): Darren Walsh and I, along with our VFX supervisor Neil Riley, had developed a CG-

animated meerkat character called Aleksandr for a series of commercials which had become a massive hit in the UK. We had digitally puppeteered the meerkat, so he could 'speak' at events. Around that time, Joel Collins got in touch and asked whether we could animate Waldo. It was close to the wire, but we managed to get it all working in time and have all of Waldo's performances live in camera.

Bryn Higgins: Before, all of Waldo's scenes would've had to be bluescreen, and all the animations and timing would've been affected by that. But this amazing moment had come, where the technology was *just* good enough that you could do live animation.

Joel Collins (series production designer): The puppeteers used a rig called a Waldo rig, which Charlie named the character after. This rig goes around your head, picks up on all your emotions and facial movements and then replicates them live in a 3D character. It was ground-breaking technology.

Justin Hutchinson-Chatburn (VFX supervisor): In the end, the technical solution also became the 'behind the scenes' rig seen on screen.

Bryn Higgins: Daniel [Daniel Rigby, who played Jamie] was never fully controlling Waldo. He was using the actual puppeteers' equipment, but it took four very experienced puppeteers, who'd done stuff like *The Muppets*. One guy did Waldo's eyes, another did the mouth. Someone did his body, and someone else had all the rest. Occasionally, the eyes would argue with the mouth! And every now and then, Waldo would go wrong, which was quite funny too. There was a huge amount of data flowing around – it was a complex piece of CGI.

Joel Collins: That tech brought a kind of immediacy and reality, in much the same way as when we ran the screens live in *Fifteen Million Merits*. Waldo was clunky, but that was part of it. The weirdest thing is, we could've made it way more slick, but Charlie actually wanted it clunky, to go along with the tone. That was difficult for me, when you're downgrading it for the story!

Charlie Brooker: Waldo needed to have a PlayStation 3 level of complexity, in terms of polygons and stuff. If he'd looked too Dreamworks, or too Pixar and polished, I thought you wouldn't believe that Jamie could actually operate him live. So it's not that we couldn't do better: if you look at the gopher in *Playtest*, for instance, that's a very sophisticated CGI character. But Waldo's a Sonic the Hedgehog sort of graphic.

Bryn Higgins: Finding the voice of Waldo was quite hard. There was a concern that, if he became too much of an aggressive assassin, he wouldn't be very appealing to people. Again, Ali G was referenced quite a lot.

We took the Waldo van to High Wycombe, which we used as a traditional, provincial English town. Members of the public started turning up and they actually quite got into Waldo. They responded to the live animation quite a lot.

I had a funny discussion with our producer Barney Reisz about the scene in which Waldo's knob is supposed to appear. Barney rightly questioned whether we could do that in public. We didn't have control of the space,

'Waldo's not real, but he's more real than all the others'
– Jack

Opposite top: The sets for the newsroom and both TV studios were developed by series production designer Joel Collins and co-designer Byron Broadbent.

Opposite bottom: The puppeteers operating Waldo during a live animation sequence.

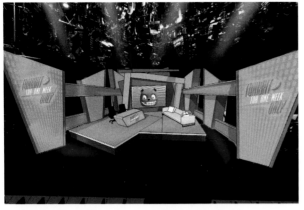

and there might have been children around. So we started having these conversations: "But it's just a blue animated knob – does that count?"

Barney Reisz (producer): We erred on the side of caution and spared the good people of High Wycombe the spectacle of Waldo's full glory.

Charlie Brooker: I now feel like I've been way too down on this episode! Any issues that I think are there exist purely at script level. Everyone else did a really good job, and there are a lot of very powerful moments. The whole *Question Time* panel scene is really strong, where Liam Monroe, played by Tobias Menzies, has done some research and he turns the tables on Jamie.

Annabel Jones: Again, we tried not to demonise politicians or make them one-dimensional. Liam Monroe knows he's the Tory on this panel and not there to be loved, but there is a conviction in him when he asks what Waldo actually has to offer.

Charlie Brooker: What is it with me and writing reasonable Tories? What's going on? Because, tribally, I fucking hate them. But then, oddly, I try and avoid that if I'm writing.

There was a moment we cut out, where Monroe's in the back of the car. He looks out, sees a Waldo poster and says, "He's making the whole system look absurd. Which it may well be, but it built these roads." And then in the script, the car immediately goes over a pot hole. Which was a nice little moment. It only got cut because it didn't visually come across like the car was going over a pothole. It just looked like a mistake, as if the camera had wobbled.

'If you were preaching revolution, well that'd be something. But you're not because that would require courage and a mindset. And what have you got? Who are you? What are you for?'

– Gwendolyn

Bryn Higgins: *Black Mirror* films are ideas-led and satirical, but the ones that work particularly well bring proper human emotions in. We certainly tried to get as much emotion as we could into Jamie and Gwendolyn's relationship, but it's a crowded story when you've got 45 minutes.

One of the main things I like about *The Waldo Moment*, though, is the energy. It makes its move towards a total dystopian future pretty quickly. It would've been great to have had a little more space to explore that, and see more of the emotional, human fallout from Waldo's actions, which was the destruction of a very promising young female politician.

Jodie Foster (director, Arkangel): I especially love *The Waldo Moment*! It's an amazing combination of satire and all of our sociological fears that seem to have come true. I do feel like Charlie has some kind of Spidey sense about what's about to happen. *Black Mirror* has so many things he couldn't possibly have known about. *The Waldo Moment* really speaks to where we are right now in politics.

Annabel Jones: I do think *The Waldo Moment* has had much more impact, post Trump.

Charlie Brooker: Yeah. When people stumble across it now, they're quite frightened. It's very prophetic, in a way that probably none of us thought at the time. Maybe I could just go back and tinker with it. Get the cast back in and add Jamie's line, "But I can't go and stand in that town, because that's where my ex-girlfriend is running for election!" Shall we schedule that? I mean, George Lucas did it.

THE CHRISTMAS SPECIAL

In Conversation

Charlie Brooker – executive producer
Annabel Jones – executive producer
Shane Allen – then Channel 4's Head of Comedy

Charlie Brooker: Again, I think the second series went well. *Be Right Back* was nominated for a BAFTA and *Black Mirror* was now going out in 80 territories.

Annabel Jones: You sort of go, "Oh! We thought these were small, parochial, very British stories. Who'd have thought other countries in the world have technology?"

Charlie Brooker: Or pigs.

Annabel Jones: Or pigs. So we began to realise that *Black Mirror* was filling a gap. There weren't many anthology shows out there, and certainly not shows that were dramatising these sorts of things. There was an appetite for it, and so we felt quite buoyed by that.

Shane Allen (then Channel 4's Head of Comedy): Unfortunately, as happens often in TV, musical chairs at Channel 4 had resulted in a new element in the creative process. Someone had flipped their nut over the budget, which was far and away above what comedy tariffs were set at, and then, to my horror, started to become involved on the editorial front.

I had to keep all this away from Annabel and Charlie as much as I could, so they could get on with making *Black Mirror* with as much creative freedom as they'd always enjoyed, whilst I made my exit plans. I have such mixed feelings about the whole thing: seeing this amazing show come to life was one of the most exciting creative experiences, but there was much to contend with on a daily basis.

Annabel Jones: Shane is now Controller of Comedy Commissioning at the BBC, and probably has the best record of supporting talent in UK TV. If you look at the companies he's worked with, and the people he's helped realise shows, he's impeccable. There was a matter of trust with Shane, based on a long-standing relationship, his instinct and his general ballsiness! Whereas I think people who don't know you as well maybe don't have that same trust, understandably.

Charlie Brooker: We were then still coming through Channel 4's comedy department, and because we were an expensive show, there was a question of whether we should've been under the drama budget. So there was a growing danger that we might become homeless.

Annabel Jones: Any show needs its champion at a broadcaster. When Shane left, the incoming Head of Comedy didn't have a relationship with us. It wasn't his show, he'd inherited it but it was taking up a huge chunk of his budget and stopping him commissioning the shows that he should have been making.

Charlie Brooker: Also, he probably wondered why he was suddenly having to give notes on a drama series. You wouldn't expect the head of drama to be giving notes on a comedy.

Very soon after the second series went out, we had a meeting with Channel 4, who said they wanted to make more *Black Mirror*. My memory is that we agreed to do four more episodes. But this time, they wanted to see detailed synopses for each film in advance. Which I found somewhat outrageous at the time! But we went off, came up with some ideas, and wrote them out. One of them was called *Crocodile*: a very different *Crocodile* to what we ended up with in Season Four, but there was some degree of overlap.

Another of the stories was a bit *Men Against Fire*, which would end up in Season Three. Very different, but with similar elements, like another evolution of that early war script *Inbound*. Then there was a story that ended up as part of *White Christmas*, the dating one. *Angel of the Morning*, it was called. Anyway, the upshot was that we handed these stories into Channel 4. And then we waited.

Then we were just waiting for a long time. When the feedback finally came, they thought these ideas weren't very *Black Mirror*.

Annabel Jones: We were trying to get a meeting to discuss why these weren't *Black Mirror*, so we could attempt to understand what the concern was, to see what we could do.

Charlie Brooker: But it turned out that they just didn't want these ideas – and were no longer going to allocate the money for four episodes. I think, at one point, they mooted the idea of doing a special, but Annabel and I felt this wasn't great. I was supposed to just go off and come up with another load of ideas? That didn't inspire much confidence.

Annabel Jones: We'd been in the industry long enough to know that some shows work and some shows don't. It's always an uncomfortable conversation, but either you're decommissioned or you're commissioned. And given that the show had won lots of awards and had been really positively received on the whole, it was strange. I think we felt there wasn't any clarity from the channel. We also felt un-championed.

Charlie Brooker: We went off and spent a year making some other TV things like *A Touch of Cloth*, and I did more *10 O'Clock Live*. But in terms of *Black Mirror*, we didn't know what to do. It was all left a bit open, and Channel 4 had shown so little enthusiasm that we thought we should focus on stuff that we thought might actually happen.

And then I bumped into someone at Channel 4, who said something like, "We miss *Black Mirror.*" So I emailed them and asked how we could make this happen.

Annabel Jones: They had the budget left for one hour. And we were like, "Well, is that a Christmas special, if it's the same length as a normal episode? Could we possibly get 90 minutes?" We told them we were feeling slightly unloved here. Could we get another half hour, just so it felt as if we were giving something different – an extra bit of running time that allowed us to adopt the portmanteau format?

Charlie Brooker: We wanted to do three stories in one. Weirdly, three stories feels like a full meal. You can't really do a portmanteau with two stories. So you go, "I've got these ideas. They're not a full episode, but they seem like they could be linked." Also, I like portmanteau things like [the 1983 film] *Twilight Zone: The Movie.* Portmanteau horror films always have three or four stories in them, and it just felt like you hadn't seen one of those in a long time. It felt fitting, and so did doing it at Christmas.

Annabel Jones: It took some back and forth, but we got commissioned. And then the festive fun began.

WHITE
CHRISTMAS

In Conversation

Carl Tibbets – director
Annabel Jones – executive producer
Charlie Brooker – writer and executive producer
Joel Collins – series production designer
Robyn Paiba – co-production designer
Shaheen Baig – casting director
Barney Reisz – producer
Jon Hamm – actor
Sharon Gilham – costume designer
Jon Opstad – composer

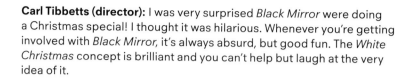

Joe Potter and Matt Trent have spent five years working together in a small Arctic outpost, and yet remain virtual strangers. On Christmas Day, Trent seizes the opportunity to get to know Potter. Over dinner, they exchange stories of date-coaching gone tragically wrong, the existential horror that lurks behind 'smart houses' and, finally, the terrible series of past events that Potter has tried so hard to forget.

Carl Tibbetts (director): I was very surprised *Black Mirror* were doing a Christmas special! I thought it was hilarious. Whenever you're getting involved with *Black Mirror*, it's always absurd, but good fun. The *White Christmas* concept is brilliant and you can't help but laugh at the very idea of it.

Annabel Jones: It was great that Carl, who'd done such a good job on *White Bear*, came back to do *White Christmas*. He can do brutal. He's not afraid of embracing the horror, but he's a very sensitive guy.

Carl Tibbetts: I came on board with a treatment that became more and more fleshed out, and eventually turned into the episode. They had four or five concepts that weren't fully formed episodes. We talked about portmanteaus and the early classic British horror movies like 1945's *Dead of Night*, which became an influence on *White Christmas*. We wanted to do our own portmanteau: several stories that spun off a central conceit.

Charlie Brooker: The Christmas aspect makes it a little more emotive and nightmarish. Christmas isn't really central, but we set one of the stories at a Christmas work party, and we keep referring to Christmas, and there's the snow.

    White Christmas is structured like a series, with three separate stories at the same time. Some of the ideas had been developed for this potential third series that hadn't quite materialised. And then the process of weaving those ideas together suggested the overall structure of it. Originally it was set on a spaceship, but not for very long.

    What we do is set up two different technologies, then use them both at the end. So we set up the stuff to do with the Z-Eyes device, which lets the user stream live video and block people. Then it brings up the cookie concept, of your consciousness copied into an egg.

    This film was the first time we chose to start reusing gadgets we'd used before. At one point, we tried to reinvent the interface device and went through different variants, but no matter what we did it wasn't as good as the gizmo we had in *The Entire History of You*, so we decided to just use that. And doing that slightly opened the door to us dropping in Easter eggs, these references to other episodes. I probably thought that *White Christmas* might have been the last one we ever did, so I thought, "Fuck it, might as well."

Annabel Jones: We were very keen for the individual films to feel they were building towards something, unlike a few portmanteaus with discrete stories that don't really pay off. I always feel slightly cheated by a portmanteau where there's no real link. So we worked hard at making sure that there was a build, that they tied in, that they came together and that it made sense of the whole world. I think there was really good craftsmanship in that film.

Joel Collins (series production designer): A *Black Mirror* Christmas special felt so ironic that there was talk of calling it *Black Christmas*! It was like giving someone a dark festive treat. We tried to design an environment where it was a London, but a new-ish London, a bit ahead in the future, because the technology was a bit beyond. It was a very complex thing to

do, and again, sometimes showing less is more important than showing more. At one point, we thought everyone could be living in boats so we'd never see any cars. But without much financial scope, the best thing to do was reduce it to a much simpler form and just work with the story.

Charlie Brooker: At no point did Annabel or I think that they would be living on boats.

Robyn Paiba (co-production designer): The challenges were not only the timescale and creativity, but geographical. In one week we were prepping and shooting in the four furthest corners of London. The set was built in Twickenham, which was also the starting point as a base for the third and fourth series.

The two lead actors for White Christmas' *were* The Big Short's *Rafe Spall as Potter and* Mad Men's *Jon Hamm as Trent.*

Shaheen Baig (casting director): During our first series especially, actors' agents hadn't understood what the show was yet, so sometimes I had to battle to explain what we were trying to do. But because the quality of the scripts was so great, people wanted to do it.

Barney Reisz (producer): But by now, people were ringing Shaheen up, practically offering to do it for nothing! Big names like Jon Hamm made it public that they wanted to be in *Black Mirror*.

Charlie Brooker: In the first draft, before Jon came along, Trent was a cheeky cockney. He was more of a Jack the Lad, a chirpy bloke to contrast with Potter. And then fortuitously, around mid-2014, Jon Hamm had seen *Black Mirror*, and was in London, and we got word that he would like to meet up. So we said, "No of course not. Not that physically repugnant idiot!"

Annabel Jones: We went out for dinner with Jon and he talked about how much he loved the show.

Charlie Brooker: And obviously, Annabel was being sick because Jon was so ugly.

Annabel Jones: This matinee idol is sitting in front of you, speaking intelligently, and I began to realise what it must be like to be a beautiful woman where a man is looking at you, but not really listening to a word you say. Anyway ... too much information. Distractingly handsome. But we didn't mention the *White Christmas* script.

Jon Hamm (actor): What I remember most about that evening was how genuinely pleasant everyone was. Very enjoyable drinks turned into dinner, and I had the nicest time just talking about stuff. I wasn't auditioning – or at least I didn't *think* I was!

Charlie Brooker: I started thinking about whether this Jack-the-lad version of Trent could translate into Jon.

'Try to blow on my face. You can't, because you don't have a body. Where are your fingers? Your arms, your face? Nowhere'

– Matt

Annabel Jones: And we were like, "Do you think Jon really wants to do it? Will we offend him by asking him?" So fucking British. Anyway we offered him the role of Trent.

Charlie Brooker: So I sent Jon a PDF of the script, went to sleep, then when I woke up he'd replied, saying that he loved it and wanted to do it. I was really groggy and looked at his email, thinking, "Fucking hell! That's a stroke of luck."

Jon Hamm: I loved the whole of that script: especially the tone, which was so right on the border of thriller, horror and sci-fi, etc. Such an exciting place to be. [The American comedian and actor] Bill Hader had originally told me about *Black Mirror* when we went to see a friend's movie. I went home, watched *The National Anthem* and was immediately hooked.

Barney Reisz: Jon is a huge star, but the sweetest and most charming man. He also has a history of doing things that he fancies. He's his own man.

Shaheen Baig: Casting Jon was one of the easiest American deals I've ever done. Normally you speak to 25 lawyers and it goes on for weeks.

Annabel Jones: It worked nicely, the idea of Jon being this Californian dating expert. This handsome man, telling these young dweeby guys how to pull.

Charlie Brooker: Jon is just incredibly hypnotic, and not just because he's good looking. You want to know what's going on in his head, because he looks like he's thinking all the time. He's really good at being sinister and charming in equal measure at the same time. He's also got good comic instincts, so he knows when to hit a note.

Jon Hamm: Mostly I wanted Trent to be a likeable, affable guy … that does these truly heinous things. I think that juxtaposition is what makes his comeuppance extra salty.

Charlie Brooker: In the original script, Trent was deliberately a little grating. Oddly, it remained in the script that he makes a terrible Christmas dinner, but you don't really notice because Jon is so charming. He's got a magnetism and this sort of sinister charming glint to him throughout.

Annabel Jones: Trent's manipulation works well against Potter, who's very convincing in that taciturn, reserved way …

Charlie Brooker: … and who then has to explode later on and be vulnerable.

Carl Tibbetts: It's the classic odd couple, isn't it? It was perfectly cast, in terms of how they're so different. You probably wouldn't have put Jon Hamm and Rafe Spall together, but Rafe plays Potter so well – he bears the weight of that thing he's holding in. And Jon Hamm is playing this flamboyant, sleazy salesman, but it's infectious because they're both charismatic actors who you can't help watching.

Charlie Brooker: We were shooting around October, at the point where the weather turned, and everyone started getting bugs. Vomiting bugs went around, which terrify me. Jon and Rafe both had really bad, heavy colds throughout filming.

Jon Hamm: Rafe and I got on like a house on fire. I really enjoyed working with him and getting to know his family. The experience of working together was not unlike being stuck in a cabin, as that one set in Twickenham was where we shot all of our things – and obviously we were the only actors in those scenes. It was very much like doing a cool one-act play. I had a fantastic time, despite being under the weather. Working on something as rich and different as *Black Mirror*, and with such talent, tends to heal all for me.

Carl Tibbetts: Rafe had the hard work. I won't say Jon had an easy time, but Rafe certainly had the headspace to get into. He had to get into a certain place, which was challenging for him. Jon's the consummate professional: great to work with, so generous. They were different from each other, but in good ways.

Charlie Brooker: I don't know quite how actors prepare, but it must be really hard to think, "My character is basically a bit of code." Both characters are actually copies of themselves in a simulation, but only Jon's character knows this. So Rafe has to play someone who can't remember exactly why they're there – and his character hardly says anything for ages. A lot of actors would flip through that script, going, "When does my character

Above: The kitchen set of the cottage, actually filmed in South West London.

fucking speak?" But you don't notice Potter's not really talking, because he's giving you so much.

Annabel Jones: You know Potter's withholding, you know there's a secret, and you know that he's troubled. And he knows that Trent is trying to manipulate him, so he's on his guard.

Charlie Brooker: It's a really difficult thing to have pulled off. You get the sense that Potter doesn't trust Trent, but he doesn't know why. He's openly disdainful: a little bit off with Trent from the start.

Annabel Jones: And yet Potter also can see the environment shifting and changing and he's aware that he's not really in control. So he is terrified.

Joel Collins: A lot goes on in that cabin, but you have to look quite carefully to see. As we go through the three stories and keep coming back to Potter and Trent, so many details change. It slowly turns into the house where Potter commits the murder, but you have to keep your wits about you.

Charlie Brooker: For instance, Potter notices the novelty bird clock on the wall. I literally once had to stay in a B&B which had that fucking clock, making bird noises and stuff.

'It's a job, not a jail'
– Joe

Carl Tibbetts: The cooker changes behind them and the work surfaces change. The fireplace changes, just slowly as it's getting closer and closer to Potter's confession. Every time we go back to them, the background is changing slightly as we flipped the set out.

Robyn Paiba: There was a strong element of back-engineering the design, so that the cabin could be turned into the kitchen for the reveal at the end.

Charlie Brooker: I wasn't sure people would notice it, and you *don't* notice exactly! You pick up on it without noticing, as it creeps up on you.

Also, things happen where you go, "What the fuck was that?" and then we distract you again. At the dinner table, Potter hears a noise and turns around and it's actually the noise of his cell sliding shut. It's the sound of somebody checking on him.

Carl Tibbetts: Originally, we were going to see the exterior of the cabin as a snowy base in the middle of nowhere. But I didn't want to see the exterior, because I thought we should stay with Potter. So with that opening shot, we stayed on Potter for a while until he turns the radio off and then that's the first time we see Trent. The idea was to know whose story this was and adopt a point of view. We didn't want to see Trent before Potter sees him. So we were experiencing Trent through Potter's eyes, because we're in a version of Potter's head.

Sharon Gilham (costume designer): The cabin location was a slightly timeless look at outback living. It could be contemporary or it could be 100 years ago. Trent's costume was designed to look a bit too squeaky clean for the environment, like he just took it out of a packet, while Potter's was more used and worn.

In the first of White Christmas' *three stories, we learn that Trent was once a dating coach, until the night he helped geeky Harry (Rasmus Hardiker) bed the enigmatic Jennifer (Natalia Tena), only for her to fatally poison him.*

Charlie Brooker: Really the first story stemmed from an observation that literally everyone in the world had, when Bluetooth headsets first became a 'thing'. Walking down the street, you'd pass someone who seemed to be talking out loud to themselves, as if they had a mental illness, whereas they were actually conducting a hands-free call. It took a while to get used to. And I thought, "Could we do a story about someone with literal voices in their head encountering someone with delusional voices in their head"? The whole murder-suicide thing is quite a melodramatic twist for *Black Mirror*, but we wanted *White Christmas* to have a touch of Stephen King about it. You get away with that stuff in a portmanteau, in a way you wouldn't in a standalone episode.

The story about the man on the horse came from me reading about the bullshit ice-breakers that pick-up artists come out with. Actually, within the episode, it works when Jon Hamm says it to someone, because he's Jon Hamm, but when Harry does it at the office party he's a bit less successful. I think if you went up to somebody and said that horse story, they'd go "Have you been reading these pick-up artist websites? Fuck off."

Carl Tibbetts: The three stories had to stand alone, but there also had to be some kind of overarching identity for the whole piece. Jon Hamm and Rafe Spall's characters gave us that, but also if you look at the colour palettes and the costumes, they're all a nod to each other. When you've got these separate stories, you don't want them to spin away from each other too much, so that they feel like a different show. There was definite style and design cohesion in there.

Sharon Gilham: In the same way Charlie's writing presents a world we know is ours but with a slightly exaggerated truth, I wanted the costumes to feel familiar, yet strange. For the first story, I used monochrome tones and small details, like the shape of the men's collars – rounded rather than pointed – to move them to their own world. Jennifer's dress was specially made in navy leather and mesh, signposting her as a dominatrix reeling Harry in.

Jon Opstad (composer): I wanted to give each of these three stories a different character musically, but in a way that still gave the score a sense of wholeness and unity. The music of this first story has a lopsided weirdness to it, shifting into outright horror once the two characters are back at Jennifer's flat and Harry's being drugged.

Sharon Gilham: Trent's costumes across these stories were designed to show him as a sleek, fast living, fast talking manipulator of other people's lives, effortlessly slipping in and out of situations like an upmarket door-to-door salesman.

Carl Tibbetts: It was a challenge to get the point-of-view shots right. Trent's live feed was technically challenging, and for Jon Hamm too. I'm one of his perverts on Trent's side-screen, by the way: I'm Popcorn! People always commented how I did it so well. I was like, "What do you mean by that?"

The second story sees Greta (Oona Chaplin) sign up to have a digital copy of herself surgically extracted from her brain and tasked with running the minutiae of her home system. Greta's new digital incarnation is appalled when Trent outlines her new existence.

Charlie Brooker: This whole story is basically just someone arguing that they exist!

Annabel Jones: It started as quite a comic idea: you just want your toast exactly the way you want it, so we'll put your digital consciousness into a toaster. It's a crazy idea, but when you see it, it's harrowing. Oona is trapped in there, just so you can have toast the way you like it!

Charlie Brooker: An idea had been knocking around for a while: what if you put a consciousness into a toaster, and it falls in love with you? I couldn't work out what the story was, until I realised it wasn't a love story at all but a fucking nightmare. In one draft, Oona's character Greta had kids. She saw her own kid playing with the real her, and she immediately realised that she would never hug her own children again. And she fucking wept, and so I cut it out completely, because it was just too weird and nasty.

Annabel Jones: But we kept it for *Black Museum* in Season Four, where it's more poignant.

Carl Tibbetts: For me, this story was the most disturbing. It established the concept of what was really happening to Potter in the cabin, while being a standalone story. I always liked the idea that, when you heard this voice in Greta's head, you thought it was her. But actually it was this chip, and then they remove that chip in the surgery room, and the chip sees itself in the reflection! It sees itself leaving the body. That felt like another crucial decision when it came to establishing point of view, because it was about establishing that concept of 'removal of self'. Or a version of self.

Barney Reisz: Oona was another great example of late casting – I think we cast her literally two days before. She was in Los Angeles, so got on a flight to London. She was brilliant, but totally knackered.

Carl Tibbetts: Because Oona's first scenes involved lying down a lot on an operating table, she fell asleep due to jet lag.

Sharon Gilham: Greta lives in a world of clean lines and expensive gadgets. She aspires to live a zen-like existence and so I put her in a kimono-like robe in her house. The virtual Greta's costume was made of neoprene, a fabric that is used to make diving suits – a man-made, robust, practical substance that fits perfectly into the world that has been created for her.

Jon Opstad: For this second story, I wanted to give the music a crisp, clean, sterile nature to fit the narrative. I used digital synths, contrasting with the more analogue sounds used in the rest of the score.

In the third and final story, Potter confesses how he argued with his pregnant girlfriend Beth (Janet Montgomery), leading her to 'block' him. His subsequent discovery of her affair then led him to kill Beth's father.

Charlie Brooker: The blocking storyline was a classic example of a humorous 'what if' discussion in the office turning into a story. Years earlier, 2001 or so, I'd done a thing for *Unnovations* – a *TV Go Home* spin-off, full of ludicrous inventions – with a pair of high-tech glasses that turned homeless people into cartoon characters, so you could selfishly walk from one artisan coffee shop to the next without getting depressed by social inequality. With the advent of stuff like Google Glass and augmented reality in general, that sort of tech looked closer to reality. We were chatting about the idea and it fused with a discussion of the practice of 'blocking' people on social media. And bingo: we had Potter's story.

Jon Opstad: The third chapter is more emotional, veering from romance to tragedy, and so the music needed to help support this wider emotional range. I added solo viola to the palette for this chapter, to bring a more human emotional quality to the music, which I then processed heavily to fit with the electronic nature of the score. As well as the different instruments there are also different themes developed in each, so in a way it's like an individual score for each of the three stories, but it all fits together.

At the end of White Christmas, *Potter admits that he also accidentally caused the death of Beth's daughter. When Trent celebrates having extracted Potter's confession and disappears, Potter finds himself alone in the virtual cottage, effectively doomed to stay there for eternity.*

Charlie Brooker: I do seem fond of eternal horrendous torments, which is a bit of a problem, because I've got some other eternal horrendous torment ideas that I feel like I can't do! I loved the short 1981 Stephen King story *The Jaunt*, about this new teleport system that takes people from Earth to Mars. It works instantaneously, just as long as you don't open your eyes. Because if you open your eyes, you experience infinity. It's blood-curdling, and such a horrifying concept.

I don't think I'd ever seen [the 1979–1982 British sci-fi/fantasy series] *Sapphire & Steel* as a child – it struck me as too weird and creepy. But by chance, I later saw the last ever episode. My memory of it is that they're walking around a motorway service station or a roadside cafe in the 1950s. Some kind of time anomaly has happened and they realise they're going to be there forever. There's something about the horrific mundanity of being stuck in one place, so you can draw a direct line – whether you call it inspiration or downright copying – from that to *White Christmas*' notion of being stuck in one room for millions of years. It was so horrifying, that the only thing that could make that more so to me, would be having one piece of music playing over and over on a radio.

Quite often, I'll come up with a nasty ending, then wonder what makes it nastier. Okay, so the child's corpse is always there, outside the window. And then Wizzard's [1973 hit] *I Wish It Could Be Christmas Every Day* is playing and Potter can't switch it off, and we deliberately crank the music each time until it's cacophonous. Oh, and we've got that time-thing we set up earlier, so he'll be there for millions and millions of years.

Carl Tibbetts: Once again, like *White Bear*, it's crime and punishment. It's about what's criminal and what's not. Potter's an unfortunate man who did something wrong, but how they extracted the truth out of him. You can torture things that aren't people, but when do they become people?

Charlie Brooker: We get very involved in the edit, and I love that process, because you can keep changing and massaging things. You can alter the course of the story and the tone so hugely. That's why I'd find it really fucking hard, now, to write a movie script, then hand it over and go, "Bye everyone!" It'd drive me mad, because I'd feel that what I'd get back would be a random series of images and sounds.

On *Black Mirror*, you go through the whole birth process, seeing all the rough cuts, and seeing it again and again. And then finally you're in the dub, in a big sound studio watching it on a big screen, in 5.1 Surround Sound at cinema volume. Before watching the endings of *White Bear* and *White Christmas*, I'd lost sight of how horrifying they were, but then when you finally saw them with everything polished, you thought, "Fuck me, that's so nasty." *White Christmas* is so powerful when all the bells and whistles are going.

Barney Reisz: I never want to hear that Wizzard song again, but that's why it was the best choice. It was supposed to be complete madness by the end, and I think we achieved that.

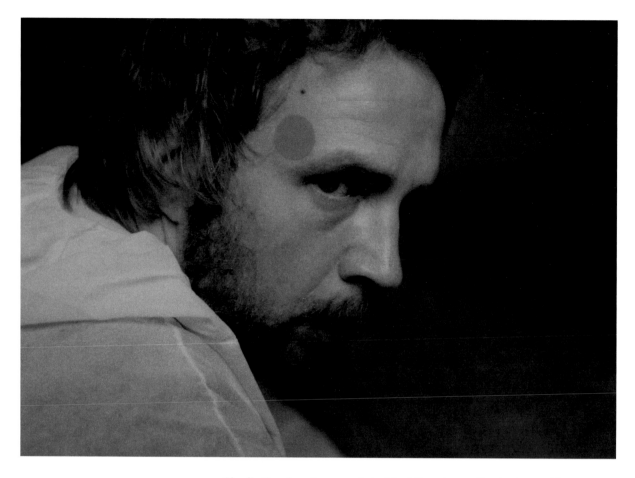

Charlie Brooker: It was scripted that there's a radio playing and Potter smashes it, and then he turns around and the radio's come back. That was done in-camera, which was someone's idea on the day. We only had a limited number of those radios he could smash, too. The camera follows him around, and then somebody just out of shot puts another radio there. I think there was another take where you just see the hand, and you're like, "Oh fuck!" There was something else we ultimately cut out, where he smashes the snow globe against the wall, only for that to come back as well. In the edit, we decided we didn't need that and we'd just use the radio.

And then, while we were filming, I suddenly had the notion of constantly pulling out of the snow globe at the end.

Carl Tibbetts: We wanted to sell the horrific, cyclical nature of Potter's punishment. The torture of it. I remember us all thinking, "Wow, wouldn't it be brilliant if we could do that?" And we did, but it wasn't an easy shot. It was a combination of VFX and camera trick.

Charlie Brooker: We probably used the poor man's method because we didn't have motion control cameras and stuff. It was literally patched together from lots of different takes.

A lot of people ask why Potter deserved such torment. In a way, he did and he didn't. He's basically in a hell – quite a lot of hell goes on in our stories – which is of his own accidental making. Part of the horror is that, to the police, this is a very abstract thing going on inside a device. For no real reason, the guy cranks it up to 1000 years a minute, just because why not? It's a bit like deliberately running over a pedestrian in Grand Theft Auto.

Potter loses our sympathy pretty early on in that third story, I think. We hint at him having a drink problem several times throughout the story, and we see him being obnoxious while Beth is trying to sing karaoke — that's the point at which we realise he's an unreliable narrator, as is Trent. Originally there was also a quick scene where Potter's throwing up outside the bar while Beth struggles to get him into a cab, but we ended up not shooting it because of time constraints. I think it's clear that his rosy description of the relationship doesn't tally with the reality. Beth is somewhat afraid of him. He's possessive and has an explosive temper. She's not a saint herself it turns out, but for my money he's the root cause of the problems between them. Whether he deserves eternal damnation is a different matter. It just amused me greatly as an endless box of torment.

People also ask whether Trent deserves to get blocked by all of society. First of all, we're saying this is quite obviously a very punitive society that we've created here. There's even a visual nod to *White Bear*: a lot of the police things have little *White Bear* symbols on them. There's one on Potter's cell door, when they look through and see the real him. So there's this vague back story of a future dystopian Britain. But also Trent's been filming people without their knowledge and doing lots of other stuff.

Annabel Jones: "Lots of other stuff"?! Trent witnessed a young man being poisoned to death and abandoned him! Even Jon Hamm can't get away with that.

Charlie Brooker: Trent's really nasty, but because he's charming, that must be why people find it quite harsh. Trent's punishment is surely not far off, though: a bit like someone with a conviction on their record, which you'd see if you were Googling them to employ them. So it's a hellish representation of that going on in real time.

Jon Hamm: I'm a big believer in redemption and forgiveness, so I think Trent should be punished, but also be able to access a path of redemption. *White Christmas 2*, anyone?

Charlie Brooker: I do remember being very worried that *White Christmas* would be disjointed. I remember going, "But it's not about anything!" And (a) like that matters; and (b) it is about something. There's a lot of stuff covered in there, like punishment, and whether AI is a form of life. It's also about two quite flawed men and Facebook stalking. So there's actually loads going on: I don't know why I thought it wasn't about anything. Also, karaoke gets covered.

Annabel Jones: Do you remember what happened on the day of the *White Christmas* press screening?

Charlie Brooker: I do remember! So, shall we say? Okay then ...

SERIES THREE

In Conversation

Charlie Brooker – executive producer
Annabel Jones – executive producer
Cindy Holland – Vice President of Original Content, Netflix
Lucy Dyke – producer
Joel Collins – series production designer
Jina Jay – series casting director
Peter Friedlander – Vice President of Original Series, Netflix

Charlie Brooker: The run-up to Christmas 2014 was a horrible, horrible time. My dad was quite ill and I was supposed to be doing my end-of-year *Wipe* show for BBC Two, but that kept getting delayed because we were still in the edit on *White Christmas*. It was a nightmare.

We literally worked on *White Christmas* up until the day of its press screening at the Channel 4 building. In fact, I think one FX shot was still missing. But we got to the end, and we thought it was strong and that Channel 4 would be happy. And then, right before the press screening, we had a meeting with the channel, which we assumed would be about making more *Black Mirror* episodes.

Annabel Jones: We also probably expected a pat on the back, because we'd just delivered *White Christmas* that very morning, there was a press screening happening in an hour and we had Jon Hamm at this event, giving his all to the press.

Charlie Brooker: Now, I'm not good at knowing how meetings are going. I can't quite read the chess moves, when someone says one thing but actually means something else. It's like I can't hear it. Also, I'm too busy jabbering.

Annabel Jones: Not jabbering. You're performing a little bit, in terms of ...

Charlie Brooker: Like a little monkey in a waistcoat, doing a dance? That's what you think I am, isn't it: a chimp in a fucking waistcoat with a little fez.

Annabel Jones: I wish you were that articulate. Anyway, for that whole year, we hadn't been able to get a meeting with Channel 4 about a third series ...

Charlie Brooker: ... and in this meeting, they said they'd like more *Black Mirror,* but anthologies are expensive, so it would have to be a co-production. So that felt deflating.

Annabel Jones: Channel 4 already knew that, at their request, we'd been to LA a few months earlier to try and secure co-production money, but had failed.

Charlie Brooker: And then they said, "But here's what we *are* doing ... "

Annabel Jones: Big news!

Charlie Brooker: They told us they were working with Bryan Cranston on this anthology show called *Electric Dreams*, adapting Philip K. Dick stories.

Maybe, they suggested, I could write one of those? And I thought, "I'm not good at gauging what's going on in meetings, but I'm feeling angry. Am I wrong? Am I misreading what's going on here? Is this insulting?" They'd just told me they couldn't afford to do our show, but what they *were* doing sounded conceptually similar.

I couldn't believe it. I remember coming out of there, looking at Annabel and she was furious. And upset.

Annabel Jones: I don't often show when I'm upset, but there were actual tears from me. They'd just basically told Charlie his show was going to be cancelled, an hour before he went out to do a big press meeting. And they were replacing it with another sci-fi anthology show that looked to us like it was more expensive to produce, with more episodes and probably filming overseas.

Charlie Brooker: I was shell-shocked as we went downstairs. Jon Hamm, Rafe Spall and our director Carl Tibbetts were there, and [the journalist] Andrew Collins was going to do an onstage Q&A with us. So I'm standing there and everyone's in a good mood. It's Christmas, there's champagne and mince pies, and we're about to have the screening for this thing that everyone's happy about.

I went straight into the end-of-year *Wipe* show for the BBC, immersing myself in the edit. The *Black Mirror* situation was all very depressing. We'd had a really good thing going there, making these little mini movies with a lot of creative freedom, and we were doing quite well. And now we'd stumbled and stopped. We were absolutely convinced that this was the end of *Black Mirror*.

Annabel Jones: But then, before Christmas, everything changed. The first two series of *Black Mirror* went up on Netflix in the US and the show caught fire. Everyone was talking about it. We were being contacted by all the networks. Suddenly there was going to be a bidding war.

Charlie Brooker: By January 2015, we were in a good position. Now it was like, "Which American network do we go with?" And this seemed to solve the problem with Channel 4, because they wanted us to find someone like HBO or AMC or Netflix to help fund *Black Mirror*. But that was when stage two of the Channel 4 discussions began.

Annabel Jones: Netflix were showing *Black Mirror* and it had gone huge for them. So they led the bidding war, offering us a commitment of two seasons, each with 10 episodes. They said, "You're green-lit; don't present us with any ideas, just start."

Charlie Brooker: They basically told us just to carry on doing what we were doing.

Annabel Jones: That is unheard of, in the UK or the US. If you make a two-season commitment to a drama series that is a big, big deal, but you know what you're committing to, because you've got continuous characters and a story arc. To commission essentially what could be about 20 films, off nothing, is nuts!

So we both recognised what a huge turning point this was. With Channel 4 being the original commissioner, they had to be involved because they took the financial risk in making the show. Which was perfect for us, because then it meant we'd keep Channel 4, our *Black Mirror* DNA. We thought Channel 4 would be delighted because we thought we'd delivered the money that they'd said they needed. Netflix respected that Channel 4 were the original commissioners, seemed happy to be equal creative partners with them. It was a very grown-up approach. Because Netflix were so keen to get the show, I think they would have done anything to find that marriage.

Cindy Holland (Vice President of Original Content, Netflix): There's simply nothing like *Black Mirror* on television anywhere in the world. It really stands alone in its creative approach, its voice, the look and feel and the format – it's utterly inventive, groundbreaking and moving. We were huge fans of what Charlie and Annabel had done. We also had Seasons One and Two on Netflix and saw how the audience responded.

Annabel Jones: For whatever reason we could not seem to get Channel 4 to engage with the idea. We couldn't even get a meeting. I think it was at a time when Netflix represented a challenging future and it threatened Channel 4's streaming platform 4OD.

Charlie Brooker: It was incredibly annoying.

Annabel Jones: We now had two-season commitments from all of the big American players. Didn't matter what ideas we did, it was totally there for the taking. And the message we heard from Channel 4 was, "Well, maybe we could commit to three episodes."

When we finally got into the room with them, we didn't even get to discuss a co-production deal. I suspect Channel 4 might have been reluctant to work with Netflix but I also suspect they were nervous about our ability to deliver such a long series. Charlie and I knew it was unlikely we could go from doing three films per series to ten individual films in one year, while maintaining the quality.

Charlie Brooker: Usually when we'd done three, we'd been doing other things as well. So I realised that if I wasn't doing other things, we'd have more time and could probably do six.

Annabel Jones: I think it came down to nervousness, but no one articulated that. If they had, I'd have had more sympathy for their position. So there was some confusion at their end, I think.

Charlie Brooker: Then they said they'd do it if they could get all six worked-up treatments in advance ...

Annabel Jones: ... which is a *lot* of development work. And would mean us turning down all of the offers from the US networks because we only had a few weeks to respond to their offers. Instead, we'd have to work up all these ideas and then cross our fingers hoping that Channel 4 would like them and then green-light us ...

Charlie Brooker: ... which of course was worrying, given how they'd rejected ideas apparently outright in the past. Still, I desperately wanted it to work. I sent Channel 4's chief exec David Abraham an email, saying, "Can we please make this work?" I would have loved it if everyone was happy and *Black Mirror* could still go out on Channel 4 *and* Netflix.

Annabel Jones: Eventually, we realised this was not going to happen with Channel 4. We had to push ahead and do this deal with Netflix. So that's why it sticks in our craw when we occasionally hear people say, "Oh they took a load of Netflix money and ran away from Channel 4." You can see why, from outside, it looks like the Americans came in waving a load of dollar bills around and we all jumped. It wasn't that at all. But once again, I do have to say that if it wasn't for Jay Hunt and Channel 4, *Black Mirror* would never have existed.

So, you suddenly find yourself going from three episodes to six episodes. Suddenly your budget and your aspirations are a lot bigger and you're filming overseas. Suddenly, the operation becomes fucking huge.

Lucy Dyke (producer): I joined *Black Mirror* at the start of Season Three, when there was a lot of recalibrating to do. Laurie Borg and I were among the show's new producers, and together with Annabel we all had to work out how this new season should break down in term of budget and episodes.

There was definitely an expectation from Netflix to make it bigger and better, more international in its conception, and Charlie was already responding to this in the writing. Some of the ideas were clearly more expensive than others, but we were aware they needed to fit together as an anthology series, so we couldn't blow the budget on one particular episode and leave nothing for the rest. It's a balancing act, because you don't have consistent sets, characters, familiar locations to fall back on like you would with a linear series. So while the budgets were bigger, so were the ideas, and therefore so were the production challenges.

Joel Collins (series production designer): Moving to Netflix wasn't really a transition on any crazy level at all. In fact, it was quite remarkable – a big support network. If we wanted to go bigger, Netflix were there to help, and if we wanted to stay the same, they were equally happy. There was no obligation to do certain things. Introducing American settings to *Black Mirror* wasn't so much a mandate as it was a good idea.

Jina Jay (series casting director): Netflix brings a global audience and that feels so meaningful. I like the idea of a shared experience all around the world, and from the moment I arrived on *Black Mirror*, the show was a joy to cast. It's so liberating to work with Annabel and Charlie. When we're flushing out who is best for a role, the conflict is always constructive and my taste feels very in sync with theirs. It's a completely free and confidential space to say whatever we like with passion and commitment.

Peter Friedlander (Vice President of Original Series, Netflix): We were confident that, with Netflix's tech origins and love of tech, we could be great partners with Charlie and Annabel. We told them that we were enthusiastic to explore these powerful themes without any restrictions. We were happy for them to play with running time – as seen with the episodes *Hated in the Nation* vs *Metalhead* – to set and shoot the stories in locations around the world and other narrative innovations yet to come ... what could *Black Mirror* look like without any borders?

Charlie Brooker: *San Junipero* was a deliberate raspberry-blow to people who said we'd gone all American now. So it was quite amusing to me to go, "Right, okay, we'll set this one in California."

That was the first script I wrote for Season Three, and so it was a real relief that Netflix liked it! And while writing that, I was consciously aware that this was a departure. I did partly want to stick a flag in a new bit of territory. I thought, "If we can do this, and broaden the tone of the show, then that actually makes my job easier, because I'm not having to think of six variations on the same identical tone and theme every time."

We don't want viewers to continually wonder when the main character's iPhone is going to fuck him up, or when he'll turn out to be a child murderer!

So instead, they're wondering that five times out of six.

NOSEDIVE

In Conversation

Bryce Dallas Howard – actor

Charlie Brooker – original story writer and executive producer

Annabel Jones – executive producer

Rashida Jones – co-writer

Mike Schur – co-writer

Joe Wright – director

Joel Collins – series production designer

Laurie Borg – producer

James Foster – co-production designer

In a world where everybody's socioeconomic standing is dictated by their star-ratings given by other people, Lacie Pound is desperate to move into a luxury apartment. Having been invited to the wedding of her top-rated childhood friend Naomi, Lacie spies an opportunity to boost her own score, but her increasingly frantic cross-country trip to the wedding does not go according to plan.

Bryce Dallas Howard (actor): I went to New Zealand to shoot a film and was away from my family and friends. I told my husband I was lonely and he recommended that I watch *Fifteen Million Merits*.

Now, I really have to police what I watch. I don't know whether it's because I get so immersed while watching something, or my imagination goes wild afterwards, but I'm sensitive and can get very affected by it.

To say I had a nervous breakdown would be way too dramatic. However, I had quite a night, let me tell you! Owing to the time difference by the time the show ended, I couldn't get hold of my husband. So I sent him a series of videos of me crying, saying, "How could you do this to me? Why would you make me watch this? This is the stuff of my nightmares!" I just felt total betrayal.

In one of the videos I sent, I actually said, "I've just taken a real nosedive." So I didn't watch any more of the show. And then *Black Mirror* reached out to me to star as Lacie in their film called *Nosedive* ...

Charlie Brooker: This one started as a movie idea, yonks ago. It was substantially different but we went out to the States and had meetings with various movie companies, some time after the first season of *Black Mirror*.

This is a common experience for writers. You go out to the States, have all these really positive meetings with lots of studios, and you think, "Wow, this is the big time. I'm going to be the king of this town in a week!" And then nothing happens.

Annabel Jones: Because these Hollywood execs are worried that everyone else is having the same meeting, they have to have the meeting. And so everyone spends a lot of time telling each other that they're great. That's how it works. And by accident, some things get commissioned.

Charlie Brooker: Back then, *Nosedive* was more of an outright comedy, set in a world in which the economy was run on your personal score. It centred on a celebrity who's got a really high rating, but he's blackmailed into reducing it to zero in twenty four hours. It was like *Brewster's Millions* for reputation. He had to shred his own reputation, but there were certain rules, like he wasn't allowed to break the law. So he could walk around saying offensive things to people. And yet, the more he tried and went around being offensive, the more he become a folk hero in this Charlie Sheen meltdown sort of way, so he could never get it down to nil. If someone makes that film, they owe us some fucking money because it was our idea.

Annabel Jones: This was back before Uber, before people's rating had become a kind of currency. Before you'd get in a car with a total stranger because they've got a high four.

Charlie Brooker: Thanks to TripAdvisor and Amazon reviews, you were used to the idea of things being rated out of five, but not so much people. So then, when Season Three came along, we felt it should be more about a waitress or somebody. What if we followed somebody who's teetering on the brink of being downgraded? So that was the new starting point.

Annabel Jones: For added variety, we thought we should take an approach more like [the 1987 comedy film] *Planes, Trains and Automobiles*, where she's got to get somewhere. We'd plot her journey and have the system throw more obstacles at her.

Charlie Brooker: Originally, our main character Lacie had been invited to give a work presentation, somewhere where lots of influential people would be. At that point, we started talking to Rashida Jones and Mike Schur, because we knew it would be set in America and we wanted that authentic American voice. *Nosedive* also felt more comedic than some of the episodes. Rashida actually contacted us.

Rashida Jones (co-writer): Oh yeah, I approached them ... if by "approached" you mean "begged to be a part of it in any way".

The multi-talented Schur and Jones had plenty of experience in US TV. Mike had created Parks and Recreation, Brooklyn Nine-Nine *and Netflix's* The Good Place. *Rashida Jones co-wrote the 2012 film* Celeste and Jesse Forever *and had starred in the likes of* Parks and Recreation, The Office *and* Boston Public.

Rashida Jones: I had been a fan of *Black Mirror* and Charlie's show *Newswipe*, because some UK friends had introduced me to his work. No one quite has a brain like his: twisted, hilarious, prescient, and singular. So he and I became friendly and talked about what we could work on together. Then he and Annabel called about their first Netflix series and how they wanted to take a stab at the show's first comedic episode.

Mike Schur (co-writer): I've been friends with Rashida forever: we met in college 25 years ago. One day, when we were talking about shows the other one would like, I told her she had to watch *Black Mirror*. She then informed me that not only was she already a fan, but she had started a correspondence with Charlie and he had mentioned the possibility of her writing an episode. This is usually how it goes when you're friends with Rashida – she's eleven steps ahead of you at all times. I had just finished the final season of *Parks and Recreation*, so the timing was perfect, and we ended up just volunteering for duty.

Annabel Jones: When Rashida said Mike would like to work on *Nosedive* with her, we were like, "Okay, a comedy god? Great!"

Mike Schur: Our only goal was to try to serve the show Charlie and Annabel wanted to make. Charlie's treatment wasn't fully fleshed out, moment by moment, but the entire idea and narrative were there. It was such a clean idea: a world where the five-star rating system had gotten out of hand, and was now determining social standing and access to resources. Such a haunting and perfect *Black Mirror* idea. So perfect, that all of China is apparently now actually using it.

Above: The development work for the tech devices used throughout the film, designed by Joel Collins and co-designer James Foster, and developed by Painting Practice.

Rashida Jones: We all had several phone calls about character and plot. Mike and I pitched some new ideas and then went off to write a draft. One big shift was to make Lacie less of a mercenary game player and more

of a people-pleaser. That's a very American archetype that I can relate to – I vacillate daily between people-pleasing and misanthropy – and we thought it would help you follow her demise with empathy.

Mike Schur: A wedding seemed like a better place to have a total meltdown than the original work presentation, because Lacie yearned for social standing and snapshot perfection above all else. We also liked the idea that Lacie had a real talisman from her past with Naomi – the little doll, Mr Rags. Lacie's brother was originally a boyfriend, I believe, who broke up with her because she was too consumed with the points system.

Charlie Brooker: I remember they had an idea I was really taken with that didn't end up being used. It was the idea of rage rooms, where people go to just smash stuff up, because it's the only place they could vent any anger. It was sort of like needing to go to the toilet somewhere. So it was a funny idea, but then we realised that it just destabilised everything, because why doesn't Lacie just go into a rage room?

Annabel Jones: While *Nosedive* would end up being the first film in the Netflix running order, it was the third film we shot. Obviously we were curating the series and trying to make sure that there's range within it. We'd done *San Junipero* first, then *Shut Up and Dance*, which was obviously bleak and small and gritty and suburban. Then *Nosedive* became the big pastel, Americana, aspirational-living episode, so we could afford to be slightly heightened with it.

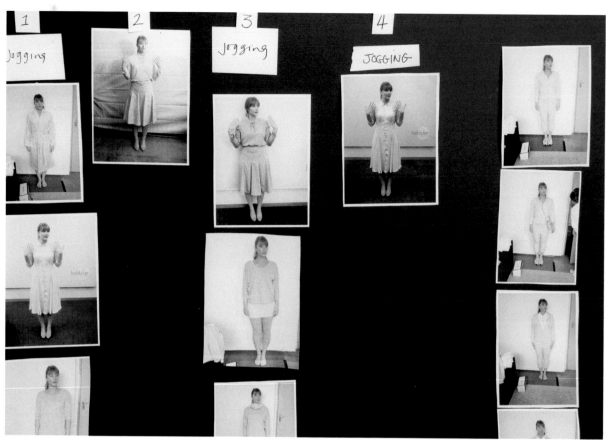

Charlie Brooker: There was a point at which *Shut Up and Dance* was set in America and *Nosedive* was potentially set in a non-specific Britain, but then they swapped around.

Annabel Jones: If you are going to live in the idealised world, it's going to be hard to sell that when it's in Hounslow. No offence, Hounslow! But, you know, when you're controlling your life to such a degree, you want the beautiful weather, you want everything to feel manicured. And that's when Joe Wright came on board.

Joe Wright is the award-winning British director of Pride & Prejudice *(2005),* Atonement *(2007) and* Darkest Hour *(2017).*

Joe Wright (director): I'd just made this film *Pan*, which had been universally slagged by the critics. The whole star-rating system can lead to you validating yourself, based on how other people think of you. And so *Nosedive* kind of spoke to me, in terms of that experience.

The only social media I've ever engaged in was Instagram. I was on that for about six months, and then realised I was becoming completely obsessed and addicted by it. Instagram was just a disgusting lie, really. I found I was judging myself based on the appearances of other people's lives and constantly comparing myself to others. I would either become vain or bitter, based on those judgements. It's a desperate, soulless endeavour that concerns me greatly.

The interesting thing about Charlie's work on *Black Mirror* is that he's completely obsessed with all the tech and high-concept stuff. It's pretty much all he talks about and it appears, on the surface, to be all he's interested in. And yet he writes these incredibly emotional, and tender, portraits of human fallibility. He seems to do that without really realising he's doing it, as if that's easy to him. So the thing that's most difficult to most people comes quite naturally to Charlie. He does it without really paying very much attention to it. Which is very odd.

Charlie Brooker: That's a very perceptive quote from Joe. I'm pretty sure I could be diagnosed as being on a spectrum somewhere, because I am quite socially awkward and obsessed with little details of things. You should see me trying to follow a recipe. If it says 450 grams, I have to measure and if it's 449 grams, I'm like, "Oh no, it's a fucking disaster." I had to be trained in how to do small talk once, because I'm so bad at it. If it's a Monday you say, "What did you get up to the weekend?" If it's Friday, you say, "Have you got any plans for the weekend?" If it's the rest of the week you're fucking lost.

I feel like I know exactly what characters are thinking emotionally when it's really clear. For example, when the stakes are life or death, or someone's child has gone missing, or they're about to see a loved one die. I find that relatively easy, because that's a strong flavour, so I can imagine what that would be like. I find it harder to work out how people would be feeling when it's less of an obvious emotional cliff edge. Maybe it's more that I'm just desperately unsubtle, but when it's something like, "How would an old lady feel about seeing a sail boat?" I have no clue.

'Naomi and I were best friends. I wish her well and I wanna express that best I can. And yeah, if I nail the speech and get 5-starred by hundreds of primes, so what, it's win-win'

– Lacie

Opposite top: Behind the scenes in the wardrobe department, keeping track of the different outfits worn by Bryce Dallas Howard's character, Lacie.

Opposite bottom: Director Joe Wright onset giving notes to Bryce Dallas Howard.

Annabel Jones: Yes Charlie is obsessed with the tech details, as increasingly am I – he's dragged me over to the dark side – but the obsession is with making the tech as backgrounded, unobtrusive and subtle as possible. Working with Gemma Kingsley, we spent a lot of time designing the *Nosedive* phone interface to ensure it was as simple and beautiful as the rest of the world. It needed to feel unassuming, like a friend you'd invite into your life. That's what makes *Black Mirror* sometimes feel so insidious. Similarly, Max [Max Richter, composer] and Joe had the idea to make the reward-sounds from the phones part of the score. So these ringtones which were driving the narrative also became very subtly and sinisterly part of the soundscape.

Charlie Brooker: A pet hate of mine is ostentatious computer interfaces in movies and TV. You know, when someone opens an email and it triggers a 30-second animation of an envelope spinning around. It'd drive you absolutely bananas in real life. It's just silly and actually bumps you out of the story, because it doesn't tally with your everyday experience of computers and so on.

I understand the impetus: it's based on a fear that screens are boring, or viewers won't understand what's happening unless icons are the size of picnic blankets. But in the real world, the successful interfaces are minimal. Apple's interface, at its best, is graceful and understated. So a frequent refrain from me when it comes to our fictional user-interface design is to strip out absolutely anything that either wouldn't be necessary or would hog processing power. Less is always, always more.

Joe Wright: There wasn't a *Nosedive* script yet, but I signed up on the basis of that synopsis, knowing that the writing would make it something really special. I'd been wanting to work with Bryce Dallas Howard for ten years. We'd met, once, and I thought she was great, but wrong for that project back then. And then I thought Bryce would be perfect for *Nosedive* so I asked her, and she signed up on the basis of this synopsis also. Getting Bryce to do that part was by far my most important choice.

Bryce Dallas Howard: When I read *Nosedive*, I had only recently joined social media. I was never on MySpace or Friendster or Facebook or anything, and then at the age of almost 35 I joined. It was the most agonising process to figure out what my profile picture should be, or what my little tagline was. I started doubting myself and worrying about it. And then I thought, "I can't get too wrapped up in this because, Jeez Louise, I'm playing Lacie! I don't wanna end up with a microphone, covered in swamp and losing my shit at a wedding."

I let myself eat what I wanted, when I wanted, to get to the point where I didn't really look like ... an 'actress'. But the real key choice I made was Lacie's laugh. It wasn't so different from my own laugh – I added 15 per cent fear, 30 per cent disingenuousness and 25 per cent depression! When you're faking laughter, it feels awful, like a nightmare. Everything else really fell into place after Lacie's laugh.

When I got to South Africa, where we shot, I pulled out one of my 'nosedive' videos to show Joe and I freaked out, because my real-life nosedive had happened exactly one year prior.

Joel Collins (series production designer): I'd found this town called Knysna on the Garden Route of South Africa. You had to fly to Cape Town, get on another plane for an hour-and-a-half, then drive for two hours. The new relationship with Netflix was exciting on that level, because I was able to find something amazing online, then get on a plane and say, "Shall we do this?" When I showed Charlie and Annabel this place they were enthusiastic. So I had to convince all the people living there to let us shoot.

Laurie Borg (producer): Whilst I was prepping *San Junipero* in Cape Town, Joel and I went to location-scout Knysna, which has a wonderful feel of an American coastal town with white clapboard houses and immaculate gardens. Think *The Truman Show*! We knew we had found our key location and, with some clever set dressing, created a perfect American world. Filming all of *Nosedive* in South Africa was a great decision for both creative and financial reasons.

Joe Wright: All these houses looked the same, so it's this really weird, homogenised little community. And that felt really appropriate for contemporary and near-future America. Especially California. I spent a bit of time travelling back and forth between Los Angeles and San Diego, and it all kinda looks the same.

Joel Collins: Joe and I recced around the island on bikes. It was hilarious. We shot there for no more than a day or two, but it set the tone for the feeling of the world that Lacie lived in.

James Foster (co-production designer): The enforced social conformity put me in mind of the 1950s, or a near future version of that at least. I saw the painted smiles on the people in old adverts for modern homes, telling you this was the way you needed to live, and to fit in. Keep up, don't fall behind. Joe was also liking certain late-1980s modern styling, reminding me of the 'upwardly mobile' and showy side of successful individualism. I really liked the idea of a mix of the two.

Joel Collins: In true Joe Wright style, he took ownership of our key *Truman Show* ideology, went for the jugular and pushed and pushed. He made it more pink, more blue, more pastel.

Joe Wright: I don't do things by halves, and I guess the colour range was based on the palette of this community that Joel had found. I wanted people to be camouflaged within their own world. No-one wants to stick their head out too much, and yet they all want to be noticed at the same time, which is a weird visual oxymoron.

Above: Recce shots taken in Knysna, South Africa by series production designer, Joel Collins, whilst scouting for locations.

James Foster: We aimed for an almost digital-looking reality. Perfect interiors with nothing out of place, but still uncomfortable. Clean and uncluttered modernist interiors with blank walls and repeated textures, confining things to the point that it could feel claustrophobic. Joe was keen to be really bold with the amount of sickly sweet pastel tones we were using, from the smallest props to entire interiors. With this veneer of colour, we gave the world a fake smile

Annabel Jones: We'd spoken about the aspirational element and sending that up by creating this saccharine world. And then Joe took it to a whole other level. We were like, "Oh, *okay* … "

Charlie Brooker: I was writing *Men Against Fire* while *Nosedive* was filming in South Africa. Because obviously, whenever we film somewhere nice, I'm not there. Not that this is a constant bugbear of mine! But I saw the rushes and immediately thought, "This is going to go one of two ways. This is a really strong flavour."

The first scene I saw looked beautiful, but way more stylised than I'd envisaged. I probably pictured something a bit near-future, with shiny glass, more *Minority Report*. I would not have thought about pastel pink, blue and peppermint green. So I thought, "Christ, I've taken my eye off the ball slightly there. Does that alter things?" I was really nervous about it.

Joel Collins: At the time, those colour choices felt like risks. But when you watch the show, it doesn't feel like a risk at all. It feels just right.

Joe Wright: I think people might have been a bit surprised. But Charlie and Annabel find people who they want to realise these stories, and then do give them a large degree of autonomy in doing so.

Charlie Brooker: The more I saw of what Joe was doing, the more I understood. And then when you get the final product, with Max Richter's score, you see this saccharine world, but then there's this very sad, contemplative piano score that's quite mesmerising.

Annabel Jones: That audio-visual marriage suddenly took the edge off everything. You realised that Max's melancholic score had allowed Joe to go very big with the aesthetic. And there was the emotional punch.

Charlie Brooker: That's very clever. Imagine how annoying *Nosedive* would be, if it looked like that and the music was jaunty! You'd go, "Fuck this." But the whole thing also looks dreamlike, like a weird Disney nightmare.

Annabel Jones: You can't talk about *Nosedive* without mentioning Seamus McGarvey, the director of photography who normally works with Joe. He just made it look painfully beautiful and cinematic. Seamus normally works on big, big Hollywood movies, so we like the fact that people who normally work on features for nine months can come and do what's essentially a short film with us for three or four weeks. They can take an idea, have fun with it and enjoy blowing it up.

Joe Wright: At one point in the original script, Lacie drove from her suburb through the desert, and through different landscapes, to arrive at the wedding party. But we couldn't afford to go to those locations. And then it struck me that she should drive for 12 hours or whatever, then arrive somewhere that looked exactly the same, as a comment on American homogenised culture.

For me, to a large degree, *Nosedive* is about sincerity. What is sincere? The characters in this story believe, in the moment, that what they're saying is true. It's just that, in the next moment, something else is true.

'Pelican Cove …
What is this, a
eugenics program? …
No-one's this happy.
A two-year-old with
a fuckin' balloon
isn't this happy'
– Ryan

Opposite top: Promotional material for Pelican Cove, designed by series raphic art director Erica McEwan with a matte painting backdrop provided by Painting Practice.

Opposite bottom: Posts from Naomi's social media feed, developed and animated by Painting Practice.

LIMITED EDITION LIVING

Pelican Cove
★★★★★

Naomi Jayne Blestow
Weekend on the Ocean *with Paul Mathesen*

★ *26 People rated Naomi's post*

Lacie Pound
4.2
★★★★★

People **Naomi Jayne Blestow, Paul Mathesen, Anthony Johnson, Sally Johnson**

Comments
Anthony Johnson
Great weekend guys!!
Jon Mckenzie
Invite me next time buddy?

Naomi Jayne Blestow
I love spending the evening with Paul, he's so wonderful and such an amazing bf :) *with Paul Mathesen*

★ *17 People* Paul, James and Julie have all rated 5 stars

Comments (3)
Nicole Blestow SOOOooo Lucky Sis!

Paul Mathesen
Weekend on the waves again baby? *with Naomi Jayne Blestow*

★ *9 People* Naomi, Sally and Anthony have all rated 5 stars

Comments (3)
Naomi Jayne Blestow Anytime baby, love you xx

I find it very difficult to figure out whether I'm really being sincere. We're told we should have fixed characters, and that having one is somehow an important quality in people. But I'm not sure I do have a fixed character. I mean, I'm not a murderer ... but put me in front of a Nazi, with a rifle, and that Nazi's trying to kill me, and I'll murder him. So our characters are formed by the circumstances in which we find ourselves. And so when Lacie and Naomi have that first video chat, for instance, they are both being totally sincere.

Annabel Jones: You do want Lacie's mission to reach Naomi's wedding to feel sincere. People want to have some validity to their childhood and feel that these things were formative. But the reality is that lives have changed and that's probably an upsetting truth. You hanker to get it back.

Charlie Brooker: I remember having that conversation with Rashida and Mike at one point: why does Lacie think she's going to the wedding? Does she feel great about going to her childhood friend, or is it a transaction? And I think it's both. She's genuinely touched that Naomi has asked her to do it, but she also can't escape the excitement of it being her ticket to a new apartment.

Above: Bryce Dallas Howard and her stunt double consider the tumble ahead.

Bryce Dallas Howard: I think that Lacie and Naomi sincerely ... need each other. They are sincerely using each other.

Joe Wright: It was Bryce's birthday on the day I flung her into a muddy swamp. And so when I called cut, and she stood up out of the swamp, covered in mud, we all sang happy birthday. Bless her.

Bryce Dallas Howard: Happy birthday to me! They sang really, really well. The best part was when we broke for lunch. I was getting back into the swamp after lunch, and there was no way for me to change clothes. So I was just walking around like this total swamp thing. Some merciful individual gave me a wet-wipe for my hands.

When Lacie finally reaches Naomi's wedding, she grabs the microphone and inflicts a lengthy, deranged speech upon the beautiful people.

Joe Wright: Lacie's speech wasn't shot in that many takes. We spent a couple of days shooting that scene, which was very generous given the overall schedule. Coming from film budgets and schedules, a 20-day shoot was fast for one hour. *Atonement* was 64 days, so in terms of an exercise in economy *Nosedive* was really useful for me as a filmmaker.

James Foster: We wanted each environment to reflect a level of rating; the wedding was the highest level and needed to appear hyper-perfect. The reception was to be outside on the lawns of a luxurious family home in an exclusive private development. Everything had to be white, pink and green.

Joe Wright: The wedding looks horrible. The nicer it looks, the more horrific it is, to me anyway. I'd been to a wedding a few months prior to that, and *Nosedive* reminded me. So I replicated that wedding I'd been to.

Joel Collins: That wedding was a nightmare to do, and a brilliant bit of work on the set decorator Katie Spencer's part. I remember Joe telling her, "I've got a gift for you, and it's the gift of a wedding to decorate!" She was like, "Oh. My. God.", because she knew exactly what that meant.

Bryce Dallas Howard: The wedding speech went smoothly and was tons of fun, but we had a potential problem. I have really sensitive eyes, which is so annoying for everyone I work with, and on the wedding set there was this crazy vortex of bright sunlight! I told Joe I wasn't sure if I could do the scene without squinting. But no joke: a cloud appeared for the entire time I was doing my speech and blocked the sun! Oh my gosh, I was so grateful.

Charlie Brooker: Lacie was designed to be quite grating at the start of the film, but we'd put in a key moment. During the taxi scene when she's really shrieking, we have the driver groaning at her. This tells you, the viewer, that we know she's a bit much. But by the time she delivers this whole wedding speech, it feels really triumphant. You're really on her side, because she's snapped and screaming at everyone.

Joe Wright: I think Lacie is a likeable character. She's vulnerable and she wants to be loved, and most of us can identify with that.

In the final scene, Lacie has been locked up in a cell, opposite another detainee. The pair begin to trade insults.

Mike Schur: In Charlie's original outline, Lacie's big blow-up at her work presentation went viral and she accidentally achieved the status and fame she'd been craving. When I brought up that it reminded me of the end of *Fifteen Million Merits*, Charlie laughed and agreed. The four of us then worked out the new idea – I think the actual idea was mostly Charlie's – wherein Lacie managed to find freedom in being stripped of her device in jail, and that there was a small amount of optimism in the idea that we all might be able to reset – if, admittedly, someone kind of forces us to.

Joe Wright: Lacie and her fellow prisoner fall in love. They reveal their true selves. When he says, "Fuck you", and she says, "Fuck you next Tuesday", she means it. Then they both end up shouting "Fuck you" and they become one. They're gonna have sex as soon as they leave.

Charlie Brooker: So they'd be having sex on the pavement. It's really nice, that moment, because it goes from grumpy to annoyed to playful to flirty. They're both genuinely smiling in the final few frames.

Annabel Jones: Lacie hasn't been able to compete with Naomi before, in terms of body size and all of that, and suddenly she's in her element: "Let me charm you with how offensive I can be when I'm totally liberated." I think the two of them will end up together too, that's the whole idea. It's like they're having a competition of who can offend who the most ...

In this world, we're all so caught up in our own heads, it's easy to loose sight of whats real, what matters. But as I stand here today, seeing the joy Paul has brought to Naomi's life, I know she's something that truly matters to me.

NayNay. The little girl who, when we were just five years old, in art camp, started talking to me because she saw I was scared. The girl who helped me make Mr. Rags. I still have him.

He lives on my desk. And every day he reminds me of NayNay, what she meant to me then, and now. I am so honored to be here. And i wish you all the happiness this stupid world can muster...

Charlie Brooker: ... which is the starting point for all sexual encounters.

Bryce Dallas Howard: I think that moment is about euphoria and freedom. They share this connection of authenticity, almost like a religious, transcendent moment. Both of them realise that they can just be free. While that's obviously dramatic irony, given that they're in prison, they've been freed of expectations and judgement. But what Joe said about the sex is also true.

I keep pitching a version of *Nosedive* 2.0, where we're these two outlaws who go around swearing and shaking people up. But that will probably only ever exist in my mind.

For many Netflix viewers, Nosedive *would have been their introduction to the world of* Black Mirror.

Charlie Brooker: In a way, the episode order doesn't matter because it's an anthology, but equally it fucking does matter. I always assumed *San Junipero* was going to be the first one, because that was the first one written. We had a lot of back and forth with Netflix, who thought *Nosedive* should go first. *Nosedive* is a very accessible gateway drug, whereas something like *San Junipero* is more high concept.

Bryce Dallas Howard: Now, when I walk around, people see me as the girl from *Black Mirror*. To be identified at all with a show and a story that's just remarkable on every level, is exciting and inspiring. It just makes life feel really awesome. With *Black Mirror*, there's nothing to apologise for.

Charlie Brooker: A slightly adolescent bit of me thought that people who liked *White Bear* would watch *Nosedive* and go, "Oh, it's all gone pastel." So I remember being really, really anxious about *Nosedive* being a lighter episode. Then I showed it to a friend of mine, without saying anything. About five minutes in, she said, "This is a fucking nightmare." I suppose I forget: what I think is frothy and light is someone else's fucking nightmare.

Bryce Dallas Howard: My dad [the Hollywood director Ron Howard] and I watched *Nosedive* together, just the two of us. Afterwards, he shot up and started backing out the door, blurting, "Wow, that was excellent-excellent-excellent! I've gotta run, I'll see you later!" And he then told me later that he was having a panic attack! He found it so unnerving and uncomfortable. He doesn't have neuroses on the level of Lacie, but y'know, he's on social media ...

Annabel Jones: After seeing that episode, a lot of people said, "I just stopped using social media. I realised this was taking over my life." The running order definitely matters, because people get what the show is very quickly from *Nosedive*. And then the fact that we follow up with a very different episode teaches you that this is an anthology. It's like, "Don't be fooled into thinking all the episodes are going to be like *Nosedive*, because look what we've got next ... *Playtest*!"

Opposite: A copy of the speech delivered by Lacie at Naomi's wedding.

PLAYTEST

<u>In Conversation</u>

Dan Trachtenberg – director
Laurie Borg – producer
Wyatt Russell – actor
Charlie Brooker – writer and executive producer
Annabel Jones – executive producer
Joel Collins – series production designer

Cooper has travelled around the world, in a bid to avoid the aftermath of his father's death from Alzheimer's, but finds himself unable to afford a return ticket to America. When he applies for a short-term London job as a game-tester at the company SaitoGemu, he gets sucked deeper and deeper into the augmented reality world of the creepy Harlech House, which uses his own fears against him.

Dan Trachtenberg (director): I first heard about *Black Mirror* while directing [the 2016 film] *10 Cloverfield Lane*. Mary Elizabeth Winstead had binge-watched the first two seasons and was raving about it. I liked that very-much-discussed first episode, but loved *The Entire History of You* and *Be Right Back*. These were exciting futuristic concepts, taken to logical yet unexpected places and paired with powerful performances and filmmaking.

Annabel and Charlie sent me a little *Playtest* synopsis, which eventually became a more evolved treatment. I was gonna do the project no matter what, because it's *Black Mirror*, but certainly the subject matter made it all a no-brainer.

Laurie Borg (producer): Dan brought a different approach to the *Black Mirror* process. He understands VFX extremely well and wanted a cinematographer with a distinctive voice – the New Zealander Aaron Morton. I love working with people who push the boundaries.

Wyatt Russell (actor): In 2015, I was in Atlanta doing another movie, and lived in the same house as my actor friend Alex Karpovsky, who told me about *Black Mirror*. I watched *Be Right Back* and we were all like, "Oh my God, this is the best show ever." In America, it was just this show on Netflix: very culty and not mainstream at all. Because it was an English show with English actors, I never thought about acting in it. Then my agent said *Black Mirror* were interested in talking to me. Dan Trachtenberg was directing and the script existed, but wasn't entirely finished. I didn't care because I knew it was gonna be great.

Charlie Brooker: *Playtest* came about when two ideas glommed together. I wanted to do a haunted house one, a digital ghost story. And then there'd been an idea involving Whac-A-Mole, which would end up being a sequence in it.

I still think this idea was funny, but we can't do it now. Somebody answers an advert, then goes to test an augmented reality Whac-A-Mole system. He whacks the moles and gets better and better at it. The moles get faster and faster – and then they can't switch it off. So everywhere he looks in his life, these little cartoon moles pop up and he has to keep whacking them. If he stops, they fill his whole field of vision. If he sleeps, he wakes up and there's thousands of moles. He goes mad, and they have to tie his hands down. Then they just go, "Put him with the others," and they move him into this big room full of people who are all tied to gurneys, screaming and seeing moles.

Something really appealed to me about the silliness of this cartoonish idea, but it wasn't a full episode – it was a horrible 15-minute short. Still, that idea kept floating around and so did the haunted house idea. Then I suddenly thought, "Oh wait a minute: what if you had a ghost story where it's working out what frightens you on the fly, so what you're seeing is being changed on the fly?" In the same way, in video games, there used to be dynamic soundtracks that would work out if the action was exciting and so the music would get more exciting. And so those two ideas somehow coalesced.

The twist that happens at the end with the phone call, that came in late in the day. Dan Trachtenberg was already on board and we were having lots of discussions. Dan's a very big games person as well …

Annabel Jones: Dan's a *huge* games person. Bigger than you, Charlie. And much better than you, I'd say. Much more knowledgeable.

Charlie Brooker: Well, you wouldn't know because you don't know anything about games. So actually, even if Dan knew nothing about games, you as a fucking rube would be dazzled by his knowledge. He could tell you that Pac-Man was written by a dog and you'd go, "Oh was it? Gosh I never knew that."

Annabel Jones: Whatever makes you feel better ...

Dan Trachtenberg: Charlie and I hit it off immediately over Skype. We both had not realised the other's history in games journalism and fandom. Ours is a very specific love for all things video game.

Charlie Brooker: Originally, *Playtest* was set in Tokyo. We even booked a recce to Tokyo to have a look, before cancelling it. Even though Resident Evil was a reference point, and that's a Japanese game, it still felt strange to basically have a character from the west fly to Japan to stand in a house that's like a house from Britain.

Annabel Jones: Also, we hadn't shown contemporary London in all the films we'd done. We'd been hiding London, or the UK, and making it timeless, so this was an opportunity to embrace the flavour.

Wyatt Russell: We shot around London for half a day on one of those double-decker tourist buses, which was awesome. I'd been to London when I was young but had never seen it, you know, for real. One of the ad-libs they kept in was Cooper asking how high buildings were. Slipping in some American stereotypes felt like a fun thing to do. Americans can be overly nice, to the point of being annoying. They're always asking how high buildings are.

The pub scene with Cooper's date with Sonja wasn't improv: it's just the way we wanted to do it. We have a very short time to get invested in Cooper's journey through Europe, so that scene was important to get to know him a little bit. And it was important for when Sonja becomes the figment of his imagination: when he meets her again later, you trust that she's real. Because when you recall their time together, it feels real, rather than staged.

Charlie Brooker: Cooper was originally written as more of a dick. Very intuitively, Dan said we should like him, or he should have a strong flavour about him. So rather than Cooper being a bland everyman, he should have a cockiness and a spark, so we can really break him down.

Dan Trachtenberg: Once I started rehearsing with Wyatt, I very quickly clocked into how much fun we would have improvising. There was a lot of humour to be mined in Cooper's eager aloofness. I loved bringing a more naturalistic approach to the first half of the film, so that you're more firmly linked to the characters. You're on the train with them as it heads towards disaster.

Above: The logo for tech company SaitoGemu, designed by series graphic art director Erica McEwan, and an imagined future edition of *Edge* magazine featuring the founder of SaitoGemu, Shou Saito, as its cover star. The cover artwork was created by *Edge* magazine.

Charlie Brooker: I'm not too worried if actors go slightly off-piste, as long as they don't start saying anything mental. But we really encouraged Wyatt to go for broke. So, early on in the Harlech house, there are loads of different takes where he's doing all sorts of fucking stuff.

Wyatt Russell: For instance, there was my scene with the childhood bully Peters. For VFX reasons, nobody was actually there for half that scene. So when I was doing karate on Peters, that came out because there was nobody there to do karate on! We did this whole 14-minute take of me talking about how Peters' dad was a drunk, and other stuff I didn't like about him.

Cooper is wisecracking during the experiment because he's nervous. I would be! I wanted to find the humour in almost everything. Not comedy, but humour. In dark situations in life, a lot of people fall back on humour to try and relate to something unrelatable. If you tried to play it earnest, you'd run the risk of people saying how they'd never get themselves into that situation.

Joel Collins (series production designer): *Playtest* was the last film we shot for that season. It ended up being one of the most fun stories of that first Netflix season to make, but I must admit we were all quite tired. Our big build of the SaitoGemu company offices was multi-level and Japanese-inspired. We built the Harlech House on the Unity game engine [software framework], so people were actually building a real game on-set at the game company. You can see it in the background: it's all there.

Wyatt Russell: It was incredible how they transformed this old abandoned school building into SaitoGemu, but the Harlech House was an actual house. It was the home of a woman, who was 91 or something. She was there and I met her. The kitchen was dressed as this creepy witch's brew kitchen, and they took all the furniture out of the main room. But all that woodwork, the bones of that house, are the actual place, so it was awesomely immersive for me.

In one hair-raising scene, Cooper finds himself confronted with a bizarre hybrid of his childhood bully Peters and a giant spider.

Joel Collins: Dan Trachtenberg made references to the slug-like creatures in [the 2005 film] *King Kong* and the spider Shelob in [the 2003 film] *The Lord of The Rings: The Return of the King*. So I got my friend Alan Lee, who was the conceptual designer for both movies, to do some illustrations and sketches of the Peters-Spider. Then we got a whole array of other ideas, and threw them all in.

Dan Trachtenberg: The CGI Peters-Spider was a challenge, but beautifully executed by the VFX company Framestore. It was also fun to lean into the audience's expectations and genre awareness. There's a math to the 'jump scare' that I wanted to play with. Sometimes Cooper is aware that a scare is coming, and then it's delivered to him, and us, in an unexpected way.

Wyatt Russell: I said to Dan, "Doesn't Cooper know that the Peters-Spider can't hurt him now? He's knows it's not real, so why is he scared?" And then he told me it was 14 feet long, and I was like, "Holy shit, okay!" And then I

Above: The development work for the gopher, which appears in an augmented reality game of Whac-a-Mole. The character was art directed for visual effects by Justin Hutchison-Chatburn at Painting Practice.

'Who are you and what
have you done to me? ...
I don't know who I am ...'

– Cooper

enjoyed how, whatever Cooper did would dictate what the thing might do. That was really fun with the Peters-Spider, feeding it a cookie or whatever.

The film's true psychological horror arrives when Cooper enters the upstairs bedroom and suffers a full mental breakdown.

Wyatt Russell: That last scene was tough: the big switch from This Is Fun to This Is Not Fun. Dan came to me and said they were gonna do it all in one shot. So it was put-up-or-shut-up time.

Dan Trachtenberg: That wasn't some intellectual notion we had early on. Rather, we looked at the room and realised one continuous shot would be the most efficient and cinematically 'best' way to go.

Wyatt Russell: It had been a long day and everybody wanted to go home, but every single person was on point. We walked through it first, for Dan to get the idea of what things would happen where. Cooper goes from sheer terror on entering the room, to relief that he's in the room, to wanting to get out, to realising it's one step further than he ever thought, then to pure panic, then anger, then to total desperation and total loss. Every single fucking thing has to play: you have to see it. If I got stuck behind a bed post and my face got blocked, then that take would be unusable, even if it was otherwise the best take I ever did in my life.

By the fifth rehearsal, everyone was ready and it was time to go for the first of our three takes. All the energy in the room was a 10, and it was time to rock 'n' roll. One of the coolest experiences of my life was getting to be a part of, and be the focal point of, a team working together to get something right. I had to be totally vulnerable, no holding back.

Dan Trachtenberg: Wyatt kind of shocked us all when he went to such a devastating place. And he had to go there multiple times as we perfected the camera move.

HARLECH_034
19:21

Charlie Brooker: That was one of those moments, when we first saw a scene in the dub and it's almost too much. That moment where Cooper's babbling and going, "I don't know who I am." It's so horrific. You feel so bad for him.

The fact that Cooper ultimately dies because his mum calls his phone, that was partly a knowing nod to people who say, "Oh, it's the show where some British guy warns you about what would happen if you dropped your smartphone on your toe, and then the pixels went into the toenail and filled up your bum, and your bum went digital, and then your bum was emailing your ear and you didn't know about it and they were talking about you behind your back." So we deliberately did an episode where a phone does kill someone! Something as trivial as phone interference becomes the big twist. Here's a bit of audio trivia: you know that noise that phones make when there's a bit of interference, which you hear before the phone rings? That starts to surface near the end, but it keeps happening throughout the soundtrack in a slowed down, embedded way.

At one point, we wanted to break the fourth wall. We had a thing where Cooper gets told he's a character in *Black Mirror*, but that would have been a bit weird. We also wanted to do Nightmare Mode, so that if you went back and watched the film again it would be different.

Annabel Jones: This is a good example of where stripping things out makes something stronger. There's the danger that it becomes so layered it all becomes slightly meaningless. So if we ever felt we were putting too much in, we wanted to draw it back.

Dan Trachtenberg: Initially Cooper's relationship with his mom was quite different. She was overtly neurotic and his death was more her fault for constantly trying to dote on her grown son. But we realised we had it the wrong way. It was more poignant to shift it so that Cooper was taking his relationship with his mom for granted. The wall he's put up between them, his defiance against reaching back out to her, is ultimately his undoing. Basically, I have guilt about not calling my mom enough, as many of us do.

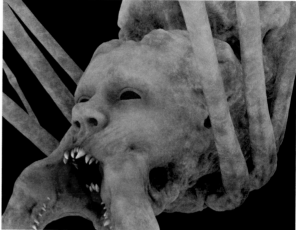

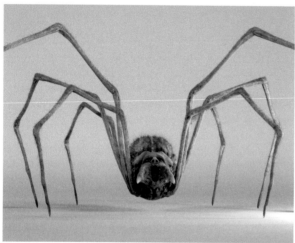

Annabel Jones: Throughout *Playtest,* there are lovely little details that I think probably still get missed. The idea was that every experience Cooper has had, to the point where he plays the game – the pubs he's visited, the places abroad – all get sucked up into his memory and then are used against him. Or he uses them as textural details within the world. So the Raven pub in which he meets Sonja – that becomes the book he's reading in the Harlech House.

Dan Trachtenberg: We devoted a lot of time to this. Sometimes it's overt, like Cooper's watching a giant spider movie on the plane and then later we see a spider. But sometimes it was subtler. On the morning he and Sonja wake up together, the placement of his scar and her head are matched later in the film in a very different scene between them. There's even a Red Sonja poster hanging in her apartment!

Charlie Brooker: Everything's referenced. The stuff that Cooper sees on monitors on his way into SaitoGemu, is actually the stuff that all feeds into the nanosecond fantasy that kills him.

Above and opposite: The development work for the giant 'Spider Peters' and 'Red Sonja', art directed for visual effects by Justin Hutchison-Chatburn at Painting Practice.

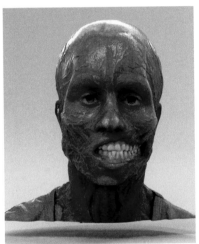

Annabel Jones: The magazine cover that Hannah shows him in the flat, with the image of Shou Saito, informs Cooper what Shou looks like.

Charlie Brooker: Sometimes people ask why Shou speaks Japanese at the end, whereas he speaks English to Cooper. That's because Cooper never actually met Shou! Shou dresses differently when we meet him properly at the end: he's actually a different kind of guy.

Annabel Jones: *Playtest* had a twist on a twist, and at script level it did confuse people. A lot of conversations went, "So how come Cooper is so good at Whac-A-Mole? How come he's so susceptible?" or "So how did Sonya actually steal his credit cards?" No. None of that happened. There are often a lot of pained expressions on a *Black Mirror* set.

Dan Trachtenberg: I'm so damn happy with *Playtest*. I'm always delighted when people come up to me and tell me how scared they were watching it. Because the making of a film like this is never scary, so you really have to rely on the craft to do its thing. It's just such a relief to hear it did!

Wyatt Russell: Genre filmmaking in its heyday was John Carpenter and those early 80s films. Because there were elements that my dad [Kurt Russell] was involved in pioneering with Carpenter, it was really fun to do *Playtest* and for my dad to see it. He really loved it and he likes *Black Mirror*. It's our generation's *Twilight Zone*. It was especially cool because *Playtest* has a lot of homage to Carpenter movies, particularly with the spider that resembles *The Thing*.

You wondered whether the second ending was gonna be annoying. How was it gonna work? But more than anything, what comes across to me in that ending, is the idea that if you skirt responsibility in life and try to run from your real world problems, it's going to bite you in the ass somehow. Cooper was trying to avoid all these inevitable things that were coming. Early-onset Alzheimer's, or death in its many forms. By going away, he was avoiding his father's death and his mother's grief over his father's death.

Charlie Brooker: That's a fair interpretation from Wyatt. It puts me in mind of the *Twilight Zone* stories where an unbelievable giant concrete block of punishment is dropped on your head, just because hard-nosed reality comes in and clobbers you.

Wyatt Russell: In my mind, Cooper's dead in real life, zipped up in the body bag. But does his consciousness live on in some other digital realm? Does he have this hellish existence for eternity, where he has to live out the rest of time inside his constant anxieties and fears? This chip inside his head might allow his consciousness to live on in some way, in an everlasting hell. Which is an absolutely terrifying thought.

Charlie Brooker: I like to think that too. Cooper could be at the point where you see reality warp and stretch – he's stuck within that plummeting sort of freefall. I like to think that could happen.

Annabel Jones: If only he'd rung his mum.

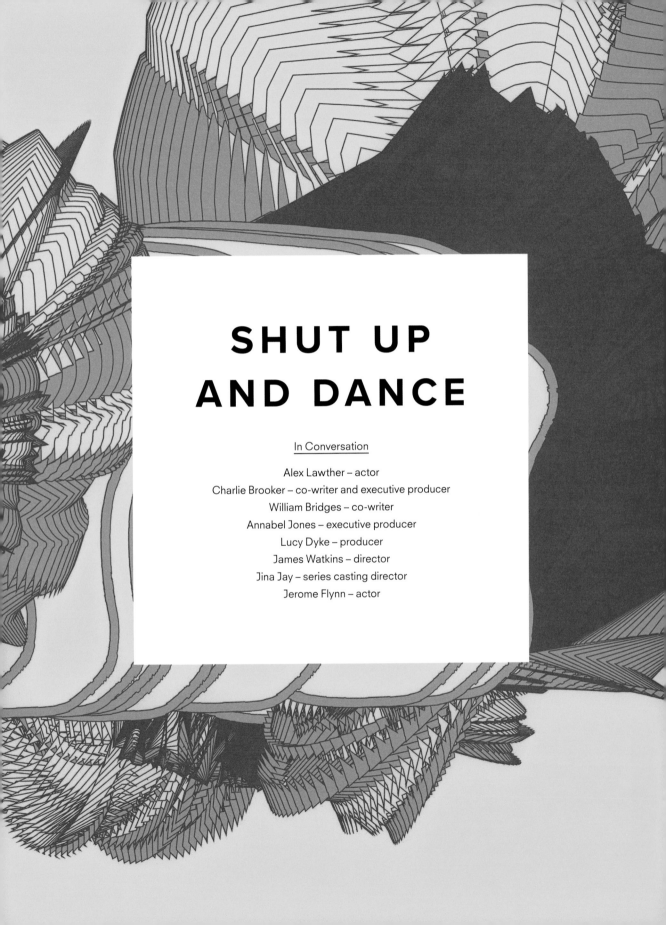

SHUT UP AND DANCE

In Conversation

Alex Lawther – actor

Charlie Brooker – co-writer and executive producer

William Bridges – co-writer

Annabel Jones – executive producer

Lucy Dyke – producer

James Watkins – director

Jina Jay – series casting director

Jerome Flynn – actor

Small-town teenager Kenny is mortified to discover that mysterious online hackers have used his laptop's webcam to film him masturbating to porn. In order to prevent the footage being made public, Kenny finds himself blackmailed into carrying out a series of seemingly random tasks, alongside the equally hamstrung businessman Hector.

Alex Lawther (actor): My *Black Mirror* experience started with the Prime Minister fucking a pig and ended with me playing a paedophile. When I was still living at home, about 16 years old, my parents said there was this new "Mirror thing" on television. It was *The National Anthem*, so that made for an incredibly awkward experience! I'd never seen anything so outrageous and yet so intelligent on TV. I became a big *Black Mirror* fan. Then an audition became available for a scrawny kid who gets embroiled in a blackmail …

Charlie Brooker: *Shut Up and Dance* reminded me of *The National Anthem* in a way. There's a seediness to it. A weird, British, colloquial nasty humour. We always say we've gone from *San Junipero* to wanking in Hounslow. Polar opposites, tonally. But that gritty British feeling felt important to have in this first Netflix season, partly to reassure people who'd watched the Channel 4 series: "Look, we're still this nasty British show with concrete and piss in it."

For quite a while it was set in America, partly because we were hung up on the fact it's easier for Kenny to have a gun if it's in America – but actually it makes the gun more frightening and unusual when it's in Britain. And initially, the idea was more *Reservoir Dogs*: a bunch of people who've been brought together to rob a bank. And then you realise they don't actually know each other and they're all being blackmailed to do it for different reasons that they don't know.

Shut Up and Dance marked the Black Mirror *co-writing debut of William Bridges, a relative newcomer to TV.*

William Bridges (co-writer): I credit Charlie and Annabel for very much giving me my break in the industry. I hadn't met them before, and had virtually no credits to my name, but I'd written a spec script for a TV show that had just been sold to a US broadcaster.

Annabel Jones: That script was a really well-written pilot. You could see there was a shared tone, with well-drawn characters and humour, so Will seemed a good fit for us.

William Bridges: The three ideas I pitched to Charlie and Annabel were shit and none of them stuck, but I think we got on enough for them to trust that my spec script wasn't a fluke. A few days later, they sent me one of Charlie's own ideas to flesh out: an embryonic version of *Shut Up and Dance*.

The treatment was very different from the finished episode. Set in America, it ended with Kenny in the desert as a hundred cop cars appeared over the horizon gunning for him. In this version, Kenny was just a sweet American teenager who got blackmailed into robbing a convenience store after wanking to harmless porn. Fleshing it out proved really tough because whenever the stakes got high enough for Kenny to face serious consequences, like jail time, it was unbelievable to have him rob a bank. Nine times out of 10, embarrassment at your peers seeing your wiener is preferable to spending a good portion of your life incarcerated.

Charlie Brooker: We couldn't work out why Kenny was being punished like this, when he'd just been wanking to porn. So, what if we made him the villain, then? And it finally made sense.

Lucy Dyke (producer): James Watkins had proven his directorial ability with films like 2008's *Eden Lake* and 2012's *The Woman in Black*, by creating tension and unease, this sense of dread.

Charlie Brooker: The final five minutes of *Eden Lake* is one of the most horrifying things I've ever seen.

Lucy Dyke: James completely understood how to take a script that felt quite small and simple and build it into something cinematic. The film had to rely on the building tension of the story-telling and the performances of the two lead actors.

James Watkins (director): At the time, I'd never done any television. Charlie, Annabel and I had a cup of tea and chatted through the script.

Above: On location, shooting the scene with Alex Lawther's character Kenny in the multi-storey car park.

We relocated it to the UK, because I'm not sure there was a reason for it to be in America. It came together incredibly quickly, the fastest thing I've ever done, which was part of the attraction. I wanted to explore the world of television and shooting on that kind of schedule. Also, the material really lent itself to that gun-and-run approach.

It's always grim and grey in the UK in February when we shot, so we particularly pushed that gun-metal palette. In the production office, I saw all these art department pictures of glamorous blue skies, as they prepped *Nosedive* and *San Junipero*. So I thought, "Right, we're gonna go the other way. We'll embrace being the ugly cousin."

The key choice was the casting of Alex. We saw quite a few actors, but he had such an understated truth. Even though he gets quite manic in the episode, he had this interesting sympathy about him.

Jina Jay (series casting director): Alex Lawther read with James and nailed the heart of the role. He's such a beautiful young actor, who's gifted with the ability to convey a secretive interior and make an audience root for this troubled character.

Annabel Jones: So much of the film rested with Alex and his performance – and him taking the role in the first place. I mean, a lot of people would have been put off taking that role.

Charlie Brooker: I know! However many pages into the script, he's pulling his pants down and wanking. It's not exactly saving an orphanage, is it?

Alex Lawther: I'd done little bits in film and theatre. My agent loves *Black Mirror*, so we were both excited. For my audition tape, I did one scene with Kenny delivering the cake to Hector's room, and also Kenny breaking down in the car – with no knowledge of what was going on around those scenes! Further along in the audition process, I read the script, and thought, "Come on Kenny, just turn yourself in – don't rob a bank or kill someone, it's not that big of a deal!" And then I thought, "Oh God!" and felt very unnerved. How brilliant that they'd made me sympathise with a paedophile for so long. And the complexity of that, because he's so young …

I really liked working with our costume designer Guy Speranza to find the right clothes for Kenny, in a way I'd paid less attention to in the past when taking roles. There was a real balance between finding clothes that were sort of sad and lonely, and someone hiding their body, but at the same time without screaming, "Oh, that's a man in a paedophile coat."

One apparently innocuous early scene, which plays very differently on second viewing, sees Kenny being nice to a little girl in the café.

Charlie Brooker: The original idea was that you think he's flirting with the mum, just as a red herring. The moment felt a bit risky, and I was worried that people would guess the twist. I guess it's like being a magician where you know the secret of the trick.

Alex Lawther: That was very creepy to play, and James was very good at keeping an eye on the balance. It came down to glancing for slightly too long, but not so long as to give the game away on first watch.

James Watkins: Alex was very attuned as an actor to his own journey, so I didn't have to police it in an insane way. Plus, if you're wary enough, you can always give yourself a couple of different colours to choose between in the edit.

Annabel Jones: We had problems casting the young girl for the café. Our producer Lucy was struggling to find any parents who were happy for their daughter to do it. She asked James whether his daughters would do it. James said, "Absolutely not!", so I got my own daughter to do it. It's what any proud mum would do.

Alex Lawther: We talked about playing it like Kenny was just a totally normal, nice, useless guy, and letting the twist tell itself. Because from Kenny's perspective, he's in so much denial about his sexuality that, to all intents and purposes, it's all very repressed.

So I decided to play it as though Kenny hasn't done anything wrong. I left the twist completely out of my mind. When I was playing him, there was always the feeling of being really uncomfortable in one's own skin. There was a squirmy feeling in his stomach, like he had an upset tummy. And that was great, because that fitted both with him being a teenager and him hiding something dark and upsetting.

Even if he wasn't a paedophile, being filmed watching porn would be social suicide for Kenny in a way. When you're in your late teens and you're already not a particularly popular chap, it could ruin your life socially and might seem like a sort of death. I could imagine people going to extreme lengths to keep that information away from Facebook and the online world. It would really just seem like the end of everything.

I can't remember whose idea it was for me to smell my fingers in the bathroom but it's really fucking weird. I bumped into Charlie recently and he said, "Why did you do that? That was so weird, Alex!" And I tried to blame it on James.

James Watkins: That's probably Alex being diffident! I would imagine that was a choice he made that I embraced. It was an odd-but-right choice – something that you wouldn't necessarily write, because you wouldn't think about it. Because an actor's very in the moment, they can bring something else to the party. To be fair, I think Charlie embraced it in the edit too. I don't think he can entirely disavow himself of that choice!

Annabel Jones: It wasn't in the script. Was it in the script? I remember us having a conversation about that moment. It just felt so weirdly unguarded and odd, that we left it in.

Charlie Brooker: Everyone's passing the buck on this one! I might pass the buck to Will. I don't think it was me.

William Bridges: I know who's responsible, but I think it's more fun to keep it a mystery. It's clearly a moment anyone who's ever been a teenage boy relates to, whether they admit it in a published book or not.

Once Kenny's blackmailers have flung him into the urban rat's maze, he drives frantically around town with middle-aged Hector, played by Jerome Flynn.

Charlie Brooker: The story originally played out over a bigger time span, and we kept cutting it back. So Kenny almost has to do that thing from the *Dirty Harry* movies, where he's running across town to answer the ringing phone.

Alex Lawther: Jerome and I spent a little time in rehearsing, but only met briefly. Then I was thrown into a two-hander in that car. We had quite a nice time in the end, but at first we were two reserved English people sitting in a car together, trying to avoid talking about the uncomfortable subject of the piece we were playing! Jerome's very laidback – he does meditation and likes being outdoors. It was funny to see him playing someone so different from the life I imagined he led.

Jerome Flynn (actor): Alex played Kenny so perfectly. The fact we didn't get time beforehand to socialise was good, because it felt very real, what we were going through with our characters.

Alex Lawther: The challenge was that it was a thriller in genre, with escalating tension, so I had to keep a gauge on where that dial was. You didn't want to show all your cards too quickly, because things just get worse and worse. But ultimately it's down to James and his editor for sustaining that tension. It could just be relentless, but there's an ebb and flow that comes down to the edit.

James Watkins: I'd just made an action film, so was able to shoot that fast and get the coverage we needed to energise it. I've worked with the editor Jon Harris on everything I've done. He's cut Danny Boyle's movies, so it wasn't shot like television. I wanted it accelerated, even through the comedic stuff. It was really good fun, but very intense across 15 days.

Jerome Flynn: The stuff in the car was really thrilling. As an actor, you're not actually driving, you're being towed, and so to compensate for that, I found myself hyperventilating, to the point where I almost fainted. It was very strange, and I don't know why I did that! Maybe I would've hyperventilated anyway, due to the tension of the situation.

Alex Lawther: Jerome was hyperventilating all the time! We kept having to cut because he couldn't breathe. Which was quite sweet, but frustrating for him – I think he was getting a little annoyed at himself.

Jerome Flynn: I did actually get in a bit of trouble and lost my head a bit, because I really got dizzy. It was stupid, because I'd have been much better with a clear head! But I was pleased with how the panic came across onscreen.

Alex Lawther: There was actually hyperventilation on both our parts – we were both just passing out in the car every five minutes. I don't think that counts as 'method', it's more sort of Heavy Breathing Acting! You'd finish the day and feel quite sick and woozy, because you'd not taken a proper full breath all day.

James Watkins: Hector was a very difficult performance: he walks a line between being a total shit and a fallible human being. Jerome did a fantastic job, because it could so easily veer into caricature. At very end, there's a real movie star moment when it's all come out in the wash with Hector's wife and everything's about to go to Hell. Those final close-ups on him, as the realisation dawns, the layers of emotion that flicker over his face ... he's doing a lot with a little. He had a real understanding of who that character was.

Jerome Flynn: Hector felt very real, full of flaws and weaknesses. I'm quite fond of him. Because of the way it was cut, I think a lot of people thought he was into paedophilia as well, but he wasn't – he was just looking for a thrill outside of his marriage and trying to feel young again. A lot of middle-aging men can identify with that, even though it wasn't a wise way to go about it and I'm not condoning that! Also, the farcical ride he went on, and his responses to it, just made me laugh, in the best darkly comic way.

There was quite a lot of laughter during the shoot, actually. At times, Alex and I had to rein ourselves in. I remember some corpsing – that old familiar feeling of having to centre and focus, otherwise you'd be in trouble.

Alex Lawther: In desperation, we had to laugh, because there was no levity in the scenes. Apart from when we pick up the brilliant Natasha Little at the petrol station. Jerome and I had been working together for two weeks solidly and all of our scenes had been about panicking and terrible things. Suddenly there was this oasis of another actor coming in to play the irritating Karen. I had a giggle with that, for sure. Maybe there was corpsing on camera and I've chosen to forget, having assumed I was way more professional.

James Watkins: Natasha's very funny and the three of them did set each other off a couple of times there. They were all throwing the odd ad-lib around and catching each other out.

Alex Lawther: My favourite scene is when Karen's asking me about Birmingham. That's what's so brilliant –it's unrelenting tension, but then Charlie always leaves room for humour. I also got a lot of joy out of Kenny's gun getting stuck in the door after he's held up the bank. Hilariously pathetic.

Ultimately, the blackmailers force Kenny to fight another of their victims to the death. They then shop him to the police for viewing child porn.

Charlie Brooker: In the original ending, the hackers had led Kenny and Hector on a wild-goose chase in order to get them arrested by the police. Which felt weirdly anticlimactic. We were also going to see who was behind this: some people in an internet cafe in Eastern Europe or something. It was people just doing it for a laugh, or they were taking part in a competition to see who could fuck with people the most.

Annabel Jones: But the film wasn't about the hackers. It was about the unknown and the vulnerability of people who are just using their laptops.

Lucy Dyke: This isn't a film about what might be, but a film about what is. This could happen to any one of us *right now*. Who didn't put a bit of Blu-Tack over their laptop webcam after watching this one?

'The pictures'd hang about on Google like a gypsy fucking curse: no cure for the internet, they'd never go away, it'd be *glued* to your name, a fucking *stain* on you'
– Hector

James Watkins: Jon Harris put that Radiohead track on the ending as a sort of temp track and I really loved it. We didn't think we'd get it, but the line producer Mary McCarthy knew Radiohead's manager. They were very generous in letting us have it, because they liked the show. Charlie was concerned that Radiohead might be too familiar, but for me that song takes it from being grim to being tragic. It acts as the moral voice in some way.

Charlie Brooker: *Shut Up and Dance* shares a bit of DNA with *White Bear*, in terms of punishment being meted out to people. I don't think we could do a third episode where a person is revealed to be horrible to children ... although Daly is in *USS Callister*. I was worried that people would think *Shut Up and Dance* was a repeat of *White Bear* – and some people did say that, but not many. I think that was because they were so wrong-footed.

Alex Lawther: I'm so proud that *Shut Up and Dance* feels part of the lo-fi *Black Mirror* that I really loved from those first two seasons. That Britishness and the mundanity. The technology is still scary and powerful, and in this episode omnipotent, but it's done in a very domestic way.

James Watkins: *Shut Up and Dance* is gruelling, but hopefully in a good way. Whenever people talk to me about it, they say they really enjoyed it. Then after a pause, they say, "Hmmm. I'm not sure enjoy is the right word ... "

SAN JUNIPERO

In Conversation

Gugu Mbatha-Raw – actor

Charlie Brooker – writer and executive producer

Annabel Jones – executive producer

Owen Harris – director

Mackenzie Davis – actor

Laurie Borg – producer

Joel Collins – series production designer

Susie Coulthard – costume designer

Tanya Lodge – hair and make-up

In 1987, self-conscious Yorkie meets flamboyant Kelly in a beach resort bar. The two women fall for each other, but there's more to the sparkling paradise of San Junipero than meets the eye. As the time nears for Kelly to leave town, she faces a huge decision.

Gugu Mbatha-Raw (actor): I was very much aware that playing Kelly was a gift of a role, and that *San Junipero* was a gift of a script. Those things don't come along very often, so I definitely wanted to do it justice. And even though this ended up as Netflix's Episode Four, it was the very first episode to be shot for that season, so there was a slight pressure of, "Ooh, this is suddenly a Netflix show and there's a bit more of that American money coming in. Let's not let the side down!"

Charlie Brooker: I'd been obsessed with doing a story about the afterlife. I wanted to do a sort of supernatural story, and was thinking of spooky, creepy story ideas. So, weirdly, *San Junipero* had started in a sort of horror movie world.

Annabel Jones: We always have a scientific explanation for things, even if it's bollocks! We introduced the idea of digital consciousness in *White Christmas*, but hadn't really explored the moral or emotional implications. There was so much untapped potential.

Charlie Brooker: Something else that we'd discussed was a way of expanding the world of *Be Right Back*. We couldn't do this now because of [the 2016 HBO TV series set in a Wild West-themed android amusement park] *Westworld*, but we had the idea of a theme park you went to that was essentially Heaven. All your dead relatives and friends would be there, and you'd pay to go and visit them. So that thought stayed around for a while: this notion of Heaven that you go to as a holiday.

Sometimes it's useful to start by thinking about what genres we haven't done yet. Partly because we were doing six films now, we wondered about a retro episode. How could we do one set in the past?

And then I'd remembered seeing this BBC documentary called *The Young Ones* – no relation to the sitcom – back in 2010. They'd taken six ageing celebrities, in their 70s and 80s, and put them in a house decorated like the 1970s, with vintage TV shows playing on the TV and everything, and the results were astonishing. They were suddenly full of life, almost tossing their walking sticks away, like they were 20 years younger.

So you can see how all these ideas lined up. At some point, they were all up on a whiteboard somewhere. The conversation became quite free-flowing as we bounced from one idea to another. And then it happened really quickly: I was talking to Annabel, going, "Ooh! Ooh! And then this would happen and that would happen!" And she almost burst into tears.

Annabel Jones: Because it was so sad. Such an emotional story.

Charlie Brooker: Back then, our characters were a man and a woman. The big twist was one of them was in a coma or dying. That was where it ended.

Annabel Jones: Once you start exploring the world, and the capabilities it offers up, you wonder what else that world might give someone that they may not have had before. Then came that idea of having a life unfulfilled, because you've been in a coma for 40 years, and going back to a time when maybe you couldn't have been as sexually free as you could today. The idea just kept giving and offering opportunities.

Above: On location at Kelly's house, director Owen Harris giving notes to Gugu Mbatha-Raw and Mackenzie Davis.

Charlie Brooker: At some point, the thought arrived of making this a same sex couple. Rather than that feeling like a gimmick, it became both relevant and irrelevant to the story. It informed a whole other layer, because these people couldn't have got married as two women in 1987.

Annabel Jones: I also love that this is a story about two mature women, finding each other and falling in love. And you forget that they're old. It's a cliché, but when you're old you're still mentally and emotionally alive to all experiences. It's just your body that's letting you down. And so to be free of that and go and fuck as much as they want, and drink as much as they want ... why wouldn't these two mature women want to be doing this? But

you don't think of virtual reality as empowering the old. So it was just such a great fusion of ideas, all coming together in an emotionally satisfying way.

Charlie Brooker: I thought people would find it more shocking or surprising, that old people had been talking to each other about fucking, but no one ever comments on it. People just accept it, which is refreshing.

As usual, I was worried, because I hadn't really written a love story before. From *Be Right Back*, I learnt that if you keep it simple and you've got good actors, people immediately root for them and naturally care about them. Still, I was really worried that people would think it was absurd how quickly Kelly and Yorkie fall for each other. But, of course, everything gets distilled down to little moments when you're watching works of fiction! So I had to fight a voice in my head that said, "It wouldn't happen like that – they've literally met for 10 minutes."

San Junipero *saw director Owen Harris return to the* Black Mirror *fold, having handled Season Two's* Be Right Back.

Owen Harris (director): Strangely, I'd had a far more immediate response to the *Be Right Back* script. *San Junipero* took longer to process, to work out what the genre was, and where the gears were. It was such a great story, but there was a lot going on. The heart of it wasn't quite so clear.

Joel Collins (series production designer): When Owen came into the office, I showed him all the visual work I'd done to express what *San Junipero* could be, and he loved it. We were going into the future, and also into the past, with the 80s. We looked at things like [classic 80s teen films] *Pretty in Pink* and *Ferris Bueller's Day Off*. Once again, the goal was to settle the audience into a place they know, and give them a stereotype that they can enjoy.

Owen Harris: Bizarrely, in the end, it was the 80s setting that excited me. If you look back to a lot of films from that decade – in particular those films written or directed by John Hughes – the mood was far more optimistic, almost to the point where you could classify it as a genre. The genre of eternal optimism! *Black Mirror* comes from a background of satire, which is by nature somewhat cynical, and that's why I liked the idea of adopting a positive genre to tell one of these tales.

The key choice was the casting of Gugu and Mackenzie. This would have been a far trickier piece to pull off without their thoughtful and confident approach. As soon as we attached them, I really felt we had the chance to make something special.

Gugu Mbatha-Raw: *Black Mirror* has always been such a dark, interesting and cool show. I loved *Be Right Back*. It reminded me of [the Roald Dahl 80s anthology TV show] *Tales of the Unexpected*, which I loved while growing up. Something about *Be Right Back* brought to mind that show's dark, twisted tales such as *Lamb to the Slaughter*!

Mackenzie Davis (actor): When my friends and I watched the first ever episode – "the pig fucking one" as it is colloquially known – we just sat in awe at what we were seeing. It felt like the first time I saw *Twin Peaks*, where the rules and expectations of what a television show was and could be were exploded. When I ended up getting the offer to be a part of the show, it felt like a *Twilight Zone* scenario, where you step through your screen and enter the world you never thought you would participate in, beyond your own passive viewing. It was surreal.

Gugu Mbatha-Raw: I first read *San Junipero* on my iPhone – an act which felt very *Black Mirror*-esque in itself. I was waiting for a bus from Oxford Circus to Brixton, so thought I'd read a couple of pages, then read the rest when I got home. But I got so absorbed that I read the whole thing on the bus. It was so original, it blew me away. I was so drawn into the vivacity of Kelly, and the whole idea of the 80s soundtrack which was already written into the script. Something about it was very inspiring and unusual.

Mackenzie Davis: Charlie wrote Yorkie as an exquisitely brave character, in such a quiet and unusual way. When we first meet her, she seems like a shy dork with some strange mannerisms, but the more you learn about her the more it is revealed how her dress, behaviour and mere presence in this world is an act of brutal honesty, bravery and authenticity. She is one of two or three characters I feel the luckiest to have been able to be a part of.

Gugu Mbatha-Raw: Kelly leapt off the page. The script didn't change from when I read it on my iPhone to what you see in the finished episode, in terms of the dialogue and rhythm of the characters. Knowing the twist of the story, I was conscious of bringing as much light and joy to Kelly as I could. I didn't want to give away the fact there was anything dark about this story.

I first met Mackenzie at breakfast at the Charlotte Street Hotel, with Owen and our producer Laurie Borg. We had a chat, then did the table-read. It was all very fast. It was a real whirlwind, so I didn't have much time with Mackenzie beforehand. As I say, thankfully the characters were so well-written and Mackenzie's a brilliant actress. We're still really great friends.

Mackenzie Davies: Gugu I first met in the hotel elevator. We were riding the elevator, ignoring each other, as you do, then I looked in the mirror at Gugu and realized she was my love Kelly! From then on, we just adored each other and I'm so thankful she was my partner throughout this whole experience.

Laurie Borg (producer): Our biggest challenge was creating period America on a tight budget, so the key decision I made was to film most of the interiors in London and most of the exteriors in Cape Town. I knew we could not afford to film in the US, but also knew South Africa could deliver 'period' Americana streets and coastlines.

Filming the Tucker's Bar interiors on a constructed set on a stage in Hayes was an effective way to control the different periods, including the management of extras in period clothing and make-up.

Annabel Jones: On the first day of filming for our new big Netflix *Black Mirror* series, we shot the interior scenes of the Quagmire. A dodgy club in North London. Naked butts, nipple tassels and pierced bits everywhere. We knew how to spend those Netflix dollars.

Joel Collins: Before we built Tucker's Bar for real, we built it in 3D. I gave Charlie and Owen a VR headset, so they could walk around the bar and

walk around the bar and look at the space. In the industry that process is just beginning, so we marched ahead a bit. We were *Black Mirror*, after all.

Owen Harris: You could walk around this VR bar and say things like, "Can we push the bar back a bit? Can we make the balcony a bit wider?" My overriding memory is feeling a bit sea-sick every time I put it on, so I gave up, but it was incredibly useful and I massively appreciated the effort!

Susie Coulthard (costume designer): San Junipero needed to feel like a simulated world without being too obvious. We discussed only having one outfit for Kelly and Yorkie in 1987, but decided it was better to have a narrative within the wardrobe, as if you could make those choices when accessing the San Junipero system. The wedding dresses, both made from the same fabric but differing 80s styles, suggested you could design your own wedding look within the system.

Above: The set of Tucker's, developed by series production designer Joel Collins and co-designer Nick Palmer with graphic design for Tucker's by Erica McEwan.

'The bond. The commitment. The boredom. The yearning, the laughter, the love of it. The fucking love. You just cannot know. Everything we sacrificed. The years I gave him, the years he gave me. Did you think to ask? Did it occur to you to ask?'

– Kelly

Tanya Lodge (hair and make-up): I wanted to tell Kelly and Yorkie's story by giving them a strong look which defined their personality but felt believable for the audience. Kelly's flamboyant appearance was a collaboration between costume and make-up. The big hair was inspired by style icons of the time such as Janet Jackson, Whitney Houston and Lisa Bonet. Her bold lipstick choice showed her confidence and ease with herself. In contrast, the pared-back look of Yorkie hinted at her innocence and social unease.

Susie Coulthard: Gugu and I kept coming back to a purple suede Versace jacket I had found on Brick Lane. We worked out we needed to razz it up with studs and fringe to make it more Kelly.

Mackenzie Davis: I loved the very first Yorkie outfit: the pleated khaki shorts and aqua sweater over a pink polo. It said so much about the character without drawing attention to itself at all – where she came from and what she thought was a nice outfit to reintroduce herself to the world. It still makes me laugh that she could have put together *anything* for this new self and she chose something that looks like her mum laid it out on her bed, the night before a charity golf tournament! But as Kelly says, it was authentically her, and there's something so beautiful about this woman choosing to be authentically herself in this moment of unlimited possibility. The thrill of her identity and her queerness is the event, the reason for all of this, not the opportunity to reinvent her exterior self and sell a coolness that would appeal to anyone else.

Susie Coulthard: Mackenzie was super happy to play the transforming geek, which is such a constant in 1980s films. With Yorkie's glasses, I really wanted the changes to be slight yet period-authentic as she jumped around the years. When she finally enters the system as a full timer, she has no glasses, as San Junipero has become her authentic life. Owen suggested that she takes them off and leaves them on the beach which I think is such a perfect moment.

Mackenzie Davis: I think they nicely undid the 'transforming geek' trope by playing with the outfit montage early on. Were they loyal to that trope, Yorkie would have re-entered Tucker's in slow-mo, modelling the *Addicted To Love* look, and the whole bar would have gone slack-jawed and silent. Instead they played through all the transformative possibilities in the mirror and Yorkie settles, once again, on a golf-mom look and lets the transformation be self-motivated and internal. Quietly, it's the most unique, least derivative of all the looks she tried on, which is Susie and Tanya's genius.

Tanya Lodge: As the two characters travelled through the decades, I kept one look for each period so each year had an identifiable look, using various hair pieces and make up. I particularly enjoyed creating the debauched world of the Quagmire, where we used crazy wigs and really strong make-up styles, letting our imagination run wild.

Annabel Jones: The concept allowed us to do *Black Mirror*'s version of time travel. When Yorkie goes searching for Kelly, she looks in lots of different years, so we had a lot of fun changing their costumes, the cars, the style of dancing. Charlie is incredibly specific, right down to the video games and

Opposite top: The costume concept art for Kelly and Yorkie, designed by Susie Coulthard.

Opposite bottom: The personalised number plates for cars driven by Kelly and Yorkie in San Junipero.

Yorkie '1987

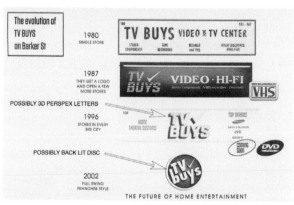

arcade machines for every year. We spent a long time, in post production, looking at archive footage and posters that would help establish these different periods as quickly as possibly – the footage that is playing in the TV shop, the film posters outside Tucker's, the music … .

Gugu Mbatha-Raw: We worked with a dance choreographer and played around with some very specific styles. We looked at the music videos of Janet Jackson. I don't think they got the rights to her song *What Have You Done for Me Lately*, but that's what we originally worked with and shot.

Charlie Brooker: Alexander O'Neal's song *Fake* actually ended up being more fitting, because *What Have You Done for Me Lately* had nothing to do with the story. Whereas with *Fake*, they were in an artificial world, so it had this additional layer. And luckily the song had exactly the same tempo, so their dance moves would still match.

Gugu Mbatha-Raw: We had so much fun! Kelly's shoulder pads, and that rhythmic shoulder thing, were totally stolen from Janet. In terms of style, I definitely took inspiration from other artists like Prince and Whitney Houston. For me, it was a great chance to be goofy and expressive. I'd come off some quite intense movie roles, so it was nice to do something playful and not take it all so seriously. The dancing was a big part of that: it was all about expressing and celebrating Kelly's life.

Mackenzie Davis: I was instructed to try to follow along with Gugu's amazing Janet Jackson homage and fail awkwardly... which I did with ease!

Halfway through San Junipero, *a throwaway comment from Kelly's fling Wes suggests that all is not as it appears in the tropical playground. Charlie worked hard to ensure the film's secrets gradually unveiled themselves.*

Charlie Brooker: I usually have to write quickly, but there wasn't an urgent deadline on this one. One reason why this script came out so fast, was that I was constantly operating under a load of restrictions dictated by the twist. Writing a script like that is like being forced to come up with dialogue that rhymes, because it's got to do two different things at once. It's got to sound like two people talking, like they might in an 80s movie nightclub scene, but it's also got to make sense as stuff that old people in a simulation might say and do. So instead of wondering what to do next, you have a constant little problem to solve. I had to get these two women to meet and fall in love, while constantly distracting the viewer from this thing in the corner of the room.

Annabel Jones: *San Junipero* is a very different film when you watch it the second time round. In the edit, we primed ourselves to wonder whether any line of dialogue might give too much away. Did it nod too much to the fact that these are 70-year-old women? And at the same time, you're trying to intrigue by adding little clues.

Charlie Brooker: I thought we gave some huge clues, but people generally didn't pick up on them! There's a moment in Tucker's when the guy shows Yorkie this arcade driving game, and a car crashes on the screen. She has

Opposite top: The Quagmire, developed and realised by Joel Collins and his team at Painting Practice.

Opposite bottom: The location used for Tucker's nightclub and the development work showing its progression through the years along with the neighbouring 'TV Buys' store.

this horrible visceral reaction, because it reminds her of the car crash that paralysed her. Once you know what's going on, it makes perfect sense. We even put the noise of a car crash on the soundtrack, so I thought people would immediately go, "Oh, she's been in a car crash in real life." But no-one ever picks up on it, until maybe a third viewing.

Yorkie runs away from the dance floor because she's overwhelmed by her new reality, in which she can walk. Everything's new to her. Which is stuff you don't need to register, but it makes sense on a third viewing. The other big clue was playing The Smiths' *Girlfriend in a Coma* over a shot of Yorkie. You see, I seem to think that viewers are writing all these small details down! But they're not. People only notice when a plot doesn't make sense. It's good to give the audience a chance to get it, though, because otherwise it might feel like a complete cheat.

In 1996, Yorkie is seen standing near an arcade game called Time Crisis. That was my little video games joke, because at that point you think they're travelling through time. There's also House of the Dead further into the future. Of course a 'house of the dead' is essentially what San Junipero itself is.

During the shoot, an unexpected debate arose: would it rain in a digitally simulated resort like San Junipero.

Owen Harris: Charlie wasn't sure about the logic of rain, but I couldn't imagine the alleyway scene outside Tucker's without it, so I clung on to it like a dog with a bone.

Charlie Brooker: It can be quite embarrassing, because I was so Taliban about that. San Junipero is an idealised version of somewhere, so why would they make it rain? As I kept saying again and again and again, the weather would be sunny all the time. Owen kept giving me all these explanations, like you might want to feel rain, and the more he said them the more I dug my heels in.

Owen Harris: I like the fact that Charlie has pretty hard and fast rules when it comes to logic. It means his ideas aren't about having a fun notion: they really have to stack up, and that's a big part of *Black Mirror*'s success. He and Annabel are pretty rigorous, so if you have an idea that is maybe more emotive than logical, you have to come with a pretty strong case. But I *wanted* rain. It was so 80s, sexy and seductive, and it briefly traps the girls, forcing them to have the conversation.

Charlie Brooker: Owen dug his heels in too, and was adamant that it would be fine, so I reluctantly gave in. And he was right, which is sort of annoying! Now, the problem is that having done that, people know that every so often I can be defeated on the Taliban front.

Owen Harris: I'm so glad I persuaded Charlie, especially because later in the shoot it started to rain for real, straight after Kelly's accident. The timing of the rain was bizarrely perfect, but it would have been a disaster if we hadn't agreed on the logic of rain in the first place!

Shooting in Cape Town and London gave us the best looks for the film, but it was a logistical nightmare. We finished shooting in London on a Wednesday, flew to South Africa that night, landed Thursday and started shooting again on Friday, with next to no prep-time. We just kept going. You get a sense you are shooting something good and it propels you forward.

I still don't know how we managed that 15-day shoot. You're constantly on the edge of not getting what you need. Probably the biggest reason we survived, on top of everyone's great skill and hard work, was the fact that the actors trusted me enough to move on after just a couple of takes, if I felt we'd got what we needed. Of course there were scenes that needed a bit more finding, and we never left a scene unless we were all satisfied, but it can be unnerving for an actor to plan and think about a scene for so long, and then it's all over in a blink. But that's what we did. And it allowed us to create a piece of filmic proportions in a fraction of the time.

Gugu Mbatha-Raw: I feel like shoots are always like that! I've never had a particularly luxurious shoot schedule, so I was used to working quickly. Most times during those night shoots, we were out in Cape Town at four in the morning, so you do have to get into the spirit of it. Plus, I try not to be one of those whiny actors who ask for another take! Unless you genuinely think you need to try something different, ultimately you have to trust the director. I did trust Owen, having seen his previous work. So my biggest challenge was to stay in the moment and be playful. I loved every minute of playing Kelly, so the challenge was more about keeping the energy up.

Towards the end of San Junipero, *we finally discover that Kelly and Yorkie are elderly, dying women. The Kelly who visits Yorkie in hospital is played by a different actress, Denise Burse.*

Charlie Brooker: Denise was brilliant. It's funny – sometimes I almost forget that there's two people playing Kelly, because when Denise shows up as 'Elder Kelly', as it said in the script, there's a through-line that you weirdly just accept. People have even have asked if Denise is Gugu in prosthetic make-up, because we were so fortunate with the casting.

Gugu Mbatha-Raw: When I first met Owen and Charlie, I said, "So, what's the deal – do I get to play it all? Am I gonna get some amazing prosthetics?" But Denise is so incredible. I'm glad it was done that way, because given what San Junipero is, it's not as if you have to look like the same person.

Annabel Jones: We only discussed old-age make-up briefly, before ruling it out. You've got to at least have the discussion, but I think that stuff just always looks fake and throws you out of the moment.

Charlie Brooker: Well, you say that, but did you know that I'm a young person in make up?

Annabel Jones: I knew there was something odd, but I couldn't quite put my finger on it.

Charlie Brooker: I'm just 24 years old.

Owen Harris: We went through the usual motions of looking for an older Gugu. Something about Denise and her choices as an actress – and also a Skype conversation where we just hit it off – made her feel right.

Gugu Mbatha-Raw: I had never met Denise, and so Owen set a bit of an exercise for us where we would read each other's lines. Not to imitate, or really do anything very technical – it was more to just listen to each other and spend time together. It was really lovely to have that time.

Owen Harris: I would love to say that we were totally instrumental in making the change from young to old feel so seamless, but a lot of it was down to the simple fact that both actresses made the part so compelling.

Charlie's original storyline had climaxed when Elder Kelly visited Yorkie in hospital.

Charlie Brooker: This was supposed to be the big emotional end: Kelly going in, kissing Yorkie on the forehead and saying, "Hello stupid, it's good to see you." I thought that was a sweet, tear-jerking ending: two dying old ladies who'd found love.

But I was enjoying the writing, so I thought I'd just keep going. And while working out what should happen next, I thought "Wait ... what if, rather than dying, Yorkie's going to be euthanised and live on in San Junipero?" It added a whole extra, deeper level. So that gave Yorkie more of a purpose. And I gave Kelly a whole back story, that I must have vaguely thought about already – things like her having been married for 40 years. So I added an end after the end, basically. And while I was writing, I thought this was much better. There was the big scene where Kelly turns on Yorkie with her big emotional speech that I'd written in one go. I was pleased with how that scene came out, because there was a lot of emotion and conflict.

Annabel Jones: I remember very clearly watching Gugu deliver Kelly's big emotional speech to Yorkie on the cliff edge in Cape Town. Kelly talks about her husband – "The years I gave him, the years he gave me" – and her daughter – "Always difficult, always beautiful" – and I was just crying. The emotion Charlie conjures up with such economy is just breathtaking and Gugu's performance was so impassioned, I knew we were making something very special. I texted Charlie to say the script was just beautiful but of course he deflected it by talking some shit. Probably something about a monkey in a fez.

Charlie Brooker: It's hard to conceive that all this stuff wasn't there to start with! The same goes for [Belinda Carlisle's 1987 hit] *Heaven Is a Place On Earth*, which randomly popped up on a 1987 Spotify playlist I put together while I wrote. Listening to the lyrics, I thought, "This is perfect. Oh my god, we've got to license the song!"

I just kept pressing 'repeat' and suddenly I could see that ending. We could show a bank of servers with lights, and it really would be like Heaven is a place on Earth. It's a joke *and* it resonates? Okay, perfect, boom.

Ugh. I just said "boom".

I have heard people say, "Oh, *San Junipero*'s the first time they've really done an emotional story." But I don't think that's true, because they're *all* emotional stories.

Annabel Jones: I think some people saw *San Junipero* as a 'first' because it was a happy, uplifting ending.

Charlie Brooker: People were worried for Kelly and Yorkie, because they'd seen us destroy people in *Playtest* and *Shut Up and Dance*. There's an extra tension in a totally merciless show like this. That's why *San Junipero* worked where it was in our Netflix running order. Across Season Three, film by film, we go, 'Bittersweet, nasty, *bloody* nasty, happy ... and then nasty, nasty.'

Owen Harris: I never read the story as being quite as positive as it ended up feeling. In fact, I'm probably a bit more like Kelly's husband: more reticent about the idea of spending eternity in a place like San Junipero. I'd worry I'd end up in the Quagmire!

Annabel Jones: Whilst there is a positive upbeat ending, it's not exactly a happy ever after. It's more about being happy for *now*, and seeing how this goes. On the cliff, when Kelly delivers that speech and says, "What does forever even mean?", that thought remains.

Charlie Brooker: But it is a deliberately triumphant ending. Quite often, we drop characters into a cage and watch them run around for a bit. And then mess with them even more. But every so often, you open the cage and let them out, like in *San Junipero*.

Owen Harris: The response has been amazing and totally unexpected. I've shot all over the world and everywhere I go I get a response. I even found out recently there's a club night in Milan called San Junipero. I think the love story and the optimism came at such an opportune time and, being an episode of *Black Mirror*, from such an unexpected place. You sit down to watch one of these episodes and expect to be thrilled, surprised, alarmed and disturbed, but maybe the biggest surprise of all was to be uplifted.

Charlie Brooker: Because *San Junipero*'s about two women falling for each other, it was doubly nerve-wracking because I hoped I'd got it right. It was gratifying when a lot of LGBTQ folk took it to heart and it resonated with them on an additional level. I was worried somebody might take it totally the wrong way, like, "What the fuck, people don't talk like this!" You just don't know. All you can ever do is imagine you are that person for a moment, and try to behave as they would for a bit, in your head. It's a form of madness, isn't it? Writing is all about sitting there and doing something mad.

Mackenzie Davis: The reception of the episode has been such an education on my own blindspots as a straight white woman. I could never have anticipated what a healthy, biracial love story – in which neither character dies – could mean to those who had experienced a dearth of positive depictions of their identities. I think that's the very thing that attracted me to the story in the first place: when I read it and while we were making it, there was never a hint of discussion about it being a gay love story. It was a love story, in which two complete characters with rich histories find each other during a second chance at life. Period. Because the writing had no agenda – or didn't feel like it was 'statement first, story later' – everyone from the cast to the creators to the audience got to experience the love story in a pure way, and process the implications of this particular love story after the fact.

Above: The cover artwork for the *San Junipero* soundtrack, by artist Billy Butcher.

Gugu Mbatha-Raw: I'm really proud and somewhat surprised by the impact the film has had, in terms of the pride and joy and inspiration I know it's become for the LGBTQ community. Many people have approached me to express how important this was: a love story between two women which was not about being ashamed of anything. It wasn't about being gay or bisexual being a problem. It was a love story about souls, and that's how I always saw it, so I'm super-proud.

It's great for a work to be fun, first and foremost, but when it's got something to say, touches people emotionally and potentially helps the culture to evolve in terms of how minorities are seen? That's a very powerful gift.

MEN
AGAINST
FIRE

In Conversation

Charlie Brooker – writer and executive producer
Annabel Jones – executive producer
Jakob Verbruggen – director
Malachi Kirby – actor
Lucy Dyke – producer
Joel Collins – series production designer
Natalie Ward – costume designer

Young soldier Stripe joins a military unit commissioned to exterminate humanoid mutants known as 'roaches', which have reportedly terrorised the local villagers. After killing two roaches, Stripe discovers his superiors are manipulating the nature of the reality seen by him and his fellow grunts.

Charlie Brooker: *Inbound*, the first ever *Black Mirror* episode fully written but never made, had been based on a true, harrowing story. Konnie had made me watch this gut-wrenching 2010 John Pilger documentary called *The War You Don't See*, about the Iraq war. There was a lengthy sequence following a grieving mother around her house, in which she was subtitled throughout, describing how members of her family had been killed. Usually you'd just glimpse a weeping relative for a two-second shot in a news report. This suddenly became more urgent and human. It got me thinking about a story in which we merely transposed a real incident from a warzone and had it play out in contemporary Britain. I read about various incidents and stumbled across one about a young boy from Iraq who was injured when soldiers mistakenly opened fire on his family's car. His parents were killed, and he was left partially paralysed. They flew him to the States, got him state-of the-art treatment, and eventually got him to walk again. He voluntarily went back to Iraq and then got blown up by a bomb. I mean, it was horrifying.

We went through various incarnations with *Inbound*, but it was hard for me to unpick. In this story, you thought an alien force was attacking Britain, but it turned out they were Norwegian. As Jay Hunt once said, it was all a bit heavy-handed and overly earnest, as well as quite humourless, given the subject matter.

Annabel Jones: Sounds perfect! There was definitely something interesting in the way war footage was now constantly being broadcast to us and the resulting desensitisation, but we couldn't find the story to make it more than that. Later, the idea became more about the future of warfare and military conditioning, and how technology could provide the ultimate propaganda tool.

Charlie Brooker: *Inbound* evolved into *Men Against Fire*, with this war in which combat is being censored for the soldiers. Thanks to these soldiers' MASS systems, human beings are being made to look like 'roach' monsters. I can't remember if our term 'roaches' pre-dated [controversial British columnist] Katie Hopkins writing cartoonishly horrible things about migrants in the newspaper and calling them 'cockroaches'. Actually, that may have been a deliberate lift, because there's a deliberately Katie Hopkins-type character in *Hated in the Nation*.

I was definitely looking for a word that could be used as a racist or dehumanising term to describe a whole group of people. At the time, I thought it was incredibly far-fetched, the notion that a future fascist government might come in and demonise a huge section of society. And then subsequently that's felt closer to home.

Jakob Verbruggen (director): We'd seen a lot of young actors, but Malachi Kirby stood out for the role of Stripe. He has a lot of star quality and a very strong physique, but he's also enigmatic, silent and observant.

Malachi Kirby (actor): I was already an admirer of the show from the first series – to the point where I was slightly conflicted by the knowledge that as soon as I read *Men Against Fire*, I would no longer be able to enjoy it as an audience member. That didn't stop me. I was definitely touched by it. A harrowing read.

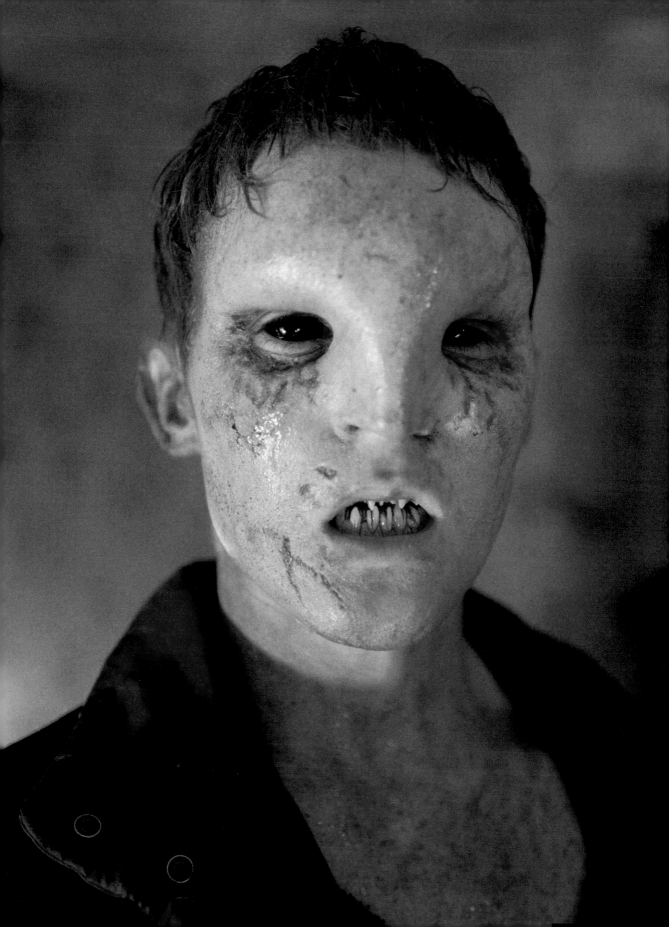

Jakob Verbruggen: Stripe starts out as an enthusiastic rookie, almost as if he's in an American football team. I was inspired by [the 1997 sci-fi film] *Starship Troopers* to create that sense of fearless high energy, so I have to thank its director Paul Verhoeven there.

Malachi Kirby: To me, Stripe didn't seem like an alpha male at all, but someone both naive and slightly aware that he may not be cut out for the journey he was about go on as a soldier. He has this chip installed in him that dulls his senses and emotions, but I still wanted to try and find some individuality and vulnerability in him.

Lucy Dyke (producer): This was a gritty film, without the gloss or sheen of some of the other *Black Mirrors*. Set in a semi post-apocalyptic world, it was intended to be slightly 'other' in terms of location, possibly somewhere in Eastern Europe. Time and budget constraints dictated we shot this in the UK, but it couldn't look like the UK or indeed 2016.

Three key locations helped us achieve the look. The first was the 'roach nest', the derelict farmhouse in the middle of nowhere. The location we found was falling down and full of grimy 70s paraphernalia which looked great but came with many health and safety warnings! A disused army barracks just outside London became our abandoned 'civilisation', which we wanted to feel urban and Eastern Bloc. And then there was the village that people had fled to when the spread of the roaches began. Joel Collins and his brilliant team built this from scratch in a forest near London. Expensive but worth every penny.

Jakob Verbruggen: Creating the roaches was a long and interesting journey. Were they a mutation, were they zombies, what were they? We looked at a lot of skin diseases and mutations. Considering our twist and how familiar everyone is with virtual reality and first-person shooter games, it was key to make the roaches as authentic as possible. There's a lot of close contact, especially for the character of Stripe. They're literally inches away from each other, so the roaches had to feel 100 per cent believable.

Joel Collins (series production designer): I came up with the idea of roaches looking as though they had hydrocephalus, as if their brains and everything had swelled. We wanted them to look scary and angry, but we also wanted you to feel sorry for them later.

Lucy Dyke: Our make-up designer Tanya Lodge brought in Kristyan Mallett, a prosthetics designer whose credits included *The Revenant* and *Everest*. We tested four shortlisted designs on camera. After a few tweaks, we and Netflix agreed on the look, but the eyes were still too human. Tanya then used full-eye black contact lenses on the adults, but we needed to VFX the boy's eyes later on.

Annabel Jones: Our reveal was that the 'roaches' the soldiers saw were just humans. So, for the story to hold, we would have only ever been able to show the roaches from the soldiers' POV. This would have restricted us cinematically, so we decided we needed the roaches to look normal from the back. We shot the first fight sequence in the farmhouse very frenetically to help obscure this.

'Humans – we give ourselves a bad rap but we're genuinely empathetic, as a species ... We don't actually really want to kill each other. Which is a good thing, until your future depends on wiping out the enemy'
– Arquette

Opposite: Set designs, including the remote farmhouse and MASS military base, by Joel Collins and Robyn Paiba with concept visuals developed by Painting Practice.

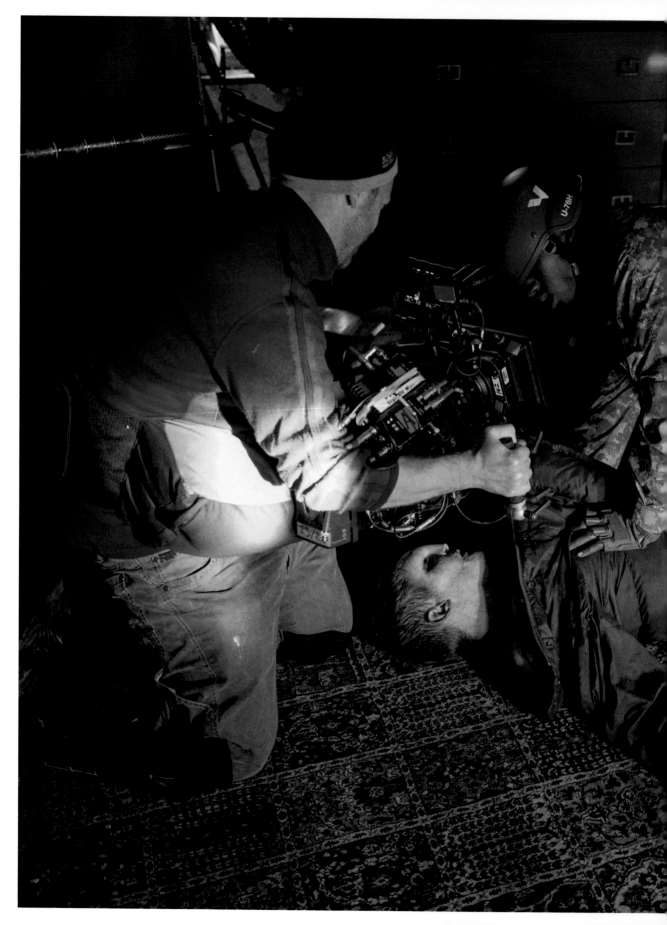

Jakob Verbruggen: The roaches had to move a certain way, so that was mainly a combination of actors and stunt people, with a few dancers too. We created a kind of choreography.

Natalie Ward (costume designer): The roaches had become like lepers in a society they were once part of. We decided they would take clothes and food from villages to survive. Nothing was meant to fit them, so they adapted things they found and wore clothes for protection against the cold. Even though we didn't see that much of them in the end, it was really important to me to make everything look believably distressed.

Lucy Dyke: The roach prosthetics required several hours in make-up, so any bad falls, scratches or nicks could see our actors sent back to the chair for several hours. We had 18 days to shoot the entire film, so the pressure was really on our actors to get it right. Malachi not only had to deal with an incredibly difficult performance, a complicated fight sequence, using weapons and very delicate prosthetics, but he was also literally shooting film using his MASS system! He did it all without breaking a sweat.

Charlie Brooker: I don't think we made the dream sequence element of the story clear enough, but the soldiers are given these sexualised dreams as a reward for doing well on the battlefield. There's some combination of mind control and augmented reality going on, but we never sit you down and tell you. After Stripe kills the two roaches, and his implant is malfunctioning, his reward-dream goes wrong and suddenly there's three of the same woman.

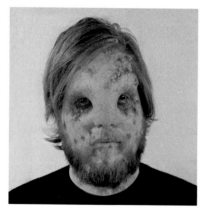

Jakob Verbruggen: To create multiple versions of Stripe's fiancée, we had this choreography where we had the actress Loreece Harrison and then body doubles with the same hair, clothes and skin tone. So everything was real and in-camera.

When Stripe learns the truth about the roaches and tries to rebel, he finds himself in a room with his quietly spoken psychologist Arquette, played by House Of Cards' *Michael Kelly.*

Charlie Brooker: Arquette was always written to seem sympathetic, but in my original version he was probably a bit more stuffy, or more of an old-school psychologist. Michael Kelly brought a lot to the role. He's very good at doing likeable warm menace!

Jakob Verbruggen: Arquette is a father figure to some of these soldiers, including Stripe, and believes he's doing good. Even in the final scene, I think, there's a fatherly element to Arquette. We always decided not to demonise him too much. Maybe he represents evil, but he believes in his cause.

Charlie Brooker: While quite a few people find this episode's twist pretty obvious, there is a complication. The soldiers literally see the roaches as monsters but the villagers don't – they just *consider* roaches to be monsters. It's easy to miss, but we explain in passing that the villagers don't have this MASS system in their eyes. So the soldiers need the system

Above: Make-up being applied to a roach onset and a prosthetic test, which was part of the make-up development work.

to allow them to kill people, but the public don't need that to demonise and hate people.

The title *Men Against Fire* came from S.L.A. Marshall's 1947 book *Men Against Fire: The Problem of Battle Command*, which talked about the low percentage of soldiers who actually fired their weapons during the first two world wars. And so what Arquette tells Stripe has some basis in reality. I was struck by the effort the military has to go to. The problem is that people don't want to pull the trigger, so what's the solution? Dehumanising the enemy.

Arquette has a lot of speeches to do, while explaining to Stripe what's been going on. There's generally a bit too much of things being explained to Stripe slightly after the fact. I should have found a different way to achieve that.

Annabel Jones: Charlie's being too hard on himself. *Men Against Fire* is one of our heavier films thematically. When you're making an anthology and it's going to sit aside films that are pure entertainment like *Playtest*, then it might appear more expositional, but I think it's a profound film. For a hi-tech world, I love the fact that the end of the film consists of two people in an empty room discussing ideas of right and wrong.

Jakob Verbruggen: We put Stripe and Arquette in a bright, uncomfortable and extremely claustrophobic room and decided not to have both actors in the same frame. Hopefully that resonates with the audience. And then, when Stripe learns the whole truth, the shape of the room seems to change, because it closes down on him.

In the final shot of the film, Stripe returns home to be reunited with his fiancée, but all we can see is a derelict, abandoned house.

Annabel Jones: Arquette revealed that, when Stripe signed up for the military operation, he knew what he was agreeing to. To enable him to return home, Stripe has agreed to have his memory of the event wiped and the military have won. Stripe's tear is a hint of him having a sense of this. We intercut MASS's idealised version of the homecoming – white picket fence Americana with the sweetheart on the porch welcoming him home – and the reality of a run-down empty house covered in graffiti. The propaganda, military and personal, continues.

Jakob Verbruggen: Everybody can make their own interpretation of our ending, because that's the only thing that hints at the society, or world, where the story takes place. What has happened? Is anything real? Was even Michael Kelly's character real? Is this just a story about a soldier dealing with PTSD? Who knows?

Charlie Brooker: What is Stripe actually looking at, in those final shots? I don't really have an answer. That is a very oblique ending. I just knew it worked as an image. The idea originally was for the soldiers to come back to a homecoming parade and then you see it's not real, and there's no one showing up to see them.

Malachi Kirby: I really enjoyed that last scene, when Stripe gets out of the car and he's in his uniform. We did quite a few different versions and interpretations of that, and it was fun to explore the possibilities. Also, I loved that costume!
   Despite how traumatised Stripe is by what has been revealed to him, he cannot bear to go back to ignorance. Here's my own interpretation: he requests an option of keeping his memories but also having the chip alter what he sees again. So when he goes back home, the chip shows him a beautiful vision of his house and this virtual 'spouse', but he knows it's not real.

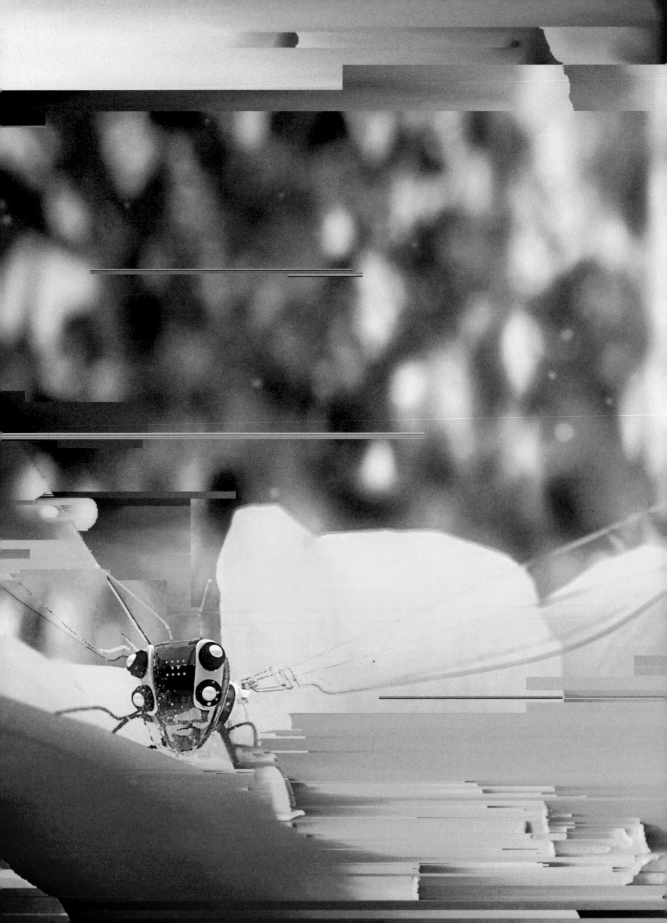

HATED IN
THE NATION

In Conversation

Faye Marsay – actor
Annabel Jones – executive producer
Charlie Brooker – writer and executive producer
Sanne Wohlenberg – producer
James Hawes – director
Joel Collins – series production designer
Morgan Kennedy – co-production designer
Dan May – visual effects supervisor

A controversial journalist is found dead, after attracting hatred on social media. A publicly shamed rapper suffers the same fate. When DCI Karin Parke and trainee detective Blue Coulson set out to find the connection between these deaths, they uncover one man's mission to punish social media's keyboard warriors.

Faye Marsay (actor): When I was in *Game of Thrones,* I played a character called The Waif who wasn't very nice. Some days, I'd wake up and people would tweet the worst things, just basically telling me to die. That didn't upset me in the sense that it felt real – it was just sad that people could hide behind a screen and say the most horrible stuff.

Social media's wonderful in terms of activism and finding out what's going on in the world, but there's a real dark side. Kids bully each other on social media and people's lives can be ruined. And that's why *Hated in the Nation* appealed to me so much.

Annabel Jones: This film plays out almost like a serial-killer story, or a conventional detective whodunit mini-series, with gradual reveals of what's going on. That was new for us. There were lots of world layers going on, and the plotting of all those things is quite complex. We'd done a bit of that in *The National Anthem,* but this was on a bigger scale.

I always thought *Hated in the Nation* was a very clever way of taking the online witch-hunt and making it feel very real. There are so many interesting themes being brought together. But for a long time, Charlie worried that the whole thing was preposterous.

Charlie Brooker: This was one of the hardest *Black Mirror*s to write, and at one point I completely gave up. It has a lot of elements which are exactly the sort of thing we parodied when we did this spoof TV detective show called *A Touch of Cloth,* a sort of British take on [the 1988 comedy film] *Naked Gun,* with that Zucker Brothers humour. Because I'd only done a police procedural in the context of spoofing police procedurals, there was a lot of stuff to work out.

This one and Season Four's *Metalhead* both sprang from the same idea: what if enough people voted for a particular person to be killed by a terrifying robot or several robots? So when we started doing the first Netflix season, I wondered how this idea might work. The next question was why somebody was being chased by a robot. Then it became a crowd-sourced assassination thing. I pictured a big thing chasing people, but I couldn't quite work out why this person had been chosen to be killed.

For a while, I thought about a robot the size of the ones in [the 2013 sci-fi/fantasy blockbuster] *Pacific Rim,* or the size of Godzilla, gigantic and unstoppable. But I didn't know how we'd do that. And then conversations led to it becoming the opposite: a robot so tiny you can't see it. It's literally the size of a mosquito and it kills you. And what if that was voted for?

Thinking about it more, I got excited and wondered why the robot would be a little wasp or a bee. Since bees are dying out, what if they invent some? I didn't know that real-life companies were actually working on drone bees, but I had the idea of this kind of programme being weaponised. So I created the company Granular to produce these bees.

Around this time, I had two conflicting thoughts. This idea seemed really silly: robot bees that kill people? Also, it could be really horrifying. But who's doing this? Why are they doing it? How do I explain why this is happening?

When I get stuck on dialogue, it's when I'm trying to capture the voice of an official who uses jargon. That throws me. So with *Hated in the Nation,* I didn't know how the fuck the police speak and I worried about that too much, because they probably speak like us when they're not spouting lingo as part of the job, and you can do research to find out what they would say.

I'm also allergic to another thing we almost did in *Hated in the Nation*, which is the evil corporation. Maybe this is naive of me, but I imagine few corporations sit around talking about how evil they are and enjoying it. Facebook might do thing that are mainly about profit, but they've probably convinced themselves they're doing it for the good of humankind. That's why we shy away from evil corporations – for a show with lots of gadgets and robots, we only allude to the companies that make these things.

So I wrote half of the script and then got really stuck. I just felt it was too silly. I said to Annabel, "I don't think I can do that one. I'm going to write another instead." The whole thing felt over-cooked. We'd spent so much time working out the logic of how it all worked that I'd slightly lost sight of things. It was upsetting, but mainly because I felt I'd squandered time. When you're a writer, there's always a voice in your head going, "You're shit." And this time, that voice seemed to have won.

Annabel Jones: We had worked out so much, including where the bees came from – originally, Scholes created his own network of self-replicating bees, before Charlie decided he should hack into an existing bee network. We established how the bees kill; the hashtag stuff and how it plays out; how the police work out the connection; the technical stuff, such as the cracking of the bees' chip and getting the IMEI numbers; how Karin works out the killer's identity. I remember us arguing vehemently about why the government just wouldn't shut down the internet to prevent anyone being named and killed.

Charlie had written 80 pages – we were so nearly there! But when he gave up, I knew he'd come back to it. I said to him, "This is brilliant, this is thrilling and intriguing!" But other episodes came in and took priority.

Charlie Brooker: I went off and worked on *San Junipero* and *Shut Up and Dance* instead. And then, at some point around the writing of *Men Against Fire*, *Hated in the Nation* became a going concern again.

Annabel Jones: Tonally, I never worry about the show's ability to land a compelling story, or Charlie's ability to write a convincing, grounded story. It's all about balance and where you place the emphasis. I think we're quite good at managing all those things, so that nothing ever tips over into being preposterous. It's all about what you show and what you don't.

Charlie Brooker: When I dug the script back out again, I hadn't looked at it for two months. I read it through, and this time I saw where I'd gone wrong.

Annabel Jones: Charlie remembered how, in *White Christmas*, we'd got through a lot of detail very quickly by having Jon and Rafe as narrators. So he came up with the flash-forward framing device of Karin and other characters giving evidence at the public enquiry, to do a lot of the narrative heavy-lifting. It also meant the film could span more time than the five-day killing spree and we didn't have to explain every step along the way.

We didn't end up using this framing device as much as we originally thought, because it actually cut into the pace of the story, but it was a really effective method for building intrigue. What happened on the day Karin is being interrogated about? We see that Blue isn't present in the flash-forward, so has she been killed? Then we're led to believe Blue killed herself, setting up the great ending.

When Charlie went back and re-read those first 80 pages, that's when I knew everything was fine, because he said, "You know what? It was all right." I thought, "Fucking hell, he must've enjoyed it, to give himself that level of praise!" Normally he'll go, "We are doomed! We are over!"

Charlie Brooker: I'm better now. A bit less doomy, thanks to experience. Because after all the times I've gone, "We're doomed!" we've always found solutions. Until of course, the one time we are doomed ... which will happen.

Producer Sanne Wohlenberg had enjoyed a varied career, but her work on TV police shows Messiah *and* Wallander *were a particularly good fit for* Hated in the Nation.

Sanne Wohlenberg (producer): Originally, Lucy Dyke and Laurie Borg were supposed to produce three films each this season. But then they realised it would be impossible for, say, one producer to be shooting in Cape Town whilst also prepping in London! So I got a phone call out of the blue, saying they needed a producer for *Hated in the Nation*. Could I start on Monday? I read the script and said, "Ooh, yes please!"

We interviewed quite a few directors. James Hawes had done a beautifully judged TV production called *The Challenger*. He had collaborated with the cinematographer Lukas Strebel, and those two really bring the best out of each other onscreen. They got the DNA of *Hated in the Nation*.

James Hawes (director): I liked how *Hated in the Nation* started with a really slow burn, moving from local to global. The real challenge was how to pace it and craft the escalation. How to draw our audience into the

Above: The design development work by Painting Practice for the headquarters of Granular, makers of the ADI bees.

world early on and then take them with us to the real darkness. *Hated in the Nation* could have gone wrong and become sci-fi horror. I wanted it far more rooted and honest than that, so that the enormous scale and consequence felt plausible.

Sanne Wohlenberg: One of our big challenges was how to portray London. It was ultimately a very normal world and terribly familiar, but five minutes ahead. We had 32 London locations to shoot in 23 days, which was a challenge in itself. It was about creating a visual coherence.

Joel Collins (series production designer): I did some Scandi-noir tonal design work, which became basically [the US anthology crime drama TV show] *True Detective* in terms of its edgy quality.

James Hawes: I often choose a reduced palette to bring a unity to the design. Lukas and I admire many of the Scandi series and sought to capture something of that aesthetic, which seemed appropriate to the story. The palette also seemed to speak of a world where the bees have died out, killed by human stupidity.

Morgan Kennedy (co-production designer): The decision to take a somewhat monochromatic approach worked really well with the idea of nature being replicated. We tried to restrict the colour palette in camera as much as possible, which gave the opportunity to use stronger colour when it was needed. My favourite example is the flowers in the foreground before the Granular HQ greenhouse scene.

Sanne Wohlenberg: We picked the right buildings, juxtaposing old with new. DCI Karin Parke's apartment had to be a bland new-build, where a divorced woman had settled. We did subtle things like lights coming on automatically when she walks in. Things that make it feel a few years forward.

> '[Online hate] drifts off like weather. It's half-hate. They don't mean it ... The hate in a marriage, that's in 3D. That's had work put into it. That's sincere'
>
> – Karin

Morgan Kennedy: One of *Hated in the Nation*'s strong themes was the mix of technology and nature. Granular HQ was possibly the biggest challenge, and went through quite a few looks to get it right. In the end, the mix of the huge greenhouse and the control room's hi-tech but simple concrete design seemed to work very well.

James Hawes: Finding locations in which to shoot Granular HQ proved hard. In the end, we shot on five separate locations to build the journey from the drive, through the reception and glasshouses, all the way to the lab. It included a salad farm in Essex and the ExCel conference centre in London.

Annabel Jones: Poor Erica McEwan, our series graphic art director, had so much to do with all of the graphics and social media interfaces. Obviously they had to be very foregrounded in the film, often driving the narrative, and so their authenticity was key. We spent months in prep and post working through it all. Luckily Erica is as patient as she is talented.

James Hawes: We spent a great deal of effort deciding what police looked like in 2024. We used existing sirens but played them in reverse. We armed 85 per cent of the officers and made all their uniforms black. The cars were BMWs but with a new livery.

Oh, the driverless car! We had this Land Rover concept car. They went to huge lengths to make it driverless, reshaping doors and so on. However, on the day, we discovered that it could only move in a straight line and then only at 15kph! Also, from the moment you pressed the button to open the doors, it took over a minute before they were wide enough for our team of super cops to be able to jump out. This meant the whole car thing ate shoot-time, and relied far more heavily on VFX than anticipated.

Annabel Jones: We had this funny moment while shooting the scene in which Karin and Blue thought they knew where the serial killer was and had

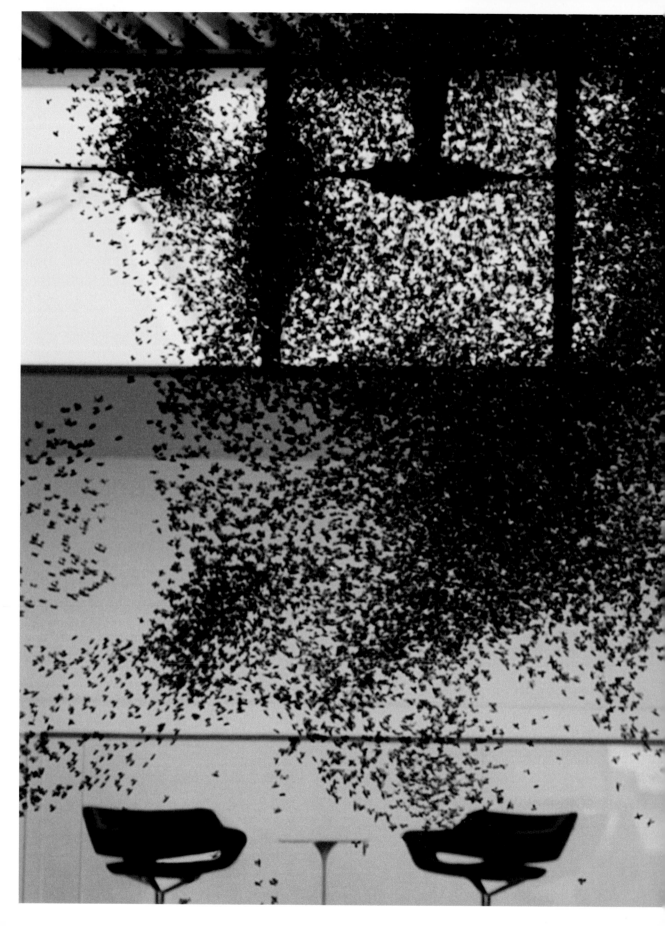

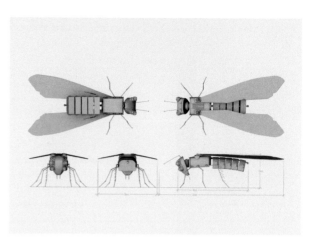

BEE ALTERNATIVES

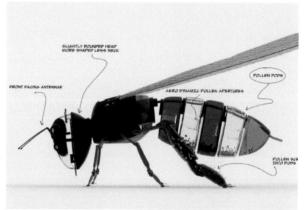

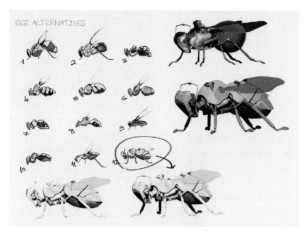

APE DESIGN NOTES

NOTE: THE BEE IS MADE OF 3D PRINTED CLEAR PLASTIC AND SCRAP ALUMINIUM

SOLAR POWER GENERATING WINGS

4 X EYES FOR GREATER VIEWING ANGLES

METALLIC STATIC HAIRS FOR COLLECTING POLLEN

CLEAR PLASTIC HEAD TO SEE IN WORKINGS AND SIM CHIP

SMALL PLIERS FOR COLLECTING SCRAP

TINY CLAWS FOR GRIPPING FRICTIONLESS SURFACES LIKE GLASS

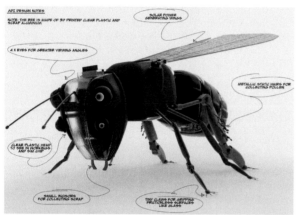

SLIGHTLY ROUNDED HEAD MORE SHAPED LESS NECK

FRONT FACING ANTENNAE

AERO DYNAMIC POLLEN APERTURES

POLLEN PODS

POLLEN SCR INTO PODS

the area surrounded by armed police. Karin and her senior team pulled up, about to jump out of the car and rush in … but had to stay seated for 60 seconds before the doors opened. Kelly and Faye struggled to hold it together.

Sanne Wohlenberg: It was wonderful to have two female leads. Charlie writes beautifully for women, which as we all know is not always the case in TV. We immediately gravitated towards Kelly Macdonald for DCI Karin Parke and were blessed that she loved it. Then we interviewed a few actors, but Faye Marsay brought Blue Coulson to life and we knew we'd found her.

Faye Marsay: I'd actually done a self-tape audition for *Men Against Fire*, which they liked, but they asked if they could see me for this other episode they were doing. I was really upset! I was like, "I wanted to have a gun and run about!" But then they sent me the script for *Hated in the Nation* and I was like, "Ooh, okay then!" Charlie writing about social media's potentially negative impact grabbed me straight away. What a privilege and an honour to get a feature-length episode, too.

I wanted Blue to be really down to earth, rather than some brooding cop who knows everything. She's quiet, quite sweet and really good at her job. I wasn't interested in how she looked and all that crap: I just wanted her to come across as a relatable person who's trying to do her best. While preparing, my main choice was to keep Blue's energy contained and calm.

I love Kelly! We're good friends: I saw her last week. We hadn't met before *Black Mirror*, but we got on so well. We're both complete dorks and constantly play tricks on each other. With some actors you get the job done and move on, but from the word go, I thought I'd know Kelly for a while.

The content was so dark, but if you saw us behind the scenes, we were all pissing ourselves laughing and punching each other! *Black Mirror* is so visceral that you have to have a laugh, otherwise you'd go a bit mad.

The film's most elaborate and thrilling set-piece sees a swarm of Granular's repurposed bees invade the remote safe house in which Parke, Coulson and NCA officer Shaun Li (Benedict Wong) are sheltering the ill-fated social pariah Clara (Holli Dempsey).

Sanne Wohlenberg: Only Charlie could bring the biggest action sequence of the entire film into a bathroom of a small house! It's such a brave choice: so unexpected and terrifying. It feels so real.

Joel Collins: *Hated in the Nation* was the precursor to *Metalhead*, in terms of the scale of the VFX attempt. Charlie was starting to integrate things into his scripts that didn't exist, at all, and we were starting to work out how to play them in the shows.

Dan May (visual effects supervisor): With the bees, we wanted to create something that was plausible, rather than being over designed. Something recognisable as bees, because within the world of the story they needed to have this kind of placebo effect, so that the population felt real bees were still there. And at the same time, they needed to be a little creepy.

Opposite: The various stages in the development work for the ADI bees, created by Painting Practice.

'It's like an unpopularity contest. Pick someone you don't like and if enough other people choose the same name, then that's who gets targeted'
– Blue

James Hawes: As soon as I read the script, I knew the safe house sequence needed to be a signature moment. Obviously there is a nod to Alfred Hitchcock, but I wanted it to feel terrifying in a real and contemporary way. It was a mammoth sequence to shoot, completed over three days: one on location and two on set, where we built the bedroom and bathroom.

Faye Marsay: Because there were so many CGI bees, we didn't even have a guide to react to, apart from James telling me and Kelly where to look. The cottage was kind of abandoned, so it had dead flies in the windows, which felt apt for what we were doing.

James Hawes: I was lucky to have actors who wholeheartedly threw themselves into believing where the bees would be and how terrifying the whole situation became. Their reactions were everything. We worked to have interactions, like the swinging light cord and the flapping fan vent – all details to help settle the VFX bees into the real world.

The early trials on the VFX bees were promising, but you never know how it will finally sit until it's on screen. We had to use various VFX techniques for the different shots. The more distant swarms were one thing, but the bees crawling on fans and faces required a different approach.

The bees gathering on the window at the safe house was a huge challenge, in as much as we needed to create the shadow of the gathering swarm to play on the faces of the actors. If I'm honest, I was never wholly satisfied with the moment of the bees inside the letterbox. However, the individual bees – like the one that crawls out of the car, or the one that hits the downstairs window – were completely brilliant.

Charlie Brooker: We had a debate about whether to cut *Hated in the Nation* into two episodes. In the safe house, the stakes suddenly go right through the ceiling and you could end Part One there, then go to Part Two …

Annabel Jones: ... But when you're trying to set up an anthology for this new global Netflix audience, having a two-parter in the middle of the season is going to harm that. I also thought the first episode might feel like a standard police procedural, rather than a *Black Mirror* ep. So I was keen for it to be one 90-minute film.

Charlie Brooker: It was a challenge to fit it into 90 minutes. When I'd written those 80 pages, I was only two-thirds of the way through the story. *Hated in the Nation* culminates with the biggest massacre in *Black Mirror* history, as 387,000 social media users fall foul of Scholes' airborne death machines.

James Hawes: The decision to keep all those deaths off-screen was wholly artistic. We had seen the individual deaths of people we had invested in, and now it was about the scale.

Sanne Wohlenberg: The image we have, of Karin and Blue walking into this appropriated hangar full of body bags, is incredibly strong. That felt like the right way to go, rather than to sensationalise it or wilfully shock people.

Charlie Brooker: There was nothing to gain by showing lots of people running around like in [1978's bee-disaster movie] *The Swarm*. And don't think I wasn't aware of things like *The Swarm*! I was thinking, "Fucking hell, the only time I've seen killer-bee movies, they've not been very good." The Hollywood movie version of our massacre sequence would have had 15 minutes of people crashing their cars into buses and screaming and running around grabbing their heads. Yet the really frightening thing is the image of one bee crawling through a keyhole, coming to find you, wherever you are.
  The National Anthem and *Hated in the Nation* both had bad guys with complicated schemes who we don't hear anything from. In *Hated in the*

Nation, with Garrett Scholes, I was thinking of people like the Unabomber or Anders Breivik, but I really didn't want us to explain too much of his dastardly scheme. The best thing to do was to keep him mysterious and give him a manifesto that we glimpse.

We don't hear Scholes say anything, so he seems more interesting as a result. Again, I don't know how that person would talk, except for the cliché of the artisan killer you get in cop dramas, post-*Silence of the Lambs*. You know, the killer who says, "Oh, hello Inspector, we're very alike, you and I ..."

Sanne Wohlenberg: Of course, how terrible for Scholes to respond to one wrong by trying to kill a whole load of other people. And yet it makes you think, "How much responsibility do I take for my own actions in the world of social media, which seems to create some kind of artificial distance?"

James Hawes: It is utterly true that people say anything that springs to mind with no sense of accountability. I am sure laws will evolve to make social media attacks sit alongside assault as a crime.

Faye Marsay: Scholes' idea that people should be held accountable for what they do on social media, that's something we need to pay attention to. But everyone makes mistakes and says things they don't mean, and obviously the way he did it was totally abhorrent.

Charlie Brooker: I don't have massive sympathy for Scholes' aims. He's being an utter fucking arsehole, killing hundreds of thousands of people.

Annabel Jones: Like a lot of deranged individuals, Scholes feels he's coming from a place of moral superiority. So it was nice to take this relatable position and then blow it up.

Faye Marsay: Like a typical actor, I don't usually like watching myself, but I went to a couple of screenings of *Hated in the Nation* and really enjoyed it. The cinematography and direction were gorgeous. One of my favourite scenes was Kelly calling the government a cunt. But in terms of us having a good old act with each other, I loved our first car scene. That was actually our first scene together in the shoot, and it was all bit awkward because we didn't know each other. I also loved spending a week in Gran Canaria.

James Hawes: Charlie originally wrote that Scholes threw his gear into a lake as he rowed across some tropical lagoon. We did not have production time to fly to the tropics, so we looked for locations within flying time that would offer something very obviously and exotically abroad. Gran Canaria offered these fabulous mountains and even a white-painted hill town that felt Andean. We also found this fantastic remote reservoir and dam. So we shaped the script to fit our assets – and even found genuinely Peruvian and Colombian people living in Gran Canaria to be our extras.

The film ends on an uncertain note, with a missing-presumed-dead Blue Coulson on the trail of Garrett Scholes in some far-flung corner of the world.

Charlie Brooker: I'm generally not a fan of completely ambiguous endings, but this one was ambiguous enough. Throughout, Blue has been so diligent that she feels responsible for the mass murder. Evidently she's been clever enough to work out where Scholes is, even though we don't show how.

Annabel Jones: If we had shown exactly what happens after our final shot, it all might have seemed too neatly wrapped up.

Faye Marsay: I think Blue does get Scholes. I don't know how, but I think she does get her victory. Might she kill him? Obviously he's murdered 387,000 people, so he's got to answer somehow. Do I believe in vengeful murder? No I don't, but then I'm not Blue.

Charlie Brooker: I can't remember if we filmed this, but originally there was a shot of Blue putting a knife in her bag as she goes after him. That was certainly in the script at one point, you knew she's going to go and knife him. But anyway, you do kind of know that Blue's going to sort him the fuck out.

SERIES FOUR

In Conversation

Joel Collins – series production designer
Annabel Jones – executive producer
Jo Kay – Head of Production, House of Tomorrow
Jina Jay – series casting director
Charlie Brooker – executive producer
Gugu Mbatha-Raw – actor, San Junipero
Mackenzie Davis – actor, San Junipero

Joel Collins (series production designer): I was in Canada when Season Three dropped on Netflix. While I was leaving a restaurant with Jodie Foster, this waitress stopped me, saying she'd heard I worked on *Black Mirror* and she was a huge fan. And Jodie Foster had just walked past her! Post-Netflix, the penny had dropped this was a fucking cool show, and that opened doors. We went from people not knowing what the show was, to people saying, "Come on in and shoot at our locations!" It changed everything.

Annabel Jones: We were happy with Season Three, and so were Netflix. Jodie Foster was directing *Arkangel*, our first new episode for Season Four, and so we felt quite confident.

Jo Kay (Head of Production, House of Tomorrow): Fortunately, the brilliant production team that worked on Season Three were able to return for Season Four, which meant we all had a shorthand. This meant that filming *Arkangel* in Canada could be dealt with quickly and efficiently.

Joel Collins: So we had *Arkangel* in Canada, *USS Callister* mostly at Twickenham Studios and *Crocodile* in Iceland. Hell on Earth! Great fun, but lots of travel. We were on planes twice a week.

Jo Kay: Either by careful scheduling or by good luck, we managed not to shoot two films back-to-back abroad. Budget-wise, Netflix continued to work with us on any demands that each script brought up, whether that was deciding to set *Crocodile* in Iceland, or the very heavy workload and cost of CGI on *Metalhead*.

Jina Jay (series casting director): I guess on Season Three, a lot of agents outside of the UK hadn't actually watched *Black Mirror*, even though they might have heard of it. It was easy to educate them, though, because the existing series was brilliant and had achieved cult status – plus everyone loves Charlie's voice, so we had a tangible foundation to work from. For me, it's all about matching talent with a role, and trusting my instinct about who might excite Annabel and Charlie. Every role cast in my office is distilled by my team, chiefly Olivia Brittain.

Black Mirror's raised profile inevitably meant that online reviews, think pieces and reaction videos grew in volume, whether positive or negative.

Charlie Brooker: I've seen so many hot takes on *Black Mirror,* and you can't keep up with it all. Maybe it's a writer thing, but it's all too easy to cancel out any positive responses and focus on the negatives. A critical thing will stick in your head more, either because you think it's so completely wrong that s irritating, or you agree with an aspect of it, which is almost more irritating. So now, I'm more prone to just shrug.

It would be really hypocritical of me to complain about criticism, when 've been quite a vicious TV critic ... but I am a hypocrite, so there you go. Occasionally it's irritating when people miss the point of the show and think t's more po-faced than I think it is. Or when they characterise it as a show warning about the dangers of technology. That slightly confuses and annoys me, because it's like saying [Alfred Hitchcock's 1960 classic] *Psycho* is a movie warning about the dangers of silverware. *Black Mirror* is not really about that ... except when it is, just to fuck with people!

Annabel Jones: Thankfully, on the whole we've been quite well received, so we're in a fortunate position. You take huge satisfaction when people want to share their favourite episode with you. And in today's climate, it's a huge plus when people have even *watched* your show, when there's so much to see.

On 17 September 2017, the Black Mirror *team attended the Emmy Awards n Los Angeles, having been nominated for three awards: Outstanding Television Movie (*San Junipero*), Outstanding Writing for a Limited Series, Movie or Dramatic Special (Charlie Brooker for* San Junipero*) and Outstanding Cinematography for a Limited Series or Movie (Seamus McGarvey for* Nosedive.*)*

Annabel Jones: We went out there proud of what we'd done, with nothing to lose. When you've got no expectations, that's always going to be the best win. n the car on the way to the ceremony, I said to Charlie, in a kind way I thought, to calm his pre-awards nerves, "Don't worry, you've got absolutely no chance of winning, because the other nominees are all big drama series writers."

When I look at the amount of ideas, detail, concepts, creativity and characterisation that has gone into all of these films, I find it breathtaking that one person can be so prolific and have such range to take on different genres so effectively, *and* have a degree of humour and warmth and emotion. t is a huge skill, and to do that across multiple genres is staggering. So while I was thrilled that we won the [Outstanding Television Movie] award for San Junipero, I was especially thrilled that Charlie won the award for writing.

Charlie Brooker: I genuinely hadn't bothered thinking of anything to say. So winning was like being smacked over the head with something, in a good way, and then immediately terrifying, because you're live on American television in front of millions. You get up onstage and in the front row there's ike Nicole Kidman and Oprah Winfrey and Robert De Niro. That's too weird so you look up, and there's just a big screen with a countdown going 38, 37, 36 ... basically telling you to fuck off!

Afterwards, it was really, really weird to walk around holding two Emmys. In LA, people act like you're a medieval soldier returning to the village clutching the severed head of one of their mortal enemies. Strangers go, "Oh my god, I love your show! What is it?"

Gugu Mbatha-Raw (actor, San Junipero): It was so, so lovely to hang out with everyone again and celebrate, even though an Emmy fell on my foot at the party. I thought it was broken at first, because it instantly went blue. I've got this ridiculous photograph of me in high heels with an ice-pack tied onto my foot with a bandanna. But I still managed to dance a little at the party, because we were so happy. Especially for Charlie.

Mackenzie Davis (actor, San Junipero): The whole reception of the episode was beyond what any of us had anticipated, particularly because it was such a cult show – in America at least – prior to getting the reach that Netflix affords. So the arc of making it, and feeling so lucky to be involved with this beautiful thing in the first place, to watching people react in the way they did, and then culminating with this very public acknowledgement ... it was a series of unexpected and lovely events.

Annabel Jones: Belinda Carlisle's *Heaven Is a Place On Earth* came on at the Netflix aftershow party. That was a big moment.

Charlie Brooker: How's this for a first world problem? I walked into the governor's ball, dying for a drink. People had trays of champagne, but I couldn't take one because I had an Emmy in each hand. So I actually had a moment of slight annoyance. What a prick! But genuinely, as somebody who tends to worry about things a lot, the Emmys was unequivocally a nice thing.

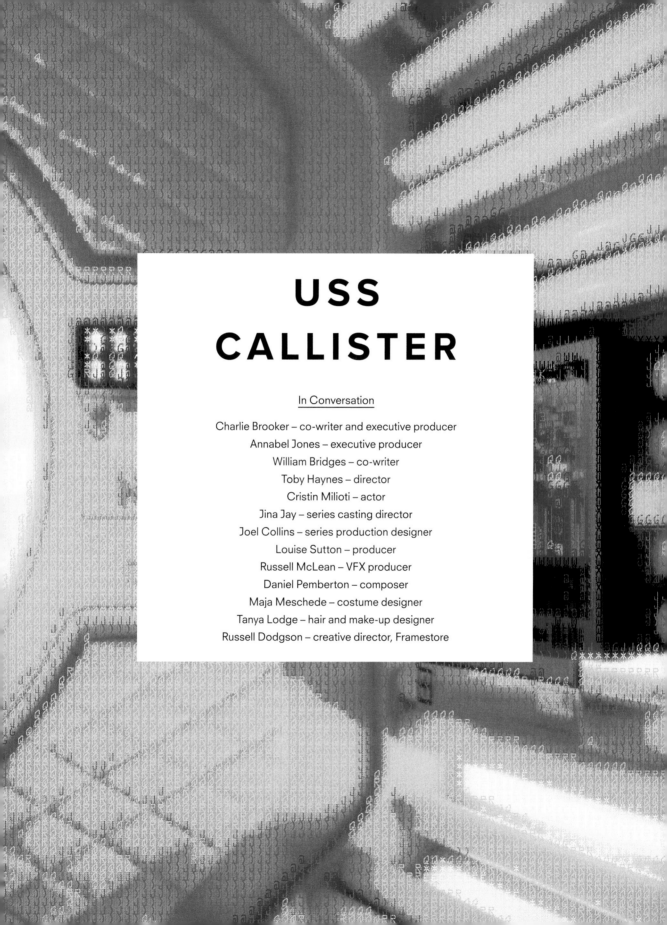

USS CALLISTER

In Conversation

Charlie Brooker – co-writer and executive producer
Annabel Jones – executive producer
William Bridges – co-writer
Toby Haynes – director
Cristin Milioti – actor
Jina Jay – series casting director
Joel Collins – series production designer
Louise Sutton – producer
Russell McLean – VFX producer
Daniel Pemberton – composer
Maja Meschede – costume designer
Tanya Lodge – hair and make-up designer
Russell Dodgson – creative director, Framestore

When Nanette Cole lands a job at the games company Callister Inc, she has no idea that chief technical officer Robert Daly has sinister plans for her DNA. Horrified to wake up as a virtual clone of herself aboard the USS Callister spaceship, where Captain Daly lives out his macho fantasies, Nanette must inspire the despondent crew members to help her escape this digital torture chamber.

Charlie Brooker: While filming *Playtest*, we'd talked about special effects in general, saying, "Wouldn't it be good if we could do an episode set in space." So one vague story at the back of my mind – normal person becomes powerful monster in VR kingdom – collided with the idea of an episode set in space.

Annabel Jones: *Black Mirror* set in space! What's not to like? We got to delve into a whole new genre for us, a space opera, and run lots of contemporary themes through it. Of course there was a nervousness, because even though the piece is about technology giving someone ultimate power, it is a classic sci-fi homage and we didn't want to mess that up! It was ambitious, it was a romp, it was our most comedic episode. A biggie!

Charlie Brooker: The notion that Daly had themed his world around this fictional vintage show called *Space Fleet* came in relatively late. That felt quite interesting because it became a comment on people going, "How dare there be female *Ghostbusters*." My co-writer Will Bridges is a big fan of *Star Trek*, which helped. I know a lot of stuff, but can't automatically pull on a lot of the tropes.

William Bridges (co-writer): If I'm being honest, I consider *Galaxy Quest* to be a bigger influence on *USS Callister* than anything from the Trek universe. That 1999 film is about a group of people unwittingly pulled into a *Star-Trek*-like world. They initially freak out and try to escape until they realise the only way to succeed is to embrace their role within that world ...

Charlie had the premise of a guy stealing people's identities so he can control them in his own digital world. He also had Nanette's character and knew he wanted her to escape in a big action set piece, but the rest was up for grabs. We chatted about the fun that could be had with your digital self trying to contact your real self, and how the best person to blackmail you is you. The first draft seemed to write itself. It's probably the first and only time I'd ever written a script and knew it was good. Most times you hope – maybe even suspect – it's good, but this one felt good straight away.

Toby Haynes (director): I'd been aware of *Black Mirror* from the first episode, but when it came on TV I was always either working on *Jonathan Strange & Mr Norrell* or doing a movie in New Zealand. I wasn't that excited to receive the script, because it seemed like familiar territory after having done *Doctor Who*. But my agent said it was one of the best he'd read in a long time, and he was not wrong! I realised we were looking at a very classy, well-thought-out and intelligent show. It was absolutely up my street.

I was anxious about meeting Charlie. I always thought he'd be quite fierce and sarcastic and angry, and he's not at all. He's quite geeky and incredibly generous with his sense of humour. He clearly has a very sharp intellect, but he doesn't need to be the funniest person in the room – he wants you to be as funny as he is. I've never laughed as much with my execs as I did on *Black Mirror*. I've also never been under so much scrutiny, but they still allow you to have your head. You can win arguments.

Cristin Milioti (actor): I was in the madness of post-production on a show I'd written, when I was asked to put myself on tape reading three pages of *USS Callister*. They were very secretive and wouldn't talk about the role of

Nanette at all. I read the scene and thought, "God, I have no idea what this means, but I'm really into it." It was beautifully written, but there was zero context. There was a scene in which Nanette blackmails herself, and also talk of a wormhole, so I was very confused.

Annabel Jones: We probably only gave her a few pages to try and minimise the chance of any spoilers getting out. That explains why she took the role! She obviously had no idea how bad it was going to be. That'll teach her.

Cristin was just so annoyingly good, it had to be her. She was everyone's firm favourite from the start. She had loads of energy, she could handle the comedy, she had a great look for the era but crucially she didn't let the mind-bending elements ever veer into silly. She kept it real.

Of course, we were thrilled when Jesse came on board ... no pun intended. He has such unbelievable range. We knew he could embrace the broader comedy at the top of the film and play the meek, invisible Daly in the office, then deliciously subvert his power and create something horribly sinister.

Jesse's fiancée Kirsten Dunst was on set with him and asked whether she could be an extra in the background at the Callister offices. Quite a few people spotted her on screen when the show went out.

Jina Jay (series casting director): I cast Jesse based on my instinct about his body of work. When Annabel and Charlie had a great Skype with him, he was clear that he wanted to commit to the role based on trusting them. We didn't have a director at that point. Jesse is able to inhabit complex roles with substantial characterisation: he elevates what is already on the page with modesty and restraint. Plus he is an actor who is never afraid to embrace the less likeable aspects of humanity.

Annabel Jones: Jina did an amazing job on *USS Callister*. We were so pleased that Michaela Coel, who had made such an impression in her role as an airport clerk in *Nosedive*, agreed to come back to play Shania. She's so innately funny she can make pressing a button on a control panel hilarious. And Jimmi Simpson so skilfully navigated his character Walton through the comedy of the early scenes, where he's the jerk CEO in the office, through the fear of being Daly's plaything on the spaceship to then breaking our hearts by sacrificing himself at the end. The cast were wonderful. It was great fun.

Cristin Milioti: When I read the full script, I could have wept. In fact, I think I did weep. I'd waited my whole life to play something that expansive – to get to play two different roles and two different genres. I remember bracing myself in case a second draft changed everything, because it was one of the most exciting things I'd ever read.

I didn't know *Star Trek* whatsoever. I was familiar with a William Shatner [who played Captain Kirk in the TV series] impression and knew who Spock was, but that was it. I watched about two seconds of the vintage episodes, but then stopped myself because actually Nanette wouldn't know.

Joel Collins (series production designer): Much as with *Fifteen Million Merits*, we were back to trying to achieve what seemed impossible for a single drama. We knew early on that we were going to go to space, so we took the time to give *USS Callister* what it needed. I brought in crew from *Star Wars* and *Guardians of the Galaxy*: people who really knew the genre.

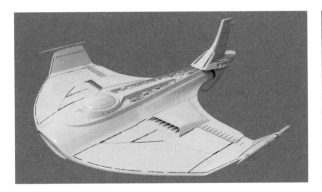

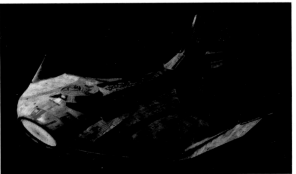

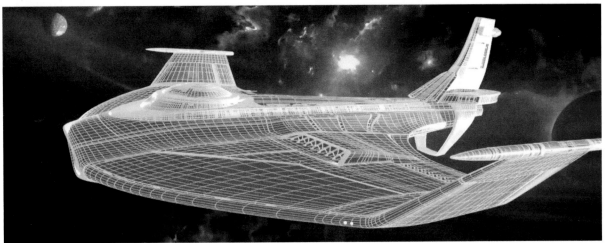

Above: Visual concept development work for the USS Callister space craft by Painting Practice, with visual effects by Framestore under the direction of Joel Collins and co-designer Phil Sims.

Louise Sutton (producer): I chose a couple of baskets for us to put all our eggs in. We weren't going to build a whole spaceship, so we put everything into the ship's bridge and corridors. Originally there was a canteen area, but the bridge became our home and stage. We did go stir crazy on that bridge, but we laughed all day, every day.

The opening sequence wrong-foots viewers by presenting Captain Daly (played by Jesse Plemons) and his crew on the bridge of the USS Callister, stylised like a 1960s episode of Star Trek, *as the villainous Valdack (Billy Magnussen) attacks them.*

Charlie Brooker: We do this little spoof *Star Trek* thing at the start and enjoy mocking some tropes ... and then we use all of them later, kind of unironically! That's the very definition of a cunt having their cake and eating it, isn't it? But if we'd had space opera tropes at the end, without mocking them at the start, it might have felt cheesy.

Joel Collins: We worried someone would think our 60s-style Callister set was rubbish and not get the joke. It's a risk, but it was meant as an homage.

Russell McLean (VFX producer): For that opening sequence, the CG spacecraft shots had to look like they were made using the same techniques as early *Star Trek*, when they filmed models on fishing wire in a studio. Making something in CG look bad on purpose felt surprisingly challenging.

Charlie Brooker: I did wonder what the logic was, of doing things like deliberately presenting Valdack's ship with shonky special effects. But Toby was right to say that the opening is Daly's perception of what happens in that game. And in his head, it emotionally looks and feels like the original show.

Joel Collins: At least, at the end, when the USS Callister becomes like the [director of the 2009 and 2011 *Star Trek* films] JJ Abrams version, you suddenly go, "Fuck me, that's a good spaceship." It's the same ship, but with all different lightings, props and details. So it goes from oranges, reds and silly colours at the start, with funny lighting, to being really slick by the finale.

Charlie Brooker: The only thing that worried me was the idea of *Star Trek* fans thinking we were having a go at them, which wasn't the intention. But I haven't really been aware of anyone thinking that, because it's clear that Daly is the problem.

I suppose you could say we took a risk by asking the audience to invest in the fates of digital characters. When Nanette wakes up in the game, if you feel like she isn't real and it doesn't matter, then you wouldn't care. But we thought that if you follow her waking up on the ship and wondering where the fuck she is, then you should care, because she'll react like she's real.

We show you Callister's crew when Daly's not around. The idea was that it was like *Toy Story*, when Andy's out of the room and all the toys are talking, and then when he comes back in, they all go, "Oh fuck!". So you're given information about the crew that humanises them a bit more.

Cristin Milioti: I tried to make subtle differences between Nanette in the real and virtual worlds, in terms of posture and mannerisms. In the office world, she doesn't allow herself to speak her mind. There's a moment when Walton puts his hand on her back and she just wants to be left alone to do her job, whereas in the space world she'd have karate-chopped his arm off.

Charlie Brooker: I think you forget that there's a real Nanette out there until later, when she tries to communicate with herself. And it comes as a surprise: "Oh fuck, of course!". Because our POV has jumped into that of Virtual Nanette, you get slightly removed from Real Nanette, who suddenly seems like an idiot who doesn't know what's going on. You're annoyed with her, because she messes things up. What's happening to her feels almost less real than what's happening to her in the game.

Cristin Milioti: One of my favourite parts of the episode is that Nanette becomes her greatest self in the space world. She realises her fullest potential because she's pushed into it.

Charlie Brooker: Incidentally, people have pointed this out, and I know it doesn't make sense: if Daly has swabbed a cup and grown a copy of Nanette from her DNA, how does she know who she is when she wakes up in Callister? We did actually work out an explanation, which used the Grain technology from *The Entire History of You*. In the original script, everyone had these Grains and we went out of our way to explain this to you.

Opposite: The creation of the Arachnajax was art directed by Justin Hutchison-Chatburn at Painting Practice, with visual effects by Framestore under the direction of Joel Collins and co-designer Phil Sims.

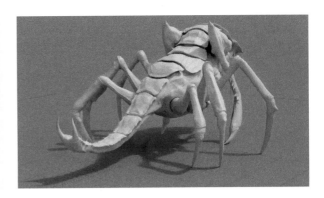

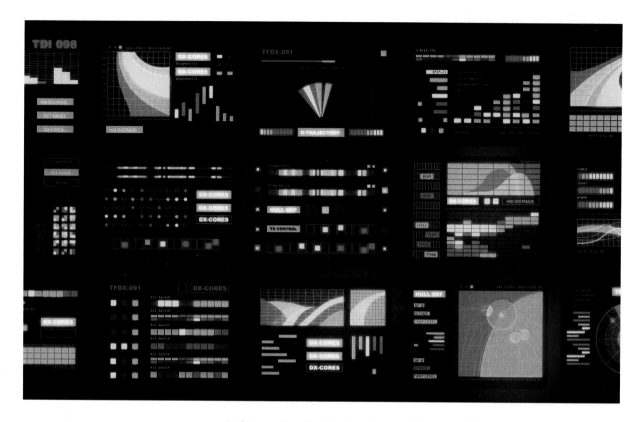

In that version, Daly had to do two things: get the DNA and download the contents of your Grain. But it was just too much business. Eventually I went, "Oh sod it, let's just say he gets their DNA and grows them all in a magic machine." When Shania says, "Whatever, it's a fucking gizmo", that was me letting on that I *knew* it didn't make sense, but still you see people complaining. I *know* it doesn't make sense! It's just that I don't care.

Cristin Milioti: It was a very charmed experience to be part of that cast. I knew Jesse Plemons, because we shot the second season of [the US TV anthology series] *Fargo* together. Billy Magnussen and I had done [the 2012 fantasy-thriller film] *The Brass Teapot* together. Me and Jimmi Simpson, who plays Walton, have a bunch of mutual friends, so it was a blast! We hung out a lot and went out on weekends.

Toby Haynes: Because of the *Star Trek* homage, we had our compliance lawyers on speed dial throughout the whole process. The way I understood it, as long as we weren't taking exact *Star Trek* colours, typefaces or whatever, it was going to be okay. I was concentrating on making the best show I could, and so I was going to carry on until someone told me to stop! Our producer Louise was the one fretting about it.

Above and opposite: Both iterations of the spaceship required enormous amounts of live playback user interface. The motion graphics were created at Painting Practice and art directed by Erica McEwan. The live playback was provided by Revolver.

Louise Sutton: You never know whether you're going to inadvertently breach copyright, but we were very, very, very careful. Every decision we made, we ran it past the team of lawyers at Endemol. That went across the board, from costumes to sound effects to Daniel Pemberton's music.

Toby Haynes: Daniel gave us this incredibly punchy, amazing score. It was one of the greatest moments of my career, sitting there in the recording studio as they played the *Space Fleet* theme! So cool.

Daniel Pemberton (composer): I wanted *Space Fleet* to have a *Star Trek*-esque theme that could be wrapped around the score, but at the same time it obviously couldn't be a rip-off of that show or theme. So I just wrote a big brass fanfare that works really well at evoking that world and time. That theme is echoed throughout the journey, culminating in the 'alive' version of it when they come out of the wormhole at the end.

From a musical point of view, *USS Callister* is possibly one of the most insanely complicated episodes ever. If the *Space Fleet* music didn't feel like it *could* be music from a show like that, of that time, it would stand out very quickly as the weak link and destroy the illusion. So you basically had to write and record a major orchestral film score or it's going to feel flat. You also had to score the other world, the modern world of this huge game company and everyone who works there. Finally, it was about meshing those two worlds as the show went on, until they became one.

Maja Meschede (costume designer): I focused on making 1960s fashion work in space. To create an artificial Barbie look, I chose neoprene as the main fabric for all costumes. The neoprene was dyed into deep, glowing colours. For the ladies, I took inspiration from 1960s high-fashion designers such as André Courrèges and Pierre Cardin, who celebrated space and future in their creations. For the men I designed fitted, impractical, generic space outfits.

Tanya Lodge (hair and make-up designer): One of my priorities was to make the characters instantly recognisable, both in the office and Daly's virtual world. I created a receding hair line and bald patch for Daly in the office, to make him appear a little vulnerable. That contrasted with his look in the game, in which he has a perfect veneer and a toupee as he pays visual homage to Captain Kirk.

Maja Meschede: The entire virtual crew had to look 'weaker' than Daly, so I designed his costume to make him look like a space Ken doll. A notably better version of himself. His costume heightens his shoulder width and chest so he appears to be very strong and well built. His top and trousers are fitted to enhance his muscular physique.

Annabel Jones: I think it's fair to say Jesse wanted to pay homage to Shatner's Captain Kirk. It absolutely wasn't in the script. He worked with a vocal coach for a few weeks to find the right cadence and watched a lot of *Star Trek*. I think he was even listening to audio clips of Shatner on set in between takes. I remember Jesse telling us that Shatner was a Shakespearean-trained actor and that he treated the *Star Trek* scripts as if they're Shakespeare. Shatner took it all very seriously and very theatrically, and you could definitely see Jesse channelling that in *Space Fleet* mode. Jesse was incredibly generous and would say things to Toby like, "If you ever need me to turn up the Shatner, I can do that for you."

Charlie Brooker: Daly is our first proper bad guy, in a way. A cartoon bad guy, so to speak. Someone who literally gives speeches about how bad he is.

Annabel Jones: What I really liked about *USS Callister* was the switch in protagonist, which you don't often see. When we meet Daly in the office he's emasculated and humiliated in front of Nanette by his colleagues and business partner Walton. We feel his pain of being ignored and laughed at by his juniors. Then when you begin to realise what he has had to do to get 'respect', to be the hero he can never be in real life, you see the monster and our sympathies massively shift. But it's a real credit to Jesse's talent that some people still feel sorry for him during the final sequences!

In the game Daly is masterful, commanding and respected. Rather than ignoring him, his colleagues are forced to play along with him, to be obsequious and sycophantic. Daly has blended reality and game into a cruel fantasy that he is living out. Unfortunately I see lots of parallels with the real world. So it was very important that we then follow Nanette. It becomes her story and she becomes the hero. She also crushes the damsel-in-distress stereotype of *Space Fleet*!

Charlie Brooker: You do feel pretty sorry for Daly early on. We actually shot a moment where he's just met Nanette for the first time and then she's chatting to her new office colleagues, and you see him clench his fist. Netflix wondered if it revealed him to be sinister too soon. I initially thought they were wrong, but to see if their note worked, we cut the shot of his fist out and it was far, far better. It left you empathising with him for longer, so it's more of a body blow when you realise he's the villain. Sometimes you get really wedded to a particular beat and then someone else comes along and suggests you kill it, and annoyingly they're right.

Above: The USS Callister logo.

Opposite: Costume concept art for the USS Callister crew by Maja Meschede.

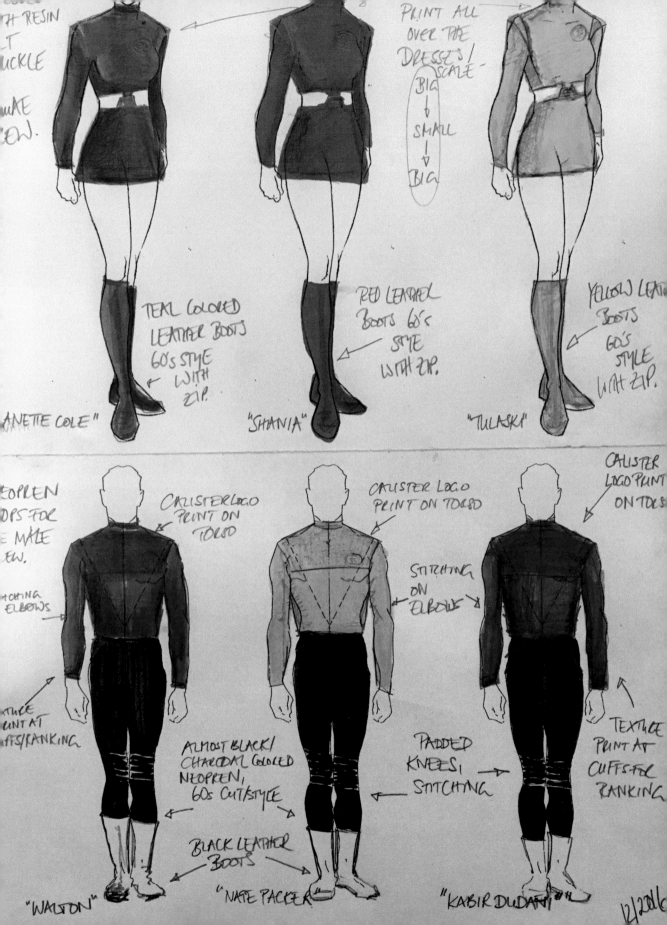

H RESIN
T
UCKLE

MALE
EW.

TEAL COLORED
LEATHER BOOTS
60'S STYLE
WITH ZIP.

"ANETTE COLE"

PRINT ALL
OVER THE
DRESSES / SCALE -

BIG
↓
SMALL
↓
BIG

RED LEATHER
BOOTS 60's
STYLE
WITH ZIP.

"SHANIA"

YELLOW LEATHER
BOOTS
60's
STYLE
WITH ZIP.

"TULASKI"

EOPREN
OPS FOR
E MALE
EW.

CALISTER LOGO
PRINT ON
TORSO

CALISTER LOGO
PRINT ON TORSO

CALISTER
LOGO PRINT
ON TOR

CHING
ELBOWS

STITCHING
ON
ELBOWS

TURE
UNT AT
FS/RANKING

ALMOST BLACK/
CHARCOAL COLORED
NEOPREN,
60s CUT/STYLE

PADDED
KNEES/
STITCHING

TEXTURE
PRINT AT
CUFFS FOR
RANKING

BLACK LEATHER
BOOTS

"WALTON"

"NATE PACKER"

"KABIR DUDANI"

12/2016

Toby Haynes: I kept saying I felt sorry for Daly, and Charlie would say, "Yeah, but he throws Walton's kid Tommy out of an airlock!" My view was that these weren't actually people to Daly, they were noughts and ones. He's a programmer who designed them for a reason, to behave in a certain way. So in some ways I had sympathies for him. But when we shot that airlock scene, Jesse smiled. He enjoyed the action. That's what he gave to Daly. He was a sadist, an evil character.

Charlie Brooker: You could argue the airlock scene is the point at which Daly's beyond redemption. He's mistreating people horrifically. Even though he feels this is some sort of virtual realm, when he's throwing a child out of an airlock, that's like Darth Vader levels of evil. It's interesting because I lose sympathy for him really early on, when he's shouting at his crew and you see how terrified they are.

There is a very clear parallel between Callister and *The Twilight Zone*'s episode *It's a Good Life*. That's about a young boy with superpowers who can make things happen just by thinking about them, and it's still incredibly uncomfortable and horrifying to this day. In our story, Daly's an overgrown boy rather than a literal one. They're both stories about superpowered tyrants.

I've got an element of sympathy with somebody wanting to lose themselves in a fantasy world, because real life is depressing. Fine. The problem is that Daly's dragged lots of other people in and he's a fucking sadist. And he *knows* he's a sadist. It's not like he's playing Grand Theft Auto where he's running people over, then accidentally finds out they've got histories and lives and relatives. He knows exactly what he's doing, because he helped create it. He should either quit, or stand up to [his real life boss] Walton, or go and set up a rival company, or tell them all to fuck off. What he shouldn't be doing is building a fantasy world and tormenting everyone.

Black Mirror flexed its growing CGI muscles with the creation of the Arachnajax monsters, which are seen both on the surface of an alien planet and on board the USS Callister.

Louise Sutton: They had to be scary but also have some comedy to them. We all loved that moment when Daly's pizza comes and he pauses the game and the Arachnajax drums its tentacles on the ground.

Joel Collins: We designed the Arachnajax, then passed them over to the VFX company Framestore. Toby wanted tentacles down the front, a bit like Davy Jones from *Pirates of the Caribbean*, which added a layer of humour.

Toby Haynes: The Arachnajax needed to be able to shrug or whatever, and I thought that would be really funny. Also, tentacles are disgusting and no-one wants to be turned into a big tentacled thing! It gave the creature a very human quality, in a really alien way.

Joel Collins: The Arachnajax were also a bit like the creatures in Starship Troopers, to be honest. There were a lot of tropes going on in *USS Callister*, so that the audience gets the tone. The art of *Black Mirror* is to stay within a box that isn't too far away from people's perspectives. So then they fall into the box with you, and you can shake the box around, bang their heads and upset them a lot.

Above and opposite: A selection of the *Space Fleet* memorabilia collected by Daly. The props were designed in the graphics department with illustrations by artists Bill Elliott and Billy Butcher, and omnicorder by Painting Practice.

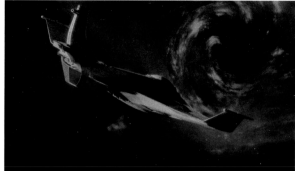

Russell Dodgson (creative director, Framestore): We had to represent a wide range of character emotion in a short space of time, with the Arachnajax's deeply non-humanoid form. The design of the creature gave us a lot to play with: we had long arms to drop as part of a sigh, and multiple tentacles to exhale through.

By the time the crew member Shania [played by Michaela Coel] has screamed and convulsed her way through the Arachnajax transformation, we're left with a pale, staggering, shaking creature. To get this look, we referenced newborn deer, who find it hard to stand after their birth and shake and shudder as they try to 'find their legs'.

Louise Sutton: There was originally talk of doing the alien planet surface in a studio, as *Star Trek* would have, but I always felt we needed to go outside to get some air and scale, because we were inside everywhere else. So we ended up in Lanzarote, which felt ideal.

Toby Haynes: We found a quarry made of red rock, but it wasn't quite right, so we transferred a whole skip-load of red sand from it to another quarry! Lanzarote was the only place within our radius that we could get to, that had a pool warm enough to put actors in. And let me tell you, it was still bloody freezing.

Cristin Milioti: The scene in the lake with Jesse was one of my favourites to film, even though it was horrible because it was the coldest body of water I've ever been in. Between takes, I was wrapped in a wet-suit by a diver, and was unable to stop shaking. They'd call action and we'd snap into character. I find that scene so scary and funny at the same time: it's this weird balance between slapstick and terror!

We improvised a lot in that scene too. From what I remember, there was one splash of water in the script but then we really went for it! I also improvised that moment where Nanette pretends something's grabbed her under the water, and maybe when she calls him a big beautiful captain! It was like being in a playground ... a freezing cold playground.

Toby Haynes: That two-second aerial shot of the planet's surface cost us about two hours on set, getting a bloody drone up there. But it did look great, and Framestore did a great job of adding a wonderful gamescape to it.

USS Callister is probably the most complete and compact piece of drama I've done. It's that lovely feature length, with such a perfect beginning, middle and end, and the climax is nice and long, keeping you on the edge of your seat. And yet it has all this subtext of fandom and toxic masculinity. We also had this great female protagonist, who surprises you by the end.

Cristin Milioti: It's rare to see a woman save the day by using her intelligence, pluck, scrappiness and skill at coding. Charlie and Annabel have a habit of being eerily prescient. I felt exactly where *Callister* was coming from, just from having been a woman in the world. When I was in London shooting that, Trump had been elected a couple of months prior. It certainly felt wonderful to see this intelligent woman take down a misogynistic bully. I don't know whether that was some retroactive wish fulfilment, but it was very potent.

Charlie Brooker: We flew to New York for the premiere. When the plane landed and everyone switched their phones on, the Harvey Weinstein story had just broken. So, obviously, *Callister* wasn't knowingly about Weinstein. I can see how that could look like we saw the news and decided to rush out a female empowerment saga, but that element was probably just a product of going for what was most dramatically interesting. If you put Daly in a world where he's strutting around like this alpha cartoon hero, what's he going to find most threatening? One of the female crew members, questioning and undermining and overthrowing his authority.

Annabel Jones: We deliberated over the Gamer voice at the very end for a long time. We did try out a few accents that were more inherently comedic, but I think Charlie was worried they were a bit patronising to gamers. Then Charlie wondered whether Aaron Paul might ever be interested and Aaron very kindly agreed. As Aaron's voice is so recognisable, it really gave the end of the film a lovely extra boost. As this was quite late in the post process we totally forgot to tell the other cast members – we're so professional – and so at the end of the premiere they were all in shock. It was a particular surprise to Jesse, who had of course worked with Aaron on *Breaking Bad*.

Cristin Milioti: I loved ending up in the captain's chair, but also that whole final scene. I just love the humour, because it's a triumphant spaceship scene and yet they're still office co-workers, who are scrappy and scrambling. I find that end very thrilling, even though there's the caveat that Nanette's stuck in virtual reality forever! But she's her best self, and what is reality anyway? It's a real onion.

'Stick us in hyperwarp and let's ... fuck off somewhere'
– Nanette

ARKANGEL

In Conversation

Jodie Foster – director
Cindy Holland – Vice President of Original Content, Netflix
Charlie Brooker – writer and executive producer
Annabel Jones – executive producer
Brenna Harding – actor

In a forgotten, post-industrial American town, concerned mother Marie Sambrell is shaken by the experience of losing her young daughter Sara in a public place. Marie decides to sign Sara up for Arkangel, the revolutionary new child-monitoring system. Arkangel allows Marie to not only locate Sara at all times, but monitor and censor what she sees. Years later, as Sara explores teenagehood, Marie finds herself tempted to get the long-dormant Arkangel back out of the closet.

Jodie Foster (director): I didn't know about *Black Mirror* until I met with Cindy Holland at Netflix. We were commiserating about the movie business, as we do every once in a while, and I said how much I looked forward to the day when we have feature-length movies on cable streaming. For me, that's the perfect short story form, with a beginning, middle and end.

Cindy Holland (Vice President of Original Content, Netflix): Jodie had graciously lent her considerable directing talents to both *Orange Is the New Black* and *House Of Cards*, but she was searching for something she could help fully realise. When I read *Arkangel* I thought it might be the perfect fit.

Jodie Foster: Cindy said, "Well, have I got a show for you!"

Charlie Brooker: The notion of a device that you can use to spy on every aspect of your child from a safety perspective almost certainly wouldn't have occurred to me if parenthood hadn't reprogrammed me. It used to really annoy me when new parents would say, "Suddenly I've got the meaning of my life!" but you do drop down in the hierarchy. You are no longer the most important thing in your world, which is irritating. Also, this constant anxiety gets augmented, where you've got to protect these kids.

I once rang NHS Direct because I thought our first child had started crying with a different accent. Suddenly his cry was completely different, because little babies are very high pitched. But I didn't know, and as a first time parent I was terrified something was going horribly wrong. And if you Google anything, it tells you that it's fatal.

Annabel Jones: So in a world of helicopter parenting and technology that can feed this neurosis, here was an opportunity for a *Black Mirror* story. And like the best *Black Mirror* technology, Arkangel is designed to help and support. A device that will tell you where your child is if they go missing: who's not going to use that?

Jodie Foster: Netflix sent me the *Arkangel* script first, before I even went back and watched any episodes! And I loved the script, so that was a good first step. Then I really saw everything I could. I love *Shut Up and Dance* with the two guys on the road, the Christmas special ... and of course we all love *The National Anthem*.

Oh my gosh, the *Arkangel* script spoke to me for so many reasons. I was raised by a single mom: that incredibly difficult, fascinating, emotional relationship between a mother and her daughter in a single-parent family. There's something almost too intimate about it, and I felt the script raised so many questions about who we are as women at this particular time in history. As mothers, we hope to raise these strong daughters who don't have to learn the feminist lessons that we did. And there's a price to shielding them from that reality.

Obviously *Arkangel* isn't autobiographical, but I really wanted this to be as real as possible. There's a trajectory, where we start off with a family we recognise, and then little by little, see the mother cross the line. I totally understand both Sara and Marie, because I was a daughter and I'm a mother! You can get away with a double perspective: it is at once the

mother's story and told through the daughter's eyes. Their relationship is so messed up, they don't know where one starts and the other ends. Marie is watching this weird, vicarious movie at all times, walking the world in her daughter's shoes.

Charlie Brooker: Before I became a parent, my response to anyone wanting to restrict content for the sake of children would've been, "Oh boohoo, fuck off. Just be a better parent, then, and don't let your kid watch *The Terminator*." And then, of course, cut to a couple of years later. I'd put YouTube on for one of my kids who was three or something, to fucking shut them up for five minutes while I do something. Being a nostalgic old prick, I'd looked up old *Mr Man* cartoons. I walked out of the room and it started playing the next video and the next and the next. And then, algorithmically, it somehow ended up showing him the trailer for John Carpenter's *The Thing*. So I walked back in and he didn't look happy. I thought, "Oh no! What have I done?" And then you think, "Oh right, I should restrict that, then. I need to start imposing controls on what he can see."

And then you think, "What if he's walking down the street and someone says 'fuck'? Or somebody gets hit by a car in front of him? Or we walk past an alleyway where a mad person's having sex with a dog? I don't want him seeing all of that stuff. I'm just describing an everyday walk in the neighbourhood here, obviously.

Annabel Jones: When we first heard that Jodie was interested in directing the episode, we were suspicious, like, "Really? Yeah but *really*?" And then we were quite intimidated. The first time we Skyped with her, Charlie and I were freaked out. Since we'd obviously only ever seen her on a screen, it was like one of her film characters had been programmed to talk to us. Like when she plays the ruthless defence secretary in [the 2013 sci-fi thriller] *Elysium* and she's sitting in the chair talking into the screen, but more terrifying.

Because Jodie had a better understanding of blue-collar America than we did, she had strong thoughts on where she wanted it to be set. She also wanted to get into Marie's character: that sense of the economic struggle that a single mum might be having. The loneliness of that world and the pressures, which all fed her reliance on the Arkangel system.

Jodie Foster: It's always difficult for directors to work with producers, and especially on something where it's so quick like this, because you don't get to know somebody. But Annabel and Charlie really want a directorial vision for the film, and that's very rare on television. So this was one of the nicest collaborations I've ever had with producers. Sometimes I think it's because they're English: they have such a nice way of disagreeing with you. They're so diplomatic, it makes me smile!

Annabel Jones: To try and give us an authentic blue-collar America, we were filming in a small industrial area outside of Toronto. We can't actually afford to shoot in America. I felt quite sorry for Jodie, because Trump was elected during our first week of filming and she desperately wanted to be with her family and friends. Instead, she was having to work with children and animals in Canada.

'Whatever she sees, I see, and I am watching *you*. So you stay away'
– Marie

Opposite: Director Jodie Foster behind the lens on set with cast and crew.

Jodie Foster: We were going to talk about America five years in the future. The question was, where is our country headed? So there was something wonderful about this idea of a rundown town, almost like the way Pittsburgh was after all the steel mills left. A place that used to have a foundation and a glory, but didn't turn out to be much. And that's really how Marie feels about herself. Her father looks at his daughter's life and thinks, "Wow, what a failure."

La La Land and *Mad Men*'s Rosemarie DeWitt was cast as mother Marie, while up-and-coming Australian actress Brenna Harding auditioned for the role of Sara.

Brenna Harding (actor): I did a two-scene 'self tape' for the UK casting agent. Jodie asked us to also do a little speaking to camera, but I stuffed up by misinterpreting the instructions. I thought she wanted us to talk to camera in character, rather than as ourselves. So I constructed this whole two-minute monologue as Sara, speaking to camera about her mum and all this stuff. It really helped me get into the character's mind, but I was so annoyed at Jodie! It seemed like a big ask, but y'know, it was Jodie Foster, so it didn't seem that surprising that she would ask for something a bit out of the box ...

Jodie Foster: Haha, oh God! Yes, I just wanted Brenna to say anything to camera as herself, off the top of her head. The poor thing, she feels like she totally made a fool of herself, but when I saw her tape I was like, "That is so brave! She's my girl."

Brenna Harding: That was probably the best example of a happy accident I've ever had in my life. Jodie is fiercely intelligent and approaches scripts, scenes and directing with enormous intelligence and insight. She's very measured and aware and focused and calm and confident, after all these years of experience. She's the only director who's ever had higher expectations for me than I've had for myself.

Jodie Foster: Brenna is an extraordinary actress, such a hard worker, a great collaborator and a lovely person. But of course, *Arkangel* is about the combination of Brenna and the three little girls. The one thing no-one can ever forget about the movie *Boyhood* is how the children all looked so much alike, because they were the same child! So it was very important that our four Saras looked alike and had this similar quality, so that the audience had that relationship with them.

Obviously, working with a four-year-old is difficult! Aniya [Hodge, who plays the three-year-old Sara] is wonderful, but you definitely get some grey hairs working with toddlers.

Brenna Harding: Jodie, Rosemary and I talked a lot about the comparisons between Marie and our own mothers, and we agreed that Marie is on the more intense end of the spectrum when it comes to being a concerned parent. That's just inherent in her personality.

Annabel Jones: The intention was never that Marie was overly neurotic or controlling – it was more about the slippery slope. Marie censors unpleasant things from Sara's life, which ultimately leads to the girl feeling

Jasmine: "I'm just pairing it with Sara's implant..."

PAIRING DEVICE. PLEASE WAIT.

a beat...

"This is Sara's current location... which his here of course"

Sara is at Hafenbauer Tech / 0 miles away

JASMINE ZOOMS IN

Jasmine zooms into the building (two-finger zoom, or a double tap could work)

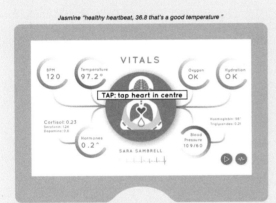

Jasmine "healthy heartbeat, 36.8 that's a good temperature "

VITALS

BPM 120
Temperature 97.2°
Oxygen OK
Hydration OK

TAP: tap heart in centre

Cortisol 0.23
Serotonin 1.24
Dopamine 0.8
Haemoglobin 98¹
Triglycerides 0.21

Hormones 0.2^
Blood Pressure 109/60

SARA SAMBRELL

Jasmine: "It's OK... the system detects a cortisol spike and scrambles the image"

Jasmine has switched the channel

emotionally detached and having problems engaging with people. And then Marie realises this has to end. But then, cut to years later where suddenly she's terrified and doesn't know where her daughter is, so what are you going to do? Marie desperately wants to confirm that Sara's not dead or kidnapped or whatever, and maybe help her. When she turns that device back on, that's the turning point of the film.

Charlie Brooker: I'm not at the point yet where I have to worry about what my kids might independently go out and do in the world, because I pretty much still have to wipe their bums. So with *Arkangel*, I was just projecting ahead. I could understand the scenario where you're terrified that your daughter has gone missing. So you'd switch the thing back on again, because of course you would.

Above: The different graphics seen on the screen of the Arkangel tracking device, developed by Painting Practice.

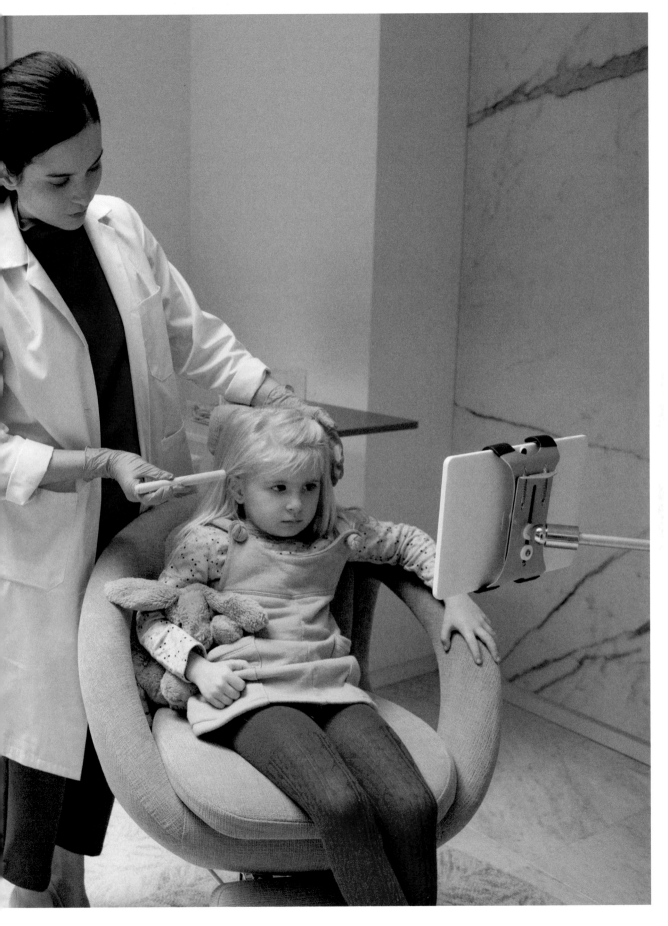

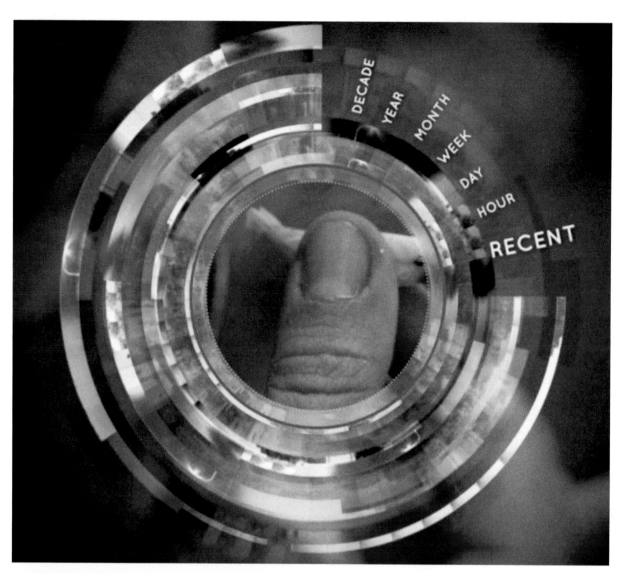

Jodie Foster: I think Marie is an unusually concerned mother. Every hint is there from the very beginning. There she is, about to give birth, and the first thing she says is how she's sorry she couldn't have a vaginal birth and is about to have a C-section. She feels such a disappointment, so we already see that she is somebody who has a terrible opinion of herself. And when they take the child away, to clean the baby, her first reaction is panic.

Brenna Harding: Once your child starts to become independent and live their own life, that's when you need to turn off the unit. The Arkangel system could be okay with toddlers, but once children get to an age when they're going to school on their own, that's when they need to be experiencing independence purely, because that's really important for development. It's hard to draw a line in the sand and specify an age, but the line is absolutely drawn at drugging your child!
 Marie isn't watching for fun: she's genuinely concerned for her daughter's well-being, but she continues to watch and that's ethically ambiguous. The teenage years are so crucial to becoming a fully formed adult and the Arkangel system hinders that so much.

Jodie Foster: Marie crosses the line, the minute her daughter starts to individuate by lying to her. We all know our children lie to us, and individuation is a good moment: it shows that they see themselves as different from you. They're assuming their own lives.

Charlie Brooker: Marie probably crosses the line when she marches into the furniture store and confronts Trick, because she's now acting on the information she has. She'd known Sara's seeing this boy and she wasn't happy about it, but now she's seen her daughter doing coke, so that's the point at which she's like, "I've got to do something about this."

Annabel Jones: Marie sees Trick giving the coke to Sara, but of course she doesn't see the intro of Sara almost forcing him to give it to her. So Marie feels that her daughter would never do something like this, and is being led astray by this guy.

Jodie Foster: The relationship between Sara and Trick always needed to feel like that messy, first-love indie movie experience.

Brenna Harding: Owen Teague's casting influenced Trick a lot as a character. Trick was not how I'd imagined him at all. There was just this beautiful connection between him and Sara. That's part of the reason it's so heartbreaking when Marie sabotages that situation, because they've found something special. They're like two old souls who connected, but it got ruined. Owen's soft, measured and polite: a genuinely lovely human.

Jodie Foster: Trick was written in a way that made you distrust him. He was a kid from the bad side of the tracks and so you were genuinely worried for Sara. But we really got the right guy with Owen: someone who looks tougher than he is, but also has that sweetness. If there were changes to the script during the process, it was because I wanted to make sure I was on Sara's side, and that she had the right to choose the boy she fell in love with. It was an imperfect, but true, first love.

Brenna Harding: Sara's final violent reaction can be read in many different ways. For me, it comes from a personal place, from the violation of her privacy and her body. The way I justified it as a performer was that betrayal by the person closest to her.

Jodie Foster: If you create a false reality for your child, under the guise of protecting them, you're altering the natural course of how a person discovers their own life. You're breaking their independence and controlling them. You're actually enabling the thing you hoped wouldn't happen, which is that they have to abandon you and leave you. And there's a necessity for the violence of that rupture, because of the control that's been exacted. So I would say that ending is more of a parable.

It was important that the violence should burst out and be as enormous as it was. We grappled with this in the editing room, in terms of how far we should go. Sara has the scrambler on, so she's not experiencing the same level of violence that we see objectively. What she's feeling is the exterior manifestation of her emotional interior.

Rosemarie DeWitt is a friend of mine, but on her first day on set as Marie I did something you're never supposed to do, throwing an actor straight into the most dramatic scene that happens at the end. We put blood all over her, then had her running out of the house screaming for Sara. We were losing the light, we only had a few minutes to get it and we were on hand-held camera. So I got a lot of grief from Ro for that!

Jodie Foster: There is an ambiguity to our final shot, with not being able to see who's in the truck. And then, when she closes the door, we cut to this Pretenders song. If there was one thing we all had a lot of conversations about, it was that song, because it changes the tone. It's a plaintive song and it's tough, but it takes us back to the mother's perspective, so there's almost this *Black Mirror*-esque wink.

Charlie Brooker: Originally in the script it was just a small car. Not that I'm implying anything about truck drivers, but getting into one doesn't seem like a good thing for Sara to do. Also, what it does imply immediately is that she's going a long way.

Annabel Jones: She's not coming back. What you want from the ending is the sense that Marie now has no control. The focus is slightly more on her, abandoned, left behind.

Brenna Harding: I feel a mixture of nervous trepidation and excitement for Sara, because there's a lot of amazing things to learn about yourself when you become independent and self-sufficient. She's an incredibly creative mind, she's wise, she's got social skills. I think she'll connect with people and find herself where she needs to be. That's a very optimistic interpretation, and I don't necessarily think it's the one that's being communicated in that final shot! Maybe one day she'll reconnect with Marie, but it's a pretty huge betrayal. She'll be just fine on her own, but I don't think Marie will. One of the hardest things about the episode is that Marie dug her own grave.

CROCODILE

<u>In Conversation</u>

Charlie Brooker – writer and executive producer
Annabel Jones – executive producer
John Hillcoat – director
Morgan Kennedy – co-production designer
Joel Collins – series production designer
Sanne Wohlenberg – producer
Jodie Foster – director, Arkangel

After a heavy night of clubbing, Mia and her boyfriend Rob run down and kill a cyclist in the middle of nowhere. Rob persuades Mia to help him dispose of the body, but 15 years later he becomes consumed with guilt. Having started a family and a successful career, Mia argues against making amends for the past. When she accidentally kills Rob, she sinks into an increasingly extreme and violent downward spiral.

Charlie Brooker: Somewhere around 2005, I was on a bike in Clapham Junction in London, waiting for the lights to change, when a man ran across the road and got hit by a car. I rang for an ambulance straight away and then had to stand over him whilst the operator talked to me on the phone, asking questions about whether he was breathing and so on. It was nasty. His head was open …

Some time later, the police came to take a statement about what I'd seen, because there was going to be a case about whether this motorist was speeding. And I realised how difficult it is. They asked how fast the car was going, and I thought it was a bit fast … but was it speeding? What colour was it? God, I couldn't even remember.

Wouldn't it be useful if there was a gadget that let you corroborate what all the witnesses actually saw? You might actually get an accurate picture in that crowdsourced Wikipedia way. And this seemed very *Black Mirror*.

The original story for Crocodile had somebody witness an accident. A magic memory machine was used to build up their picture of what happened. But when this person was two years old, they had witnessed their mother's murder, and so they became obsessed with remembering the face of the killer. That storyline felt too predictable, even though we did have a fun twist.

Annabel Jones: It also didn't feel like a *Black Mirror* set up: the mother butchered to death in front of her child. We don't tend to be that melodramatic.

Charlie Brooker: I became fixated on doing this story in a different way, because I knew there was a good idea here. Then a writers' room session produced the notion of someone having dark memories hidden away, of something bad that they had done. Suddenly the key went click in the door. Within about 30 minutes, all the basic ideas had been sketched out, right down to the twist. I went off and pretty much broke my record for writing a script. The first draft was more blackly comic, with a similar tone to [the Coen Brothers' 1996 film] *Fargo*.

Annabel Jones: It was more deliciously horrible. It played more on the humorous inevitability of the story.

Charlie Brooker: The first draft was set in Scotland. A guy called Merv and a friend accidentally knocked someone over while pissed up and drugged up, but it was much more comic.

The darker tonal shift began with the arrival of director John Hillcoat, whose work included the 2009 film adaptation of Cormac McCarthy's novel The Road. *John had been feeling disillusioned with Hollywood.*

John Hillcoat (director): The golden age of cinema was when the industry was not afraid of the dark, or of mature themes for mature audiences, or character-driven films. The Crocodile script dealt with a deeply human story that so much of cinema shies away from, so when *Black Mirror* came to my door, I was ready to jump in. I knew that I would not be under the lash for being 'too dark', or pursuing a core journey coming from the central characters' choices, their actions and reactions.

Charlie Brooker: John's got a weird habit of attaching an image to every email he sends. He had an almost inexhaustible supply of disturbing photographs or paintings of crocodiles. One was of a crocodile with a severed hand in its mouth. Quite upsetting.

Annabel Jones: John's such an actor's director, so if anyone was going to lead our protagonist through and hold onto the tone, it was him. He also does such wonderful landscapes, as seen in *The Road*: the sense of isolation and the way the environment creeps into the character.

John Hillcoat: Crocodile is a pitch-black comedy of errors. Yet crucially it's really about how human beings actually work and how we would respond to something the tech revolution may well bring into our lives, sooner than we would ever expect.

Charlie and Annabel seemed open to exploring the pros and cons of turning our male lead into a strong professional woman. Andrea Riseborough helped convince Charlie and Annabel, as she independently came to the same conclusion. She put forward the most compelling arguments for why she had to play the role of Mia. We felt a male would be more expected.

Annabel Jones: We'd sent the script to Andrea for the insurance investigator's role. She said, "I enjoyed the script, but actually I think the protagonist should be a woman." We wondered if we could believe that a woman would have the physicality to move a dead body, and Andrea's quite slim as well, but her point back was, "If you're desperate enough, you will find that inner power." She felt there was something very interesting in that, so we went with it. And you can see it in her performance, in Mia's determination. Her whole life rests on having to dispose of a body, and to carry on.

Charlie Brooker: This change made it more refreshing, because the panicking male murderer is practically a trope. And then, when we made Mia's ex-boyfriend Rob lost and broken all these years after the accident, that shifted it slightly out of the more comically heightened *Fargo*-esque world.

Morgan Kennedy (co-production designer): For the memory reader device, we offered quite a few initial designs, but Charlie had something in his mind that he wanted to emulate – an old-school 80s Space Invaders game, which is square and boxy and pretty basic-looking.

Joel Collins (series production designer): The memory reader could have been more sci-fi and over-designed, but we simplified it down to something like a slide viewer. Laptop screens are very flat these days, with everything on the surface, but with that one we wanted a lens on the front, and deep within it are your memories.

Above: The development work for the memory box, designed by Joel Collins and co-designer Morgan Kennedy, then developed in 3D for model making by Painting Practice.

Morgan Kennedy: What we ended up with reminded me a bit of the portable TVs I remember seeing as a kid in the 80s. I then went back and redesigned some of the other bits of tech – particularly the driverless pizza truck – so that it had that same boxy square design.

Sanne Wohlenberg (producer): We came to feel that Iceland was a striking and isolated backdrop that would really suit Crocodile. The country's rugged and extreme nature, together with its beauty, would be the perfect world for Mia to find herself in.

John Hillcoat: The story's coldblooded aspect fitted like a glove with Iceland during its winter. I always feel like the environment should be equal to the main characters, because people are profoundly affected by their environment. The strange, vast and primeval landscapes with blackened soil felt like they could enhance the cruel inescapable logic of Mia's fatal choices.

Morgan Kennedy: The countryside and the light in Iceland are stunningly beautiful, but it's also incredibly bleak in places. Black lava fields covered in green moss, snow-covered mountains, pink skies and steam randomly pouring out of the ground. So that was where John and I were keen to pitch the tone of the film for the design. We tried to bring some of the extraordinariness of the country to our interiors.

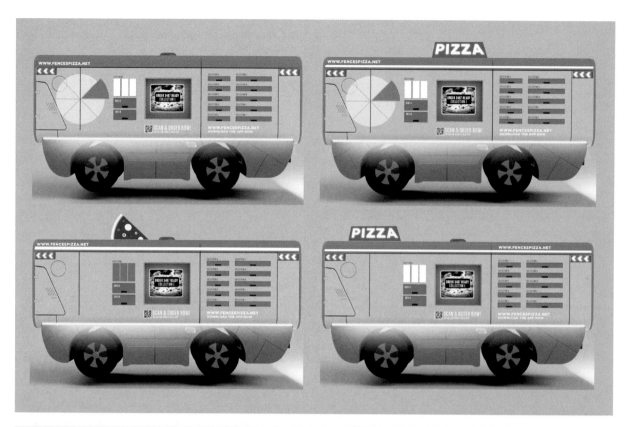

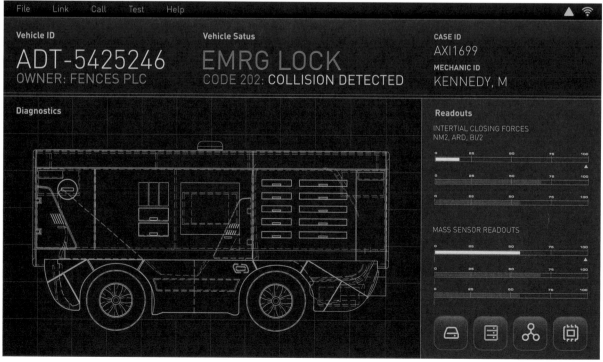

Sanne Wohlenberg: The climate was not entirely forgiving at all times. We had a terrible snowfall while filming night shoots with the pizza van outside our hotel location. We shot that sequence over two nights. On the first night, when we shot from 6pm to 6am, we had 62 centimetres of snowfall – the biggest snowfall in Reykjavik since something like 1951! We needed to keep brushing the snow all night. During our months of prep, we'd had no snow at all, ever.

John Hillcoat: The wet snow somehow seeped through every layer of hi-tech waterproofed gear. Nothing could stop it, while special effects teams with heaters and hoses tried to melt or wash away the most crucial areas within frame just before filming. An extraordinary night for sure.

Charlie Brooker: The snowfall happened while we were shooting one way, but not the other. So we built that into the story, passing it off as a nod to the slightly fluid nature of this memory technology. Basically, we explain a continuity error that no one actually ever notices.

As the story unfolds, Mia progresses from covering up the road accident, to covering up her accidental murder of Rob, to murdering insurance investigator Shazia (Kiran Sonia Sawar) and beyond.

Sanne Wohlenberg: I hope that Mia's downward spiral couldn't happen to anyone! Fundamentally, it's the story of how split-second decisions in your life can have a massive impact. When Mia was younger, she decided to go along with something that, on balance, she didn't believe in. It was a burden on her conscience, and then when it came back, she panicked. She'd thought it might go away, but of course, in life, you have to take responsibility.

John Hillcoat: Mia's deep inner flaw is her ambition, more than a hidden murderous rage. When all that ambition and success becomes threatened, along with her happy family, she unravels and lets her reptilian brain take over, like a cornered lizard or snake ... or crocodile!

Annabel Jones: I never thought of Mia as being flawed. The idea was more to explore how you come back from having been involved in something like a terrible accident. I think it was all about that one incident, after which Mia tried to protect a friend. That was the start, so it's less about her being flawed, and more the horrible logical inevitability.

John Hillcoat: The killing of Rob was almost more like manslaughter, in that it was not premeditated or calculated. Mia was trying to stop him in the heat of the moment. Even once on the ground, he yanks her hair, which has her counter by choking him too much. It all goes too far.

Charlie Brooker: Obviously, the point at which Mia really turns is when she's hiding Rob's body. What she should have done, when he's dead in the hotel room, was call the police and tell them there'd been an accident.

Above and opposite: The automated pizza delivery system, Fences, with graphics developed in the art department.

Sanne Wohlenberg: Mia takes one step, then another, and eventually there's no turning back for her. You end up going, "Oh my good lord, surely not!"

Charlie Brooker: When she's killing Shazia in the shed, there's no going back. Once that happens, it's Nowheresville for her. And then, once she's killed one person, she keeps upping the stakes for herself. She's got to keep killing people to cover her trail.

Andrea's performance is really interesting, because Mia isn't some wild-eyed, panicking maniac. When I was writing, I probably pictured somebody sweatily running around the hotel room going "Argh! Argh!" – much more like William H. Macy in *Fargo*.

John Hillcoat: Andrea was incredible in her ability to channel the most traumatic of states. She could become super-focused within a nanosecond. Her mood would change from day to day, depending upon where her character was heading, but she could still discuss anything at any given point. During the first rehearsal, she threw herself into things so forcefully that she bruised half her ribcage. Despite being in agony for the rest of the shoot, she miraculously maintained her razor-sharp instincts.

Sanne Wohlenberg: Andrea's a very focused actress. She had a hard-hitting part to play emotionally, which was difficult. Like anybody who immerses themselves in a part, there were days when she was more withdrawn, and other days, when the scenes were lighter, less so. But she was lovely to work with.

Kiran was very thoughtful and modest as Shazia, a bright light in the story. Her horrendous murder scene in the remote shed was a traumatic experience for all involved. No one wanted her to die, especially like that. Kiran was in a complete state all day, shaking like a leaf first thing in the morning and crying for real all day long. Yet she still managed to listen carefully and work with us all. Much later, when showing her the finished episode, it was the one scene she simply could not watch. I completely understood. I can't watch it anymore either!

Mia's descent reaches its lowest point when she kills Shazia's baby son, who turns out to be blind. This murder has, however, been witnessed by the family's pet guinea pig.

Charlie Brooker: Of course, the very end is quite a gag. People either go with that or they don't, so it's a really interesting one. The fact it's a blind baby – and it sounds weird to say this – was part of the joke.

Annabel Jones: It's harder to land that comic ending, when tonally you've been much straighter all the way through. So I can see why some people find it a jolt. Whereas if the tone had been *Fargo*-esque all the way through, the ending might have been less of a surprise.

Charlie Brooker: The fact that she needn't have killed the baby because it was blind, it's like, "Fucking hell." There was debate about that, and when I sent the first draft I even included some kind of caveat, because I thought everyone would say no.

Annabel Jones: There was never a question of that murder ever being seen, and we were thinking it was slightly more *Fargo*-esque, despite being very dark and cruel.

'I'm really sorry. Will you please close your eyes for me?'
– Mia

Above: Kiran Sonia Sawar in make-up during the filming of her final scenes as Shazia, the insurance investigator.

Above: Behind the scenes whilst filming key scenes for *Crocodile* in Iceland.

John Hillcoat: The twists of the blind child and the guinea pig couldn't be anything other than pitch-black comedy. The logic that Mia's actions would set up and unleash, just had to finally involve blindness and pet rodents!

Charlie Brooker: I don't think people see the guinea pig coming. It's a comic image, the idea that the cops are going to get that thing and pop it into the memory machine. Presumably they're going to waft some cheese under its nose to help bring about the memories.

Sanne Wohlenberg: Crocodile is relentlessly dark and that's probably not for everyone. It's one of those pieces that people either love particularly or feel it's too bleak. Which is a compliment in itself, rather than somebody saying, "That was nice."

Charlie Brooker: I suppose I can understand some people feeling we'd gone too far, because of the tonal shift, but I do still get surprised when people don't see the dark humour going on there. I thought if people were going to say anything, they'd say it was a sick joke, but they seem to instead say it's too much.

John Hillcoat: I was both a little surprised and proud to have further cracked that Mirror and pushed the envelope. Perversely, one of the great joys and reasons for the show's success is unquestionably all about pushing that envelope – pushing that mirror up in front of us to gaze into that blackness. Perhaps more than ever, we need to embrace all that we are. The show is a rare treat in allowing for that space to unapologetically explore a side that is normally blocked out, to our peril.

In the final scene, a haunted Mia and her husband watch their son perform among others in a school production of the 1976 musical film Bugsy Malone, *which starred a young Jodie Foster. As the police close in, the children sing the film's song* You Give A Little Love.

Jodie Foster (Arkangel director): That was such a crazy surprise when I watched Crocodile! I don't think Charlie and Annabel told me about that in advance, but it was so perfect. Only people in England understand that, because in the United States *Bugsy Malone* just came and went, but I loved the homage.

Charlie Brooker: That song is a weirdly haunting feel-good number. I first chose it as a darkly ironic counterpoint, because the kids would be singing something so upbeat. I didn't think about all the lyrics, but then realised they were singing, "You're going to be remembered for the things that you say and do," and it just felt like fate.

I've never told anyone what the title Crocodile means. John Hillcoat kept asking, and I kept saying, "Oh it's a bit complicated. I'll explain it at some point."

John Hillcoat: Here's my interpretation: the story's cruel logic has a deadly vice-like grip, akin to a crocodile's jaw.

Sanne Wohlenberg: There is a theory that, when crocodiles kill their prey, they have tears in their eyes. I don't think that's what Charlie intended, but it's fun to speculate.

Charlie Brooker: The genesis of the title actually relates to that previous incarnation of the script, about the person who'd witnessed their mother's murder at the age of two. She'd grown into this very anxious person, who saw the world as incredibly threatening.

Here's the analogy: imagine that your life is a simulated boat ride down a river. If you started playing that, as a VR experience, it could be sunny and beautiful and you love it. But if it's scripted that occasional random events will happen, such as a crocodile attacking you, well now that's slightly different. And if you are really unlucky, and a crocodile attacks you in the first minute of you playing that game, then you think you're in a horror game. You think, "From that point on, I could get attacked at any moment," and you can never relax and enjoy the rest of that boat ride, because you think it's a crocodile attack simulator.

So that's what Crocodile is: an analogy for somebody who'd been traumatized at an early age, and might be troubled by life forever and never be able to relax. The title stuck even though the story completely changed, and then the title didn't actually make sense. But it's also weirdly fitting.

HANG
THE DJ

<u>In Conversation</u>

Charlie Brooker – writer and executive producer
Annabel Jones – executive producer
Nick Pitt – producer
Georgina Campbell – actor
Joel Collins – series production designer

People in a walled-off society have signed up to a system which decides with whom they form romantic relationships and for how long. Amy and Frank develop a clear bond on their first date, but the system chooses to part them the next morning. As the pair head off to experience other relationships, will they ever be given another chance to realise their potential as a couple?

Charlie Brooker: We had a wrap party for Season Four, with a lot of actors from different episodes mingling in a room. They'd say to each other, "Oh you're in the space one? I'm in *Hang the DJ*", and someone else would go, "Is that the one with all the sex in?" There *was* a lot of sex in it, but no nudity. I think there's just a man's bum at one point.

Annabel Jones: Charlie's first cameo.

Charlie Brooker: See how stony and mirthless my face is right now? The good news is I'm laughing on the inside. Somewhere. Maybe.

Anyway, you don't want to write graphic descriptions of sex because, apart from anything else, that's probably quite off-putting to an actor.

Also, I do really like *Game of Thrones*, but in Season One of that show there was quite a lot of arched backs, tossed-back manes of hair and heaving buttocks. When that happens, it all goes a bit like a cross between a screen saver and a butcher's shop window. I'm like, "You're just showing me people's bodies for the sake of showing me people's bodies, and I feel cheapened by your expectations of what I want to see!"

Nick Pitt (producer): *Hang the DJ* is that hen's tooth of *Black Mirror*s – a happy one.

Charlie Brooker: In a way, *Hang the DJ* is a companion piece to *San Junipero*. While I was writing it I was nervous about the light and playful comic tone, and thought some people might hate it. Yet it's turned out to be a lot of people's favourite episode.

Having done *San Junipero* I was confident people would like Frank and Amy as a couple. I didn't think we needed to see them for very long, to want them to get together. It does seem that, as soon as you put a couple on screen, people are pretty much clapping their hands and going, "Fuck! Fuck! Come on, hurry up – fuck like dogs!"

Hang the DJ is also similar to *San Junipero* in that it's not really happening. We literally have a scene in which Frank and Amy say, "I think this is all a simulation!" That was me trying to pull off a double-bluff. Hopefully that worked. On some level, you might go, "Well, that's not the twist, because they've said it, so it won't be."

The story started with this idea of a Spotify for relationships. Here's what we couldn't work out: when everything's dictated in advance, how does that work as a story? Also, we didn't have the 'It's Not Really Happening' twist. You'd think with *Black Mirror* that'd be the first thing we'd think of, but it didn't occur to us for a very long time.

Annabel Jones: Oh my god, we spent months working through this idea. We wanted to do something about dating in the modern world. When Charlie had the Spotify idea, we knew it had great potential to support lots of funny contemporary observations. In the beginning, the 'Playlist' was going to be predetermined: a series of formative relationships that you should have before you settle down – scratch the itch before you commit. Have I just created a dating catchphrase?

Then we discussed changing it so the algorithm is so sophisticated it can learn from each relationship. But narratively, how can we drive Amy and Frank apart and then bring them back together at the end? So

Charlie's new twist ending allowed us to have our wedding cake and eat it. The digital Coach device merely claims the algorithm is learning from the relationships, when actually it is testing Frank and Amy to see if they'll rebel and run off together. It's a digital version of *Romeo and Juliet* but with a happy ending.

Georgina Campbell (actor): I loved the script, which felt so close to the dating experience so many of us are subject to. Endless dating seems normal these days, with all these apps and virtual ways of meeting people. It's more normal to meet someone on a dating app than in a bar! In a way it's fantastic, because you meet so many people and don't perhaps feel a need to settle, but at the same time option paralysis is definitely real. There's just too much on the menu!

To be honest, having a timer would in some ways be great. I love when Amy says how strange it is that people would have to decide and go through break-ups. I could definitely do without that drama in my life, but on the other hand it might cut your experience too short. You need time to truly get to know someone, but it can sometimes only take a second to feel that spark.

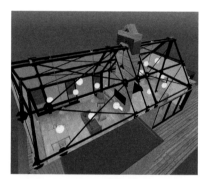

Annabel Jones: Georgina Campbell and Joe Cole, two of the most exciting actors of their generation, playing opposite each other – how lucky we were!

Given that the film tracks Amy and Frank's relationship over a number of years, and in between various other dalliances, we had to set up the romantic connection between them very quickly. They needed an immediate rapport and Georgina and Joe delivered this with such natural and honest performances – you're immediately rooting for them. Georgina as Amy effortlessly exuded warmth and likeability and Joe brought such vulnerability to Frank. The combination was heart-breaking.

Georgina Campbell: Joe Cole and I did a chemistry test together and it just really clicked. We spoke a bit before, had drinks and got to know each other a little, so it was great that we already had that rapport. I was really lucky to work with Joe: he's a fantastic actor and I think he could probably have chemistry with a plank of wood!

There was a funny moment at the pairing day celebration, when I see Frank again and kick him. After a few takes, our director Tim Van Patten came over and whispered in my ear, "Look, we're not buying the kick, just kick him properly this time, he can handle it." I kicked Joe so hard he bled … and that was the shot they used. Hopefully he can forgive me: it was a great reaction!

I really enjoyed stepping into Amy's shoes. She's just full to the brim with hope. I wanted her to be light, the embodiment of that feeling you get when you go dating, that nervous excitement. I created a little bounce in her step, to help convey her warm and almost childish energy. Even when she eventually becomes tired of the system, she still has this glint in her eye, this feeling of hope. She never gives up! I really love that about her as a character, she's so strong.

Joel Collins (series production designer): In Charlie's first draft, the people were in tower blocks. But I'd been to a birthday party in this Oxfordshire place called Soho Farmhouse. It's full of extraordinarily rich people on

Above: The concept development work for the cabins and the self-driving taxis, both designed by Joel Collins.

holiday, looking very smug. An electric milk float takes you round to your cabin, which is like a wood-shack with a bath in the middle. Then you go to clubs and bars, but all in the countryside as if in its own world. When I showed Charlie this place, he recreated the script to be set in more of a Center Parcs for dating.

I took apart a mobile phone. Inside, there's a green plate, and on that plate there's a chip, with lots of copper and brass lines leading to other nubbins. So I decided to design a park based on this mobile phone chip. There's a central hub, and all the green grass is the green plate of the chip, and all the huts are the little nubbins. Basically, I thought, "If we can't tell the audience we're inside a mobile phone, what happens if I design it like we really are?" I never told anybody that, because it's absurd, so I kind of kept it quiet! But if you look at the design, it's completely geometric. Everywhere is the same.

Charlie Brooker: There's algorithmic stuff going on in all the designs. Hexagonal grid patterns and repeated motifs that you don't really notice, woven into everything. They're there when they climb up the wall at the end.

Frank and Amy enter a second relationship of an unspecified length, having agreed not to look at their expiry date. When Frank can't resist taking a secret look, his action pulls their expiry date forward and seems to have ruined everything.

Above: The concept development work for the world within the 'wall', designed by Painting Practice.

Charlie Brooker: I always thought that was a neat little analogy for leaving things well alone, versus the human need to know everything and the insecurity that comes from worrying about how long a relationship will last. Frank ends up punishing both of them. He sours the whole thing by getting insecure.

Nick Pitt: At one point during script development, that moment gave us a structural problem and we discussed getting rid of it. But we sensed its power and Charlie found the dramatic shoehorn that eased whatever the structural problem was. Looking back, its loss would have robbed the final act of so much emotional power. I just can't imagine the show without that now, but we nearly mislaid it.

Joel Collins: When it came to designing the hand-held devices that tell everyone how long their relationships will last, I thought of Legoland. If you pay an extra fee, you can get a device that tells you when you can queue-jump a ride. So the ideology for the device was a bit like that. We needed to clarify to the audience that it was not a mobile phone. I think we called it The Oracle.

Charlie Brooker: I needed a reason for Amy to rebel against the place – something that tells her something's not right here. And if this was a simulation, there would be some things that they wouldn't bother putting a variance in. By this point, we already knew the devices were going to be round, and Amy happened to be standing by some water with a disc-shaped thing in her hand ... so it was one of those things where you go, "Oh, this is handy ... "

When Amy first skims the stones, and notices that there are four skips, you're focussing on what's going on with Frank, so it doesn't play on your mind too much. But if you did think about it, you'd think they must be clearly in a simulation, because the stone always skims across the water four times.

I'd had the idea of 1,000 simultaneous simulations producing one result for a while, but it remained an orphan until I finally found a home for it here. While we were doing *White Christmas*, someone asked whether a confession made by a virtual version of someone really would be admissible as evidence. And I said, "Well, okay, it's a simulation, so what if they could run it 1,000 times simultaneously, then say that Potter confessed in 997 of the cases?"

To rule out the argument that he only confessed because he was sent mad by the isolation of this Arctic outpost, you could have him in a different place in each simulation – the outpost, a spaceship, a cabin in the woods, 1920s Egypt. That spaceship idea, by the way, also then informed *USS Callister*.

Nick Pitt: Charlie wrote a climactic scene set in a void. This scene came after our heroes had escaped from the world of overweening algorithms, but before they reached the 'real world' bar to enjoy The Smiths – whose song *Panic*, with its 'Hang the DJ' lyrics, plays in the pub and informed the title – and each other. On the page, in this void, it was clear that stuff was turning into other stuff ... but beyond that it was hard to be sure.

Above: The various screens of the handheld digital Coach device, which is used by all participants living within the wall. The user interface was initially designed in the graphics department by Erica McEwan, then further developed and animated at Painting Practice.

Joel Collins: Nailing the ending down was very difficult, because the visual complexity was vast and Charlie's script was uber-vague. When you're coming out of a mobile phone, but you're not really coming out of a mobile phone because it's a simulation ... what the fuck does that look like?

Charlie Brooker: That script was written in quite a hurry, because of where it fell in the production cycle. I had not quite worked out how the system worked at the end, or what we should see. Frank and Amy climb up a ladder into a void. They look around and see thousands of other 'thems', then they gradually break into bits and go up into the sky. No-one, including some of the cast, really knew what was going on. They'd ask me, and I'd go, "Well, er, yeah, it's because they're in a simulation and there's thousands of them ... "

Nick Pitt: We looked at the creepy and masterful [2013 art/sci-fi film] *Under the Skin*, and drew a shiver of inspiration. Our director Tim Van Patten and our director of photography Stuart Bentley gamely harvested a crop we weren't sure was entirely edible. Actors on black floors against green screen, looking meaningfully into the middle distance, thinking, "I hope this looks better than it feels."

Georgina Campbell: I had no idea what we were doing! We were in front of a green screen changing our outfits every five seconds and trying to react differently to this unknown 'void' over and over again. By the end I was just in a giggling fit, because our reactions were getting more and more broad and ridiculous by the second.

Charlie Brooker: Annabel usually shows our films to her partner Craig, and I'll often show them to Konnie at home, and then we'll see if they understand them. They're our guinea pigs. So Craig and Konnie were really enjoying it … and then it got to the end. It was a rough cut with place-marker effects at that point, but they were like, "I don't know what happened at all." We knew this was a real problem, but it was one of those situations where you tinker away until you fix it in post. We had really abstract conversations about what we needed to see as they ascend to this heaven.

Joel Collins: We tried loads of different things, creating versions of it on the computer. Our VFX producer Russell McLean was losing his mind! It was just very complex, trying to make it not look weird. Because it just is weird. We went round in circles, because when anything's possible it's really hard to settle on something.

Annabel Jones: People weren't understanding that what they'd just seen was a simulation, so we realised we needed to see that word on the ring. Then we needed to summarise that Amy and Frank's 'rebellion' had happened 998 times out of 1000 simulations and that this revolt against the system was necessary to successfully count as a match. It probably sounds really obvious but it took forever to achieve that simplicity.

Nick Pitt: Many edits and VFX iterations later, we pulled Charlie and Annabel into a small room with a big TV. Neil Riley, our VFX supervisor, had miraculously found a way of dematerialising people so they didn't look like they were being broken, squashed or incinerated. He'd achieved a graceful leaving of their body, with elegant and fluid spheres ascending. The characters suddenly looked reassured, fracturing without fear, and happy to swap the ethereal soundtrack of Sigur Rós for the more raucous pleasures of Johnny Marr's guitar.

Charlie Brooker: That final void became more like *Tron* [the 1982 Disney film set inside a computer]. The words and figures you see in the sky took an awful lot of working out, after the fact. Then I rewrote quite a lot of Amy's dialogue in the last scene where she and Frank are in the restaurant, adding lines for her to say about what was going on. Previously in that scene, there'd been more confusing back-and-forth, so it was easier and shorter when Amy basically said, "I know what's going on, just trust me, let's go."

Georgina Campbell: On the day, I just felt really overwhelmed by that restaurant scene. It was really beautifully written and I just felt totally in it. I kept crying and Tim had to tell me to stop, because he didn't want Amy teary – he wanted her strong and in control! That intensity really bled into the final scene in the pub.

'Ever since we've met, this world has been toying with us. It's trying to keep us apart. It's a test, I swear it is, and the two of us rebelling together is something to do with passing it'

– Amy

Charlie Brooker: Of course, in the final cut it looks like we were confident enough to do the ending that way all along, but we absolutely weren't!

When we finally cut to the real world, suddenly we see logos and bottles of beer, and you realise how different and stylised the world that you've been in for the whole episode was. Suddenly it's this messy, loud world with licensed music playing.

Georgina Campbell: I love my and Joe's reactions, when we first see each other in the real world. It's just so romantic!

Annabel Jones: When we've made an emotionally upbeat film, I often have a little cry when we watch the final cut in the edit. Mostly to make Charlie feel uncomfortable, but also because I'm pleased we've managed to realise the script so well. *Every time* I watch that final scene in the pub, my heart swells with happiness and the tears aren't far away. You understand that Amy and Frank know this is special.

Charlie Brooker: *Hang the DJ* has the kind of simple, happy ending I resisted writing for ages. I do have these adolescent urges to make really shocking and nasty things happen all the time, but in some ways the slightly more gooey stuff is harder. Because it would have been easy to have a nasty ending instead. In an alternate universe, Amy and Frank have a 99.8% match and meet in the pub … and then, round the back of the pub, she clubs him over the head with a brick, looks down the camera lens and says, "It's *Black Mirror*, what did you fucking expect?"

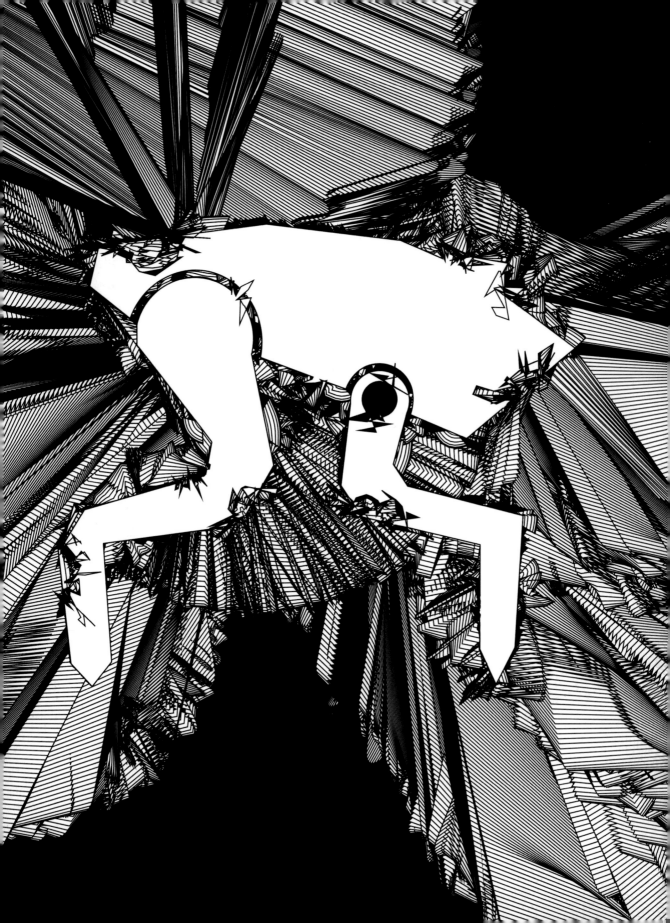

METALHEAD

In Conversation

Charlie Brooker – writer and executive producer
Annabel Jones – executive producer
David Slade – director
Joel Collins – series production designer
Louise Sutton – producer
Russell McLean – VFX producer
Michael Bell – VFX supervisor, DNEG
Susie Coulthard – costume designer

Bella and her friends Clarke and Anthony are hunting for something across an endlessly barren landscape. When they search through an abandoned warehouse, a deadly, resourceful and seemingly unstoppable dog-like automaton starts hunting them instead.

Charlie Brooker: *Metalhead* felt like the best way for us to do robots. We'd wanted to do a robot episode, and *Be Right Back* was sort of that. But there are so many robot shows around …

Annabel Jones: … and they're usually about a robot suddenly acquiring feelings, which I don't ever understand. So this was a way of doing the exact opposite: a robot that has zero feelings.

Charlie Brooker: Robots usually tend to want only two things. They either want to be free or they want to fall in love. What boring bastards. Although I suppose they do occasionally decide humanity is a virus that must be destroyed.

Annabel Jones: We wanted a relentless chase. The idea was to take the spirit of [Steven Spielberg's 1971 film] *Duel*, but make a scarier version with a solar-powered robot predator that would stop at nothing to follow you. That dread was the starting point.

Charlie Brooker: It was *Duel*, *Jaws* and [the 2013 film] *All Is Lost*, which I'd enjoyed. That's basically Robert Redford on a sinking boat for an hour and a half. Things go wrong on the boat and because he's the only person on board, there's not really any dialogue. I think he says "Shit" to himself and that's about it. You don't even know his name.

Annabel Jones: We loved that simplicity. We didn't want *Metalhead* to be a film about outwitting an AI robot, because that would have felt very different. We wanted this to feel basic and raw. One woman stranded, with this thing pursuing her.

Charlie Brooker: Originally, I did think we needed something else going on. So in the first draft, you discovered the robot was being controlled by a drone operator across the ocean in America. When our main character Bella was in the tree, the operator put the robot on 'automatic wait' mode then walked out of the room, and you realised he was in his house. So he's a freelance drone operator, who goes off to put his kids in the bath. His wife's pregnant and he helps her with something, then makes himself a drink … this stuff was all written. There was a point where something distracted him, and one of his kids went into the room and started playing with the robot, which is how Bella escaped from the tree. I thought that was a nice moment: a five year old unwittingly starting up a death machine.

Annabel Jones: Except, this sequence took you out of the film. There were nice details, but it wasn't really giving us anything. And then it felt unexplained. An unnecessary layer.

Charlie Brooker: It also felt like it was saying, "Drone operators, eh? Tsk!"

Annabel Jones: There was something far scarier in the robot having autonomy. There was nothing to stop or control this dog.

Charlie Brooker: Partly because we're at a warehouse at the start, it feels like the robot is guarding the goods, but that wasn't the intention. It doesn't matter why it's there, but about 50 per cent of viewers assume it's a security dog for that building. We never explain this, but it's meant to be a military robot. A war has happened and these things are all over the place, having killed everything. They could have been unleashed by some other country or whatever.

David Slade (director): Our actors asked a lot of questions about what exactly had happened in the world, but Charlie and I said, "It's just the end of the world." We weren't really interested in that part, even though the script had the essence of a number of post-apocalyptic ideas that I gravitated towards. It reminded me of black-and-white films like [Chris Marker's 1962 short film] *La Jetée* and [George A Romero's 1968 film] *Night of the Living Dead*, but also *The Terminator* and [the 1994 Japanese-British sci-fi film] *Death Machine*. So I knew exactly what *Metalhead* was, but I also knew it had to be something heavy and serious.

Annabel Jones: We thought very carefully about the design of the dog. We didn't want it to look too sophisticated or over-designed, because why would it be? It just needed to look functional. A pragmatic killing machine.

Joel Collins (series production designer): I wanted our robot headless. The most terrifying thing is to be hunted by something without a face, because how does it know where you are? But it doesn't need a head to hunt you.

Charlie Brooker: I'd been inspired in part by the [US robotics company] Boston Dynamics videos. Those robots are nightmarishly familiar, in terms of their shape and some of the movements they make. And at the same time, there's something completely unknowable and alien about them – they don't have any kind of face, or anything you can project any sort of feeling or emotion onto. Sometimes they move in a way which gives you this horrible sense of vertigo.

David Slade: Charlie and I were both terrified by the Boston Dynamics robots. Not only are these things very much a reality, but there's a menace to them. The reptilian part of our brains finds them very scary, because they're the first big threat to human civilisation.

Louise Sutton (producer): We needed to make our robot dog look terrifying without anthropomorphising it. But as soon as you start animating something, it has a character! We went through so many different versions: four legs, two legs, a dome on the top ...

Joel Collins: I believe military robots will have Kevlar in the future, because robots are quite fragile. So we put some of that armour on our robot's back end, like fabric covers. Our director David came along with ideas, wanting the design more angular. We'd got quite far with the dog and David pushed it to the final hurdle with me. We carried on working until we nailed it.

Charlie Brooker: We wanted the robot to dispatch people in a very brutal way. When it shoots the top of the guy's head off in the warehouse, it feels

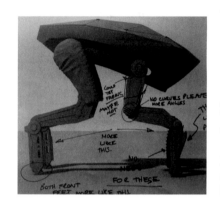

Above and opposite: The development work for the robot dog, by Joel Collins and the concept team at Painting Practice with VFX specialists Framestore and DNEG, including the dog's point of view.

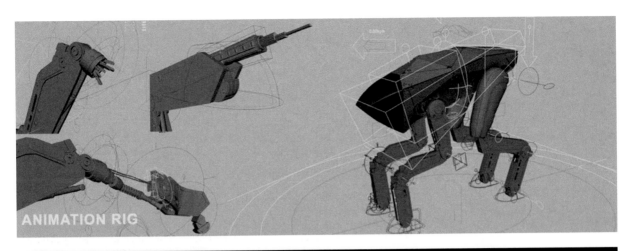

ANIMATION RIG

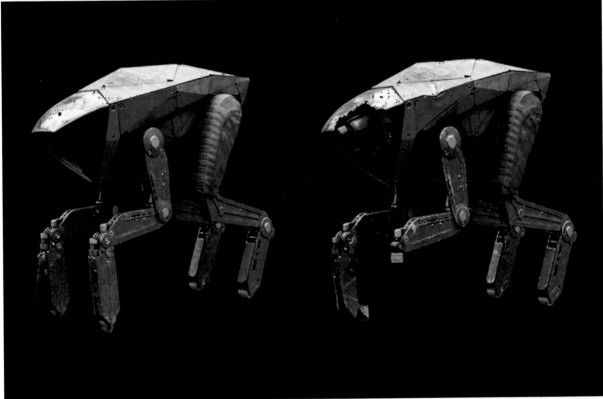

ROBOT POV

Above and opposite: The costume concept art for Bella, Clarke and Anthony, designed by Susie Coulthard.

very real and horrible. We've had gore before in things like *Playtest*, but there's something extra nasty about the matter-of-fact nature of these killings.

There's something nice about it being a completely unceremonious and brutal slaying device. It just goes *bang*, which is scarier than if it delivered a speech about how it was going to kill you. It doesn't even try and cool look, by playing rock music while it kills.

Louise Sutton: Having agreed what the robot would look like, we went to the VFX company DNEG and started to build on top of that. If the robot didn't look terrifying or believable, the whole film would just not stand up. So we went to somebody who we knew would deliver that level of intricate animation.

Russell McLean (VFX producer): DNEG's CG character work is excellent. I think they had people fighting within the company to work on *Metalhead*!

Michael Bell (VFX supervisor, DNEG): Having been a massive fan of previous seasons, I instantly wanted to be involved.

The more challenging the project became, the more excited I got. I knew we were doing something completely unique.

The legendary British actress Maxine Peake, from TV's Shameless *and* Silk, *was cast as Bella.*

David Slade: Once we'd got Maxine, I knew the camera would largely be close on her face. My goal was to access her astonishing ability to reach inside of herself and pull out truth. To do that, she needed to trust me. I needed to trust her, and set up an environment that was immediate and uncomplicated.

While flying from Los Angeles to London to start prep, I decided *Metalhead* had to be black-and-white. All of the visual themes I was trying to orchestrate – weight, heaviness, metal, stains, scratches, rust – were pushing me towards taking away all the colour. There would be utilitarian advantages too, such as a clearer and sharper image, and it helped streamline the choice process.

Annabel Jones: David felt this was a world that had collapsed and there was no hope or colour left. In black and white, it just feels more desolate and destroyed.

Charlie Brooker: Shooting in monochrome suited the spartan nature of the story. And that helps bed the CGI in, in a way.

Russell McLean: The film being black and white actually made the FX a bit harder. But it was exciting to do it that way, because I'd certainly not seen anything with that kind of CG character in black and white.

Louise Sutton: It was nerve-wracking, because we actually shot *Metalhead* on two of the few monochrome cameras in existence. There was no going back! It took an enormous leap of faith.

David Slade: I don't ever worry about that. I figure that if I'm passionate enough about something, then everybody will get on board. And after about three weeks of convincing, they did. Then, once the decision was made, I basically made the entire production monochrome, so we could start thinking that way. When the wardrobe or location photographs were coming in, I'd make sure they were all monochrome photographs. Even my memories of this production are monochrome!

Susie Coulthard (costume designer): As we only had three human characters, we needed to make sure our choices were correct, as so much screen time would be given to the 'hero' outfits. We went for a gold shiny coat as one of main layers for Bella – something which would not have been chosen, had we been shooting in colour. We also took some great Richard Avedon references from [Laura Wilson's 1985 book] *In the American West.*

Louise Sutton: We went off to shoot with stunt drivers, stunt coordinators, puppeteers, cameras on the backs of trucks, drones … we had all the equipment in the world. For the scenes where you see Maxine driving the car, we had a pod built on top for a remote driver, who could then steer the vehicle. One of the things that really draws you into the film is that you're right up and close to the action. David's a very intense director, who really captured the relentlessness of that chase.

David Slade: The word I kept saying, over and over, when asked what I was looking for, was, "Life!" There are many ways to shoot people in cars, and I wanted something fast and loose, but also quite simple. Using a pod driver on top of the car enabled me to sit with Maxine and say, "There's no-one in the car but you." When she's in the driver's seat of this car going at 30 miles per hour, it's quite easy for her to access her fear.

Annabel Jones: Obviously, we shot the whole film without the dog there, and the great Maxine Peake had to act against nothing, putting her faith in David, DNEG and our post-production team, to be able to create this robot character.

David Slade: There was one physical dog prop that we used, so Maxine knew the size and the scale. But there was no greenscreen, and everything was kept as far away from that antiseptic studio experience as possible. It was real locations, with no built sets. We were shooting in fields, climbing over fences while carrying gear, rather than flying around in helicopters.

Russell McLean: The hardest VFX scene to do was probably the robot going through the window at the back of the van.

Charlie Brooker: In one of those Boston Dynamics videos, they put a banana skin down and this thing slips on it. The robot looks ridiculous, like a plastic lawn chair that's fallen over. You go, "Haha!" … and then it rights itself, like a nightmare.

David Slade: That almost seemed like a Hollywood movie moment that had been engineered by a robot company.

'If there is anyone there ... This is just to say that I'm not coming back. Say I'm sorry to Ali and that she should give Jack a kiss from me. I'm sorry I didn't get the replacement like I promised'

– Bella

Annabel Jones: We absolutely borrow that moment for our scene with the van window.

Charlie Brooker: The script specifies that the robot comes through that window, lands unceremoniously and looks a bit pathetic for a moment. Then it gets up and blows the driver's head off.

Michael Bell: The window's glass breaking was a practical SFX effect, shot for real on the day. So when we put the CG dog in the shot, we had to make sure it looked like it was causing the break. That meant painting the glass back over the dog as it smashed through. Once it hit the floor of the van, we added an extra layer of CG broken glass over the top, so the dog had shards of glass bouncing off it as it lay there.

In April 2018, Metalhead *won a BAFTA Craft Award for Special Visual & Graphic Effects.*

Louise Sutton: *Metalhead* was up against some huge shows at those awards, so that was a really big coup for us. We're so proud.

Russell McLean: I've had people asking "which bits" were CG! DNEG totally nailed it. This was the smoothest VFX process I've ever worked on. DNEG were great and David was very clear with his vision. With animation, it can be very expensive if you start trying different options for the same shot, so you have to be quite certain about what you want to do.

Michael Bell: Some reviews said they were pleased we'd used 'a practical animatronic robot', so we knew we'd done a good job. Just in case there's still some uncertainty out there: it's all CG. My favourite type of VFX is used primarily as a tool for storytelling. *Metalhead* couldn't have been done without the VFX. It was needed to tell the story, but it's also not singing, "Look how clever we are!"

Charlie Brooker: Among viewers, *Metalhead* is a divisive one, partly because of the expectations some people have of *Black Mirror*. They might sit down and go, "Right, what's the message here?", but *Metalhead* isn't a traditional story. It's more of an experience: a relentless chase. That wrong-foots some people. Also some people are like, "Black and white? What?" or they expect a big explanation that doesn't come.

David Slade: Pride is a sin, but I'm guilty of it with *Metalhead*. It was all of the things I wanted to do. I was really blown away by Maxine. Listen, DNEG did an amazing job, but the best visual effect was Maxine.

Metalhead's final image reveals that Bella and co had been searching for a new teddy bear for a terminally ill child.

Annabel Jones: At the beginning, it had seemed that the film might lend itself to having no dialogue. But once the ending had been decided, you needed the set-up. The biggest distinction between Bella and the robot is humanity. She could hunt for survival, but the thing that undoes her is the quest to give some comfort to a dying nephew. Once we had that, you couldn't really set that up without any dialogue.

Charlie Brooker: Hopefully, by the time you get to the end you've sort of forgotten they were at a warehouse at the start, looking for something. The best kind of twist is like, "Remember that? It was only 40 minutes ago but you forgot, didn't you, you fuckin' idiot. Don't you want to know what was in that box? Here it is – pay attention next time. Now fuck off."
Ahem. That's *not* how this show speaks to its viewers.

Annabel Jones: Neither should this book.

Charlie Brooker: Right, let's leave all of that in.

BLACK
MUSEUM

<u>In Conversation</u>

Charlie Brooker – writer and executive producer
Annabel Jones – executive producer
Penn Jillette – co-story writer
Colm McCarthy – director
Letitia Wright – actor
Douglas Hodge – actor
Joel Collins – series production designer

Nowheresville, Nevada. While British tourist Nish waits for her car to charge up, she visits the nearby Black Museum run by Rolo Haynes. This master of ceremonies tells Nish three stories, each of which corresponds to a ghoulish exhibit. These are the tales of a well-meaning doctor who is doomed to conflate pleasure and pain; a man who regrets having his dead wife's consciousness installed in his head; and a Death Row prisoner who chooses a torturous digital afterlife to benefit his family. This last story resonates particularly strongly with Nish ...

Charlie Brooker: I had a bit of trepidation in essentially following *White Christmas* with another portmanteau. Annoyingly, I wanted to do this portmanteau when we were at our busiest on Season Four, just at the time when it would've been great to do something comparatively easy. But no, the idea in my head had shitloads of stuff going on in it.

Annabel Jones: And set in America! Episode Six was supposed to be our very simple British two-hander. And then: oh, here's *Black Museum* ...

It was quite involved, finessing all the individual stories so that they build and interlock at the end, having Rolo feature in them all, ensuring all the tech felt as plausible as it could be, holding back the twist, and the final twist. And the detail! We agonise over every detail. And at the same time we're in the final stages of editing *USS Callister*, in the mix for *Arkangel*, working on the VFX on *Crocodile*, filming *Hang the DJ*, casting and prepping *Metalhead*. Why would anyone work like that?!

I remember stepping off the set at Painshill Park in Surrey, where we were filming *Hang the DJ*. Charlie and I sat in the park café, desperately trying to grab some time to finish the outline of *Black Museum*. We're both tired and we're both stressed. In this public café, we're having, for us, quite a heated debate. Because we've worked together for so long now, we can be totally honest with each other. It's so important creatively to be able to disagree and argue passionately and know that it's not going to destabilise anything.

He probably wasn't even bloody listening. Probably thinking about the most scatological thing he can say in that moment. But God, it was a great script! A really good script.

Charlie Brooker: We'd been discussing some of these ideas for a while. For a long time, I'd been trying to work out this ghost story: the notion of a digital prisoner you could electrocute again and again. There was also 'Dead Wife in the Head', as we called it, which was the idea of someone having an ex-partner installed in a dormant part of their brain. And then the magician Penn Jillette and I had discussed this 'Pain Addict' idea before Season Three ...

Penn Jillette (co-story writer): In 1981, while touring with [art collective] The Residents in Barcelona, I became as sick as I've ever been in my life. I developed an extremely high fever and was in a huge amount of pain. During my stay in a filthy hospital where no-one spoke English, I hallucinated the entire story of *The Pain Addict* – the prose version of which ended up being used as filler material in a magic book that [my magic partner] Teller and I wrote.

Because I loved *Black Mirror*, a friend put me in touch with Charlie. We met at a cafe along the Thames, right in the shadow of Big Ben. I blew him for half an hour about how great he was and how *Black Mirror* was the greatest show ever. I mean, I told the truth but it was still fairly embarrassing. After about 45 minutes, I told him that I hadn't intended to pitch him anything, but I had an idea that didn't fit anywhere. With a great deal of humility, Charlie said, "Feel free to pitch – I've been out of ideas since the first season!" So I told him the whole story of The Pain Addict.

Charlie Brooker: When people pitch us ideas, often they'll over-think it. Or they'll tell you what it's about in the first paragraph, when you want the elevator pitch. Penn was one of the few people who actually just told a story that was refreshingly high-concept and a popcorn movie crowd-pleaser. We had to work on his story to make it fit. If you read his original story, it's quite different. I mean, it's incredibly grim.

Penn Jillette: Charlie was wicked-honest. He said that after months and months of no contact, he'd get in touch with me in a panic and say they had 10 days until they shoot, then he'd suck everything from me that he could and disappear again. I thought he was being cute and hyperbolic, but it was literally true!

To give you an idea of my input, we kicked around the ideas for a few hours of Skype and phone. It was so glorious to feel understood and to have someone build on your ideas, instead of acting like they haven't heard a word you said!

The final credit very kindly says, 'Story by Penn Jillette,' but Charlie changed the original story so much that it should really be a co-credit. He made it different from my idea, and 1000 times better for *Black Mirror*.

I will add I'm not as gracious as I sound. If someone else had taken that story and changed it as much as Charlie did, there might have been resentment and sadness. But his vision is so pure. He took my idea, and turned it into his idea, in such a completely pure way, that what I personally see in that story is a conversation with Charlie, about what it means to share pain with someone else.

Colm McCarthy (director): I think Penn also seeded something into *Black Museum* about Rolo Haynes – the idea that any showman is trying to frighten and entertain an audience in equal measures.

Charlie Brooker: Because of Penn, I thought, "What if the person who binds these three stories together is a bit like someone running a sideshow?" A larger-than-life character who's a bit like a carnival barker – or 'carnival talker' as Penn told me they're called. So we wanted a showman.

Penn Jillette: Charlie did talk about the framing mechanism he wanted to do, and we talked about museums in Vegas, but whatever is great about *Black Museum*, that's Charlie.

I desperately wanted to play the lead character Rolo, even though it would have cost an extraordinary amount of money for me and Teller to cancel our Las Vegas shows during the *Black Museum* shoot. My carnival background is that guy. I'm a fire-eater, a talker, I'm all of that stuff. Charlie and Annabel were so kind. Charlie basically told me they had a really great director and they wanted to let him do whatever he wanted. Also, reading between the lines, the actor Colm McCarthy wanted was better than me! I do fancy, though, that Charlie took a few of my rhythms and style in the way that he wrote Rolo. Please do not disabuse me of this, because it's an important part of my life!

Charlie Brooker: Not only will I not disabuse Penn of this notion, I will reaffirm it. Rolo's rhythms were heavily modelled on the way I'd seen Penn speak, both in the Penn & Teller stage act and their Showtime documentary series *Bullshit*.

Above: The logo for Rolo Haynes' Black Museum, designed by head of graphics, Erica McEwan.

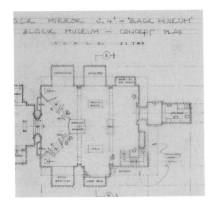

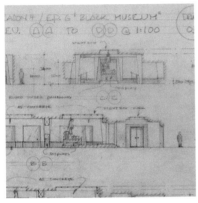

'Well, just us two this morning. You sure you wanna do this? This place ain't for the faint-hearted'

– Rolo

Above: Detailed architectural plans for Rolo Haynes' Black Museum, which was constructed in its entirety for filming.

Annabel Jones: Douglas Hodge is a multi-talented actor, who's won a ridiculous number of awards for his theatre work including *La Cage Aux Folles* and *Charlie and the Chocolate Factory*. For a lot of the film, Rolo is in his museum and quite stationary, presenting the story behind an exhibit. From a directorial and performance point of view, that's quite limiting, so we needed an actor who could give a big performance and own his space. Doug had to hold the narrative of the film together with Letitia Wright, who was also just amazing.

Charlie Brooker: Letitia and Doug are good examples of very different performers, from very different acting backgrounds, who are both just so watchable every moment they're onscreen. There's constantly something going on. We'd wanted Letitia before for a part in Season Three, but something happened with her availability, so it was really fortuitous that the role of Nish came along at the right time. She'd just finished shooting in [the 2018 Marvel superhero blockbuster] *Black Panther*.

Annabel Jones: When Letitia did a self-tape audition for us, we were mesmerised by her performance because she gave it so much more than what was on the page. Like most actors, she had someone off-screen reading in the other lines, but we were distracted by this person's voice … because it was Daniel Kaluuya, who was starring in *Black Panther* with her!

Letitia Wright (actor): We were two or three weeks away from wrapping on *Black Panther*, and I needed someone to read with. Who could've been better than Daniel? I call him "the O.G. of *Black Mirror*", because he's one of the first people to be in that show. The 'pig' story kinda threw me back then, so the first time I really paid attention to *Black Mirror* was *Fifteen Million Merits* with Daniel, which I really liked. The more the show went on and gained that cult following, the more I understood it.

Altogether, I'd had six months on *Black Panther*, then went straight into *Black Museum* with one week to learn everything and early morning call-times again. I was knackered, man! There were times when I thought I was gonna fall over, but I didn't say anything, because I really wanted to play Nish.

Douglas Hodge (actor): I couldn't have been more of a *Black Mirror* fan. Just like everyone else, I binge my way through the great things that turn up on TV in this era, and *Black Mirror*'s top of my list. Having said that, there are episodes that I watch from behind the sofa. I'm a huge, huge fan of Charlie Brooker and I think the writing's phenomenal. So I was already on board, before I even knew *Black Mirror* was coming to me.

When my agent phoned up about *Black Museum*, I said, "Oh yes! Is it an interesting role, though?" And she said, "Oh, it's an interesting role, yeah … "

With film and TV scripts, it so often feels like trying to polish a turd, but *Black Museum* arrived complete and perfectly formed. It was as good, if not better, than any script I've ever been given in theatre, film or TV. There was nothing to change: the rhythms were great, the plot was there and it was laugh-out-loud funny. Absolutely terrifying too, with a political thrust.

Rolo is a wonderful creation, an extraordinary person – a storyteller with an empathic disconnect. He's probably the most toxic person I've ever had to be. Just after *Black Museum*, I played Nixon and I'm currently playing a Guantanamo Bay torturer, but none of them come close to Rolo Haynes' unempathetic glee. Playing him was like swallowing a small thimble of poison each morning. Every day, the whole thing felt more toxic – especially as it was essentially a black cast and Rolo was a white supremacist.

Joel Collins (series production designer): Doug literally became Rolo. I thought it was really funny, because I knew he was going Method. He'd got just into the character so deeply. And when you're used to actors doing that, you just avoid them before they tear you apart.

Douglas Hodge: I kept myself to myself on set. I didn't get made-up or get dressed in the same place as anyone else. I was just sort of mumbling and salivating in the corner. It's not Method at all: I don't stay in character the whole time, because I don't believe in that. But especially when you're playing someone who's American and unlike you, you do try and stay in character as much as you can.

On the first day, Letitia came up to me and asked if I wanted to rehearse our lines. I just said no. She said, "No-one's ever said that to me before," and I said, "Well, there we are," and walked away. After that, I think she was quite nervous, but I did it to help me inhabit Rolo and to help her hate him. Also, I don't tend to want to rehearse lines much, because I'm prepared and I want to do what we do on camera, not off. If I'd been playing a different character, I'd certainly not have been so unforthcoming. But I just stayed in that mode, and whichever actors I met, I was just like, "Yeah, right, let's just do the scene."

Charlie Brooker: Fucking hell, that's quite hardcore. I always find it odd when actors do that sort of thing, just because I'd find it so socially awkward I'd collapse! Letitia must've thought Doug was a real prick ... which I can see would be helpful.

Letitia Wright: When Doug refused to 'run' our lines, that's when I knew that this was getting real! I felt a bit heartbroken, but I just had to learn that Doug is Doug. He didn't wanna hear how I was going to play Nish – he just wanted to do it in the moment, so I had to suck it up and do it. Sometimes before takes, he would look at me and growl! I was jumping out of my skin, but it really added to the whole thing. From the moment I read Rolo on the page, I hated him. Doug had to go Method, because you cannot come in and out of that character. We really got into our characters a lot, because it was so deep and there had to be so much focus and concentration.

Colm McCarthy: Letitia very much avoided Douglas between takes, but not in an arsey way – she just did what was necessary to make it real. Here's the truth: they're both really committed to what they're doing, to the extent that it could be perceived as – I wouldn't say 'difficult' – but not everybody would have an appetite to go there with them, when they're really committed like that. I would work with either of them again in a heartbeat. They're amazing actors. Even though we did some big stuff, the real tension in that episode is all in the museum. The rest of it is a story that Doug's telling – and he had so many words, the poor guy!

Above: Annabel Jones onset at the Black Museum in front of a selection of death masks, which were cast from the faces of crew members.

Letitia Wright: Doug had to juggle my scenes, plus every single scene within the story. I gained a lot of respect for him by the end, because he is a master of what he does. He and I did have moments where we could have a laugh, but everything was so intense and we spent the majority of our time filming. Any time we had a break, he had to go and learn another five paragraphs for the next scene! So I never really got to connect with Doug outside of work, but what a phenomenal actor. If we work together in the future, I wanna get to know Doug and not Rolo Haynes!

Joel Collins: I probably didn't help Doug's Method acting by building that museum as a complete set.

Douglas Hodge: We walked in and the whole place was there! It was a great set, so beautiful that you could've literally sold tickets to the general public.

Joel Collins: By the time I'd finished with it, a lot of people thought I was utterly mentally ill, because I filled it with this hidden celebration of six years of *Black Mirror*.

As you went into reception, I reused the phones from Nosedive as the museum guide devices. Along the corridor, a wall of screens showed historical footage of murderers, including the couple from *White Bear*. There was a print on the wall of *Playtest*'s Harlech House and a dummy wearing the dress from *San Junipero*. Then there were the plaster-cast faces of the crew, plus military gear from *Men Against Fire*.

Inside the museum, the smaller cabinets in the middle of the room included *Playtest* mushrooms, the bath from *Crocodile*, the scanning device from *USS Callister* and the *White Christmas* cookie-egg and headgear. One wall display had the beds from *Men Against Fire* with the dead bodies from *Metalhead*, in a set that looked like the cabin from *White Christmas* complete with bird-clock. We had Domhnall Gleeson's body from *Be Right Back* in a padded cell. And then there was a bloated pig from *Metalhead*, next to a hanging man which was a recreation of the set from *The National Anthem*. The pig was eating sweets that Bella drops on the robot's head in *Metalhead*. To be honest, I just went fucking mad.

Letitia Wright: The room I stayed away from the most, was the room that my dad Clayton was in, because I wanted to have a fresh experience when we moved behind those curtains. Other than that, I was all over the museum! It was really, really creepy: murderers, court cases, knives and stuff from *Black Mirror* episodes like the bees from *Hated in the Nation*.

Douglas Hodge: That museum became my little home, so it didn't take much to stay in character. I would come into work, get into costume on my own, put my mic on, mumble a bit, growl at a few people, then walk into my museum! And I never left it until we finished, 12 or 14 hours later.

Colm's a fantastic director. I really appreciated how we shot Rolo's scenes in chronological order, starting with him younger during the 'Pain Addict' story. One of my favourite scenes was Rolo showing the rats to Doctor Dawson [played by Daniel Lapaine].

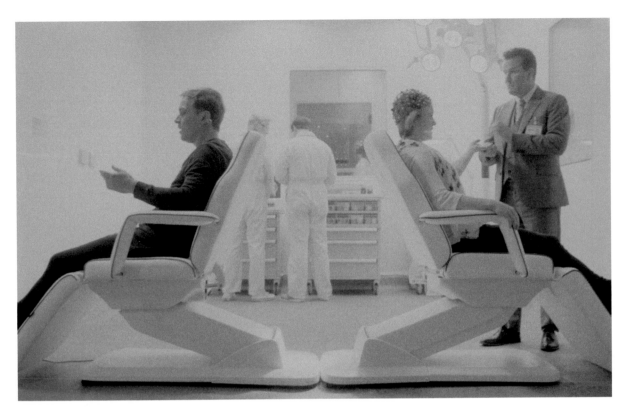

Joel Collins: We couldn't harm animals, so we used frozen rats that would have been fed to pythons. We stuffed them and put devices on their heads.

Colm McCarthy: A lot of people talk about how they couldn't handle the moment when Dawson "whittles" away at himself while looking in the mirror. What makes that scene work more than anything, is a brilliant make-up team and a fantastic performance from Daniel.

In pre-production, the thing Charlie wanted to talk about most was all the ways that somebody could damage themselves. As often happens with Charlie, these conversations became quite competitive! He won, by talking about somebody falling and hooking their eyelid over a coat-hook, while trying to maintain their balance on an icy floor. It was the most hilarious but disgusting thing I'd ever heard.

I was conscious that the sex in 'Pain Addict' was pretty extreme, but also key to the storytelling. It's always a bit awkward on set, but I think it helped that the two actors were Australian and American! Actors tend to be very uptight about doing that type of stuff, but they were more chilled-out. You just have to be upfront about what you need from the scene. It was important to the story and it's definitely not titillating. It's actually quite brief in its time onscreen, although it took a long time to shoot on set.

Annabel Jones: There was so much mileage to be had from the second segment, 'Dead Wife in the Head' – a lot of fun in taking petty domestic grievances and amplifying them. Aldis Hodge and Alexandra Roach are great as Jack and Carrie.

Charlie Brooker: That story is a bit like a divorce. *Be Right Back* played out like an internet romance, where they go from exchanging emails, to phone calls, to meeting up in the flesh, whereas 'Dead Wife in the Head' is about familiarity breeding contempt. Carrie's stuck in Jack's head with no free will, so inevitably she becomes a back-seat driver who complains about everything. It became a sort of claustrophobic relationship break-up analogy, with people fighting for custody of the kids at the weekend.

There were all sorts of other ideas I'd had around that concept, such as people who would walk around renting space to about 20 different dead people at once. So you'd be like the landlord to a whole houseful of lodgers in your own head.

Carrie ends up trapped inside a toy monkey which can only say either "Monkey loves you" or "Monkey needs a hug".

Charlie Brooker: I used the toilet in an airport in Singapore. And as I was walking out, there was this sign saying, "How was the toilet today?" with happy-face or sad-face buttons. Immediately, I thought, "Urgh, I'm not touching that, because it's in a toilet!" And then I thought, "Look at that fucking dystopian imagery they've put in my eye-line there – that'll come in handy some day." And sure enough, it did.

The stuff with the monkey in this second story is deliberately played for laughs. And then the third one gets darker, with this ghost story about people paying to electrocute Clayton Lee [played by Babs Olusanmokun] over and over again. The notion that you could still be brain-damaged, as a digital ghost, isn't very nice! But at least they haven't edited you into a new body where all your limbs are dicks, and you're constantly falling on your own balls. Or you've got 50 arseholes over your mouth that keep shitting onto your own lips.

Annabel Jones: Emmy-award-winning writing, right there.

Colm McCarthy: At what level do you sell Nish's lie, before you reveal she's actually here to take revenge on Rolo for torturing her father? That's always tricky in a story. At first, the situation seems to be: here's a creepy guy in a museum, and here's Little Red Riding Hood. So that's the bushel you're hiding everything behind in plain sight, as it were. I always talk about making things surprising but inevitable. The reveal is a shock, but you're also going, "Of course it was that, I should've known all along."

Letitia Wright: I decided to start off by believing my own lie. I deluded myself into believing that Nish really was on a tourist adventure, and really did want to find out about this museum.

Colm McCarthy: With scenes like Nish first seeing the museum, giving Rolo the water and seeing her father for the first time, we cut those moments to death, sixteen million different ways! When Nish sees her dad, she's being restrained, but it's all going on inside her.

Letitia Wright: Rolo was so carried away by his own achievement and his own ego. He was giving Nish an education, not knowing that she already had an education on how to transfer a soul and make it digital. So she just

Opposite: Pages from the *Fifteen Million Merits* comic, specially created by graphic artist Billy Butcher.

lets Rolo talk, because she's missing certain aspects of the story. She didn't know, for instance, about the racist people coming in to execute her dad.

Colm McCarthy: Charlie's really, really good in the edit. He uses reasonableness incredibly aggressively, in order to get what he wants! He's incredibly entertaining and charming, too, and understands how that process works. So there were a lot of creative conversations and debates which made the show better. It wouldn't have been made better by Charlie and Annabel just agreeing to everything.

Interestingly, during the edit Charlie and Annabel wanted to investigate the more dramatic performances. Rolo is quite comedic and larger than life, but they were keen to play away from that and find the humanity, which made it much better. Doug is an incredibly flexible actor and so he gave a range of performances.

Some of the darker elements ended up on the cutting room floor. Charlie and Annabel were weirdly interested in a tonal thing about what would be too much for an audience, and they were dead right, because loads of people have said, "Oh God, it was so dark" and loads of people have said it was so funny, but not to the point where those things broke the episode. So Charlie and Annabel were really good guardians of the audience.

Annabel Jones: I think it's more selfish than that. It's not guardians of the audience, it's ...

Charlie Brooker: ... Guardians of the Galaxy? Sorry, I'm such an arsehole.

Annabel Jones: You can only ever go with what you think feels right for the script and the character.

Doing a portmanteau with an enthusiastic and sometimes unreliable narrator allows the individual stories to go very big and melodramatic. And it allows us to have fun with concepts that wouldn't necessarily extend to a full *Black Mirror* episode. But tonally you need to keep the framing story as grounded as possible, otherwise you risk losing your audience.

Colm McCarthy: One of the tricky things with a portmanteau story is balancing all the different elements. The comedic stuff and the dark stuff all need to make sense in the same world. You have to find Rolo repulsive enough that you want him to die at the end, so you get what you're rooting for as an audience, but not so repulsive that you don't want to watch at all. In one take, for instance, we had Rolo relishing Clayton's execution, but we thought it was enough that he was there, and complicit in killing the guy. So we steered away from him revelling in that as much as he did in certain performances.

Douglas Hodge: I never tend to do the same take twice, even though you're doing the same lines. Colm wanted this Nicolas Cage or Jack Nicholson level of glee in the performance – a real showman, risking being over-the-top. So at times, I was laughing my head off and singing songs like, "Every time we say goodbyeeee, I die a little … " People were taken aback, I think.

Annabel Jones: Yes, there were moments when Rolo was being very flippant, or singing to himself. It slipped maybe too far into evil caricature and you go, "Hmmm, Rolo's mercenary, but I still think he's human."

Douglas Hodge: I hated doing the electrocution scene, if I'm honest – it was very difficult to do. It's hard to believe execution still happens in a civilised world and thank God it doesn't happen in Britain. I was very relieved to let Rolo go, when it was finished. And I never got a chance to apologise to Letitia or any of them, really …

Letitia Wright: At the end of the film, that scene when I get Rolo in the electric chair? That was me giving Doug everything! "You don't wanna run lines with me, Doug? Haha!"

Charlie Brooker: I really, really like *Black Museum*. Whereas *White Christmas* had this chilling sort of *Dead Of Night* nasty tone, *Black Museum* is a bit more DC comics, a bit more [the 90s US horror anthology series] *Tales from the Crypt*. There's literally a guy taking you round a museum of nasty things, so it's heightened and slightly Stephen King. Everything's ramped up and it's quite playfully ghoulish in places.

But also then, on another level, it's about punishment and racism. It's a bit *White Bear*. There's a lot of thematic stuff going on, but at heart it's a popcorn, campfire story. A ghost story with a nasty twist. So what I like to find, I guess, is the popcorn story that's fun to write, but will also make me look like I'm clever, because it's thematically interesting.

Penn Jillette: I was so very happy to be a tiny part of it, and have this imagery I've been obsessed with for 35 years used in *Black Museum*. If you asked me whether it was worth going through all that intense pain in 1981 to contribute to *Black Mirror*, the answer would be absolutely yes, because the story is very well-remembered, and remembering pain is very, very difficult! But if you'd asked me in Barcelona in 1981, I'm guessing the answer would've been no.

'Never accept drinks from strangers. My daddy taught me that'
– Nish

THE FUTURE OF BLACK MIRROR

In Conversation

Charlie Brooker – executive producer
Annabel Jones – executive producer
Cindy Holland – Vice President of Original Content, Netflix
Peter Friedlander – Vice President of Original Series, Netflix
Barney Reisz – producer
Shane Allen – Controller of Comedy Commissioning, BBC

Charlie Brooker: Season Four went down well, and the number of people seeing it seemed to have exponentially swollen.

Annabel Jones: "Swollen"! You have to put it in bad terms, like an infection! We'd been nominated at the Producers' Guild Awards, so I went to LA a few weeks after Season Four had launched. Usually, the immigration officers realise you're not very interesting and move you on to try and spot Tom Hanks. But this time, not only was the woman who dealt with me a *Black Mirror* fan, but everyone she worked with was too! Normally I'm either in a development bubble or a production bubble, so I don't often come up for air to see or hear the reception. It's little moments like that when you realise your niche show has become more of a global thing.

Cindy Holland (Vice President of Original Content, Netflix): What's been enormously gratifying to see is that not only has the show kept growing and finding new viewers each season, but that it's done that in countries around the world. The show and its themes have crossed borders and resonated despite geography or language. It's also become a true pop culture touchstone. When people say something is a '*Black Mirror*' moment, everyone now knows what that is. We're also proud to see the show being recognized with awards, including the Emmy awards in 2017.

Charlie Brooker: Season Five will see … the usual departures from the norm.

Annabel Jones: We're taking on new genres again. In Season Four we deliberately avoided doing anything too contemporary or politicised.

Charlie Brooker: At the time Season Four was being written, I had no idea of what state the world was going to be in by the time we went out on Netflix.

Annabel Jones: You don't want to look reactive or dated. There was so much debate anyway, about the political climate, that what could we possibly add?

Charlie Brooker: So Season Five might reflect that a bit more, because it turns out that fucking lunacy is the new norm. We just needed the dust to settle first.

Annabel Jones: We'll only continue to do the show if we think we're bringing new stories and elements to it. The great thing about being on Netflix is you can continue the show without it having to stick rigidly to being six hour-long films. They can take different forms, so that's quite exciting. If we wanted to, maybe we could do a *Black Mirror* feature film with Netflix and take the time we needed to do that. Not that we have a huge burning desire to do a big blockbuster film, because sometimes it's more creatively freeing not to have the commercial pressures that would come with a massive budget.

Charlie Brooker: Giant blockbusters that cost millions and millions can be very emotional and exciting, but they're a different thing to *Black Mirror*. But what you want is for *Black Mirror* to keep being surprising, and ... ha, I was going to say, "fun for us to make", but it's not just fun! Well, it is fun, but we don't sit around on a yacht, watching people work.

Annabel Jones: I think we'll look back and say, "How did we manage to do that number of Netflix films in three years?"

Charlie Brooker: That assumes we're alive to think that.

Annabel Jones: A lot of people have said, "I can't believe you threw that idea away in one film – you could've done a series of that." And we could have. We've done a lot of ideas in a short period of time.

Charlie Brooker: And we've always managed to find ways of making them more complicated to make! That's one thing we can say about Season Five: we've definitely come up with something that's the most complicated thing we've ever done.

Peter Friedlander (Vice President of Original Series, Netflix): The show will continue to be everything that viewers love. It will push the boundaries on storytelling, embrace all kinds of technology and shoot in new international locales, with stellar actors and performances.

Annabel Jones: We feel positive about *Black Mirror*'s long-term prospects. I don't think there'll be a shortage of inspiration.

Charlie Brooker: The show has changed quite a bit, actually. If you look at the first series, *The Entire History of You* is closest to ones we've done more recently, with invasive technology in people's eyes. But it's morphed. It went very, very VR for a while, and now we're moving out of that into some other phase. We can revisit old ideas we've done, as long as we're building a new concept on top of it. So, for instance, *USS Callister* goes into a VR environment à la *San Junipero,* but we build on the idea of copied people. There's no shortage of ideas, but it's more about morphing what the show is.

I'm usually worried that I've got no more ideas, or I've got ideas but can't make them work. But *Black Mirror* is really only limited by the number of dilemmas you can think of. There doesn't seem to be a shortage of dilemmas, but it's difficult to know where the next idea is coming from, because they just pop up when you rub various things together. Sorry, that sounded a bit weird.

Barney Reisz (producer): The great privilege of being part of *Black Mirror* was working with people who think way, way outside the box. In fact, to Charlie, there is no box. It is more like an endlessly squidgy, expanding mass of possibility. If it is absurd, it must be tried. If it is impossible, then fuck it, let's go for it! His genius is in thinking the unthinkable and carrying people with him on the wave of his unique inventiveness and extraordinary writing talent. If he wasn't so talented, he'd be fucking annoying!

Shane Allen (Controller of Comedy Commissioning, BBC): It's been an enormous honour to have been a small part of the incredible journey of this show that started with an idea about live bestiality! Charlie and Annabel are very inspiring people – a rare blend of highly intelligent, deeply perceptive and incredibly emotionally rounded. I've been so proud of what they've achieved with all the series. They're more than a little bit mad to tackle what are effectively six feature films each year, when most people would struggle to do one well. I just wish they hadn't made me read *The Road*. That's the one thing I can never erase.

Annabel Jones: We'll know it's finally time to bring *Black Mirror* to a close ... when Netflix tell us, perhaps?

Charlie Brooker: Yeah, we'll be the last ones to know. We'll be going, "What do you mean? Don't you know how popular it is? I'm sure I met someone the other week who'd heard of it." But I think if we ever got fed up with doing it, or each other, we'd either kill the show, or each other.

Annabel Jones: Could that be a *Black Mirror* episode? No, too predictable.

Charlie Brooker: Actually, it's more likely that, if we ever got tired of *Black Mirror*, we'd just put it on hold, do something else, then go back to it. Although the joy of it is, you can reinvent it all the time. We can keep endlessly redefining what *Black Mirror* is. Which I suppose means we can never stop. We can never leave. We're trapped here forever. Like a ladybird glued to concrete. Help. Help us. For God's sake please help us.

That's probably as good a way as any to end this book isn't it? Now go away.

A list of influences that have fed *Black Mirror*, from the worlds of film, TV, books, music, games and photography.

10 Rillington Place (film, 1971)
A London serial killer poses as a doctor in order to ensnare unsuspecting women.
28 Days Later (film, 2002)
Danny Boyle's movie about survivors navigating a post-epidemic London.
2001: A Space Odyssey (film, 1968)
Stanley Kubrick's psychedelic space-epic.
A Clockwork Orange (film, 1971)
Stanley Kubrick's disturbing adaptation of Anthony Burgess' 1962 novel.
Airplane! (film, 1980)
Zucker-Abrahams-Zucker's slapstick comedy classic.
All Is Lost (film, 2013)
Virtually silent survival drama starring Robert Redford.
Paul Thomas Anderson (director, 1970-present)
Filmmaker behind the likes of *Magnolia* (2000) and *There Will Be Blood* (2007).
An American Werewolf in London (film, 1981)
John Landis' update of an old horror trope.
Anyone Who Knows What Love Is (music, 1968)
A haunting song of romantic rejection by New Orleans R&B queen Irma Thomas
Battlestar Galactica (TV, 2004–2009)
Shiny and sophisticated remake of the '80s sci-fi series.
Being John Malkovich (film, 1999)
Spike Jonze and Charlie Kaufman's magical-realist mind-bender.
The Beyond (film, 1981)
Italian horror director Lucio Fulci's nightmarish gore-fest.
Boy A (film, 2007)
Andrew Garfield plays a child killer who attempts to build a normal life.
Breaking Bad (TV, 2008–2013)
Vince Gilligan and Bryan Cranston's prestige-TV triumph.
British public information films (TV 1960s–2011)
Effectively mini horror films that scared children witless.
Broen (TV, 2011–present)
Scandinavian crime series about a murder victim found on a bridge connecting two cities.
Catch-22 (book, 1961)
Joseph Heller's satirical protest about a World War II bombardier stuck in varying degrees of hell.
Cannibal Holocaust (film, 1980)
Director Ruggero Deodato's Italian horror film, with a found footage element.
CivilWarLand In Bad Decline (book, 1996)
George Saunders' first story collection.

Gregory Crewdson (photographer, 1962–present)
Known for capturing incredible stills of American homes and neighbourhoods.
Adam Curtis (director, 1955–present)
English documentarian, who focuses on power in society.
Cutter And Bone (book, 1976)
Newton Thornburg's cult-favourite crime-noir novel.
Dead Man's Shoes (film, 2004)
Shane Meadows' British psychological thriller.
Dead of Night (film, 1945)
Ealing Studios' portmanteau horror film framed by a man's nervous breakdown.
Doctor Who (TV, 1963–present)
The undying British sci-fi show.
Dog Day Afternoon (film, 1975)
Sidney Lumet and Al Pacino's urban-crime comedy drama.
Doom (video game, 1993)
ID Studios' groundbreaking first-person shooter.
Duel (film, 1971)
A motorist is stalked by a tanker truck in Steven Spielberg's full-length debut, originally shown on TV.
Elephant (TV, 1989)
Alan Clarke's British short film set in Northern Ireland during the 'Troubles'. Features almost no dialogue.
Elite (video game, 1984)
Programmer David Braben and Ian Bell's space trading odyssey, initially released for platforms such as the BBC Micro, ZX Spectrum and Commodore 64.
Engrenages (TV, 2005–present)
French legal drama about the lawyers and judges who work at Paris's Palais du Justice.
Evil Dead 2 (film, 1987)
Sam Raimi's frenetic and 'splatstick' sequel-cum-remake of *The Evil Dead*.
Fallout 4 (video game, 2015)
A role-playing video game set 210 years in the future, after a devastating war.
Fantastic Voyage (film, 1966)
A scientist invents shrinking technology, which is then used to help a team enter his body to fix a blood clot.
Fargo (film, 1996)
Coen Brothers' Oscar-winning, darkly funny crime drama.
Fawlty Towers (TV, 1975–1979)
John Cleese and Connie Booth's post-Python sitcom about an ill-tempered hotel manager.
Festen (film, 1998)
A Dogme 95 look at intrafamily venom.
Fishtank (film, 2009)
A mother and her teenage daughter fight for the affection of Michael Fassbender.
Games of Thrones (TV, 2011–present)
Little-known fantasy show.

Grand Theft Auto (video games, 1997–present)
Controversial and morally questionable video-games.
Harold and Maude (film, 1971)
Hal Ashby's cinematic romance between a weird young man and vivacious older woman.
Hammer House of Horror (TV, 1980)
British anthology series with a distinctly nasty edge.
Heaven is A Place on Earth (music, 1987)
Belinda Carlisle's chart-topping power ballad.
Alfred Hitchcock (director, 1899–1980)
The man behind *Rear Window* (1954) and *Psycho* (1960).
The Hitchhiker's Guide to the Galaxy (radio/book, 1978)
Douglas Adams' eternal sci-comedy and novel.
John Hughes (films, 1950–2009)
Writer and director responsible for classic 80's teen movies *Pretty in Pink* (1986) and *Ferris Bueller's Day Off* (1986).
Armando Iannucci (TV, 1953–present) and
Chris Morris (TV, 1962–present)
The duo behind such twisted, surreal satires as *The Day Today* (1994) and *Jam* (2000)
I'm A Celebrity ... Get Me Out Of Here! (TV, 2002–present)
British survival reality show, hosted by Ant and Dec.
Inception (film, 2010)
Christopher Nolan's dreams-in-dreams head-scratcher.
Invasion of the Body Snatchers (film, 1978)
Starring Donald Sutherland, this terrifying remake surpassed the 1956 original.
It Follows (film, 2014)
A horror movie in which a persistent evil spirit is passed along via sexual intercourse.
Jaws (film, 1975)
Steven Spielberg's classic blockbuster.
Duncan Jones (director, 1971–present)
Jones brought us the futuristic thrillers *Moon* (2009) and *Source Code* (2011).
The Killing (TV, 2007–2012)
Danish police procedural set in Copenhagen, birthing the 'Scandi-noir' genre.
Stephen King (author, 1947–present)
The undisputed guvnor of horror fiction.
The Kingdom (TV, 1994)
Lars Von Trier's hospital-set mini-series.
Nigel Kneale (TV, 1922–2006)
Writer and creator of Professor Bernard Quatermass.
La cabina (film, 1972)
Claustrophobic Spanish TV movie about a man trapped inside a phone booth.
Little Computer People (video game, 1985)
Predating The Sims, this video game was among the first with no set goals for players.
Live & Kicking (TV, 1993-2001)
Saturday morning kids' show, featuring a digital cat.

Mad Men (TV, 2007–2015)
Period drama set in a New York advertising agency.
Manhunt (video game, 2003)
An 18-certificate survival horror with graphic violence.
The Matrix (film, 1999)
Keanu Reeves takes the red pill.
Men Against Fire: The Problem of Battle Command (book, 1947)
S.L.A. Marshall's exploration of the low percentage of soldiers who fired weapons during the two world wars.
Minority Report (film, 2002)
Steven Spielberg and Tom Cruise's Philip K. Dick adaptation, about predictive policing.
Miracle Mile (film, 1988)
A young couple try to escape Los Angeles, in real time, before the onset of nuclear war.
Monty Python's Flying Circus (TV, 1969–1974)
The British series that shaped the future of comedy.
Mulholland Drive (film, 2001)
David Lynch's oblique meditation on identity confusion.
N++ soundtrack (music, 2015)
Synth-heavy sonic backdrop to the popular video game.
Network (film, 1976)
Sidney Lumet's prescient media satire.
The National Anthem (music, 2000)
A jazz-infused track from Radiohead's *Kid A* album.
On Filmmaking (book, 2005)
British director Alexander Mackendrick's filmmaking guide.
On Killing (book, 1996)
Israeli David Grossman explores the psychological effect of killing in law enforcement and the military.
Outrun (video game, 1987)
Arcade game that popularised the moving console cabinet.
Pacific Rim (film, 2013)
Guillermo del Toro's seamonster take on Japanese anime.
Peeping Tom (film, 1960)
Michael Powell's tale of a serial killer who films his victims.
Penn Jillette (magician, 1948–present) and
Raymond Teller (magicians, 1955–present)
Popular magician-entertainers Penn & Teller are the longest-running headline act in Las Vegas history.
Planes, Trains and Automobiles (film, 1987)
John Hughes' comedy starring Steve Martin.
Planet of the Apes (film, 1968)
Seminal simian sci-fi.
Portal (video game, 2007)
Addictive puzzle-based video game.
QED: A Guide to Armageddon (TV, 1982)
Pop-science BBC documentary series.
Quatermass and the Pit (film, 1967)
Sci-fi horror. An ancient alien spacecraft is unearthed in London's Underground.

Resident Evil (video game, 1996–present)
Classic survival horror-fest, later adapted into a film series.
Ring (film, 1998)
Japanese psycho-horror about a cursed video tape.
The Road (book, 2006)
Cormac McCarthy's post-apocalyptic vision, adapted for film by John Hillcoat in 2009.
Rod Serling's Night Gallery (TV, 1969–1973)
Serling's anthology gave preference to the supernatural.
Sapphire & Steel (TV, 1979–1982)
Creepy British sci-fi show, starring David McCallum and Joanna Lumley.
Saving Private Ryan (film, 1998)
By far Steven Spielberg's most harrowing film.
Scenes From a Marriage (TV, 1973)
Ingmar Bergman's mini-series. A bad advert for wedlock.
The Sentinel (video game, 1986)
Puzzle-based video game set in a bleak, immersive world.
Se7en (film, 1995)
David Fincher's serial-killer thriller, with that ending.
Silent Running (film, 1972)
After all botanical life on Earth has died, an ecologist fights the green fight on his space station.
The Singing Detective (TV, 1986)
Dennis Potter's gem, starring Michael Gambon as a mystery writer recovering from chronic disease.
The Sixth Sense (film, 1999)
M. Night Shyamalan's thriller, with wham-bam twist.
Sleeper (film, 1973)
Woody Allen and Diane Keaton in an Orwellian future.
The Smiths (music, 1982–1987)
Iconic '80s Mancunian miserabilists.
Sombrero Fallout: A Japanese Novel (book, 1976)
Richard Brautigan's dual narrative oddball.
The Sophtware Slump (music, 2000)
California indie-rock band Grandaddy's concept album about modern alienation.
Space Invaders (video game, 1978)
Taito's legendary, endless blast-fest.
The Swarm (film, 1978)
Kitsch killer-bee movie.
The Taking of Pelham One Two Three (film, 1974)
Armed criminals hijack a New York subway train.
Tales of the Unexpected (TV, 1979–1988)
Roald Dahl's British anthology series, renowned for climactic twists.
Quentin Tarantino (director, 1963–)
The high priest of cinematic homage.
The Texas Chain Saw Massacre (film, 1974)
Tobe Hooper's savage horror benchmark.
The Thing (film, 1982)
John Carpenter's classic sci-fi horror remake of 1951's

The Thing From Another World.
Threads (TV, 1984)
Harrowing British TV movie about the aftermath of nuclear war.
THX-1138 (film, 1971)
Dystopian sci-fi from George Lucas.
Triangle (film, 2009)
Mind-boggling horror aboard a mysterious ocean liner.
Tron (film, 1982)
A computer hacker tries to escape from a digital world.
The Truman Show (film, 1998)
Jim Carrey plays a man whose entire life is a reality TV show.
They Live (film, 1988)
John Carpenter's satire about a man who discovers that the ruling class are aliens.
The Twilight Zone (TV, 1959–1964)
Rod Serling's hugely influential anthology show, which also took film form in 1983.
Twin Peaks (TV, 1990–1991)
Mark Frost and David Lynch's kooky murder mystery.
Ultimate Force (TV, 2002–08)
British military action series, taking an American approach.
United 93 (film, 2006) Movies
Paul Greengrass's bio-drama about what happened aboard 9/11's United Flight 93.
The Up documentaries (film, 1964–present)
Michael Apted checks in with the same group of British citizens every seven years.
The Vanishing (film, 1988)
Dutch-French thriller about a man's obsessive search for his disappeared girlfriend.
Paul Verhoeven (director, 1938–present)
Dutch director of films including *Total Recall* (1990) and *Starship Troopers* (1997).
The War You Don't See (TV, 2010)
John Pilger's documentary about the Iraq war.
Whac-A-Mole (1976-present)
Arcade game in which players hit moles with mallets.
The Wicker Man (film, 1973)
Classic Pagan horror, starring Edward Woodward.
Wall-E (film, 2008)
One of Pixar's bleakest creations.
Westworld (TV, 2016–present)
Series set in a Wild West-themed android amusement park.
The X Factor (TV, 2004–present)
Simon Cowell's eternal quest for new singing talent.
The X-Files (TV, 1993–present)
TV's enduring intersection between sci-fi and horror.
The Year Of The Sex Olympics (TV, 1968)
Nigel 'Quatermass' Kneale's one-off dystopian TV play.
The Young Ones (TV, 2010)
Ageing celebrities are rejuvenated by living in a '70s home.

Thanks are due to many people for their help and assistance in making this book: everyone at Ebury, especially Jake Lingwood who first suggested we do it. Elen Jones and Lisa Pendreigh who made it happen despite our best efforts. Tess Henderson, Caroline Butler and Lucy Harrison. And Zoe Bather who designed the book.

Our literary agent Jo Unwin for her perseverance and her assistant Milly Reilly for her patience. At House of Tomorrow, David Girvan and Chandni Lakhani for helping to organise everything, Jo Kay our long-standing Head of Production who kicks everything into shape and Nick Irving who makes that shape legal.

And Jason Arnopp, for enduring our tedious witterings and making sense of them.

On a personal note I [Annabel] would like to thank my parents, Susan and Glen, for their endless love and support. But most importantly I have to thank my children, Arthur, Beatrice and Magnus, for being the best huggers in the whole world and their father, Craig, for being a worthy runner-up.

Whereas I [Charlie] would like to thank MY parents, my wife Konnie for constantly withstanding my bullshit and my offspring Covey and Huxley for refusing to withstand it at all.

10 9 8 7 6 5 4 3 2 1

Ebury Press, an imprint of Ebury Publishing,
20 Vauxhall Bridge Road, London SW1V 2SA

Ebury Press is part of the Penguin Random House group of companies whose
addresses can be found at global.penguinrandomhouse.com

Penguin
Random House
UK

First published by Ebury Press in 2018

www.penguin.co.uk

Copyright © House of Tomorrow Limited, 2018

A CIP catalogue record for this book is available from the British Library

ISBN 9781529102581

Colour origination by Altaimage
Printed and bound by Firmengruppe APPL, aprinta druck, Wemding, Germany

MIX
Paper from
responsible sources
FSC® C018179
www.fsc.org

Penguin Random House is committed to a sustainable future for our business,
our readers and our planet. This book is made from Forest Stewardship Council®
certified paper.

Text: Jason Arnopp
Design: Zoë Bather, with chapter openers by Joe Sharpe, Callum Strachan and
Josh Ellis at Applied Works
Project management: Lisa Pendreigh

Image credits: All images © House of Tomorrow/Zeppotron/Netflix except pages
2 Jonathan Prime/House of Tomorrow/Applied Works; 14–15, 256–257 © istock/
Applied Works; 16, 17, 19, 20, 24–25 © Ed Miller/House of Tomorrow; 26, 27, 36, 37,
38, 53, 54, 66 (below), 67, 92, 93, 97 (above and centre), 132, 137 (above and below),
139, 153, 179 (all), 183 (below), 184 (all), 197 (all), 200 (below), 210–211, 214, 236, 238
(below), 239, 249, 252, 260, 262, 274, 275, 278, 298 © Painting Practice/House of
Tomorrow; 30–31, 48–49 © Giles Keyte/House of Tomorrow/Applied Works; 32,
33, 34–35, 40–41, 42, 43, 44–45, 47, 51 © Giles Keyte/House of Tomorrow; 62–63
© Liam Daniel/House of Tomorrow/Applied Works; 64, 65, 66 (above), 72–73, 78,
79, 82–83, © Liam Daniel/House of Tomorrow; 76–77, 204–205, 242–243, 282–283
© Painting Practice/House of Tomorrow/Applied Works; 84 © Rockstar Games;
88–89, 104–105 © Hal Shinnie/House of Tomorrow/Applied Works; 90, 91, 94–95, 97
(below), 98, 99, 106, 107, 110–111, 114–115, 117 © Hal Shinnie/House of Tomorrow;
93 © BBC Motion Gallery/Getty Images; 128–129, 172–173 © David Dettmann/
House of Tomorrow/Applied Works; 131, 133, 134 (above and below), 136 (above
and below), 140, 141, 142 (all), 144–145, 174, 175, 176–177, 178, 180–181, 186–187, 188,
191 © David Dettmann/House of Tomorrow; 148–149 © Laurie Sparham/House of
Tomorrow/Applied Works; 150, 164–165, 166, 207, 208 © Laurie Sparham/House of
Tomorrow; 152 © EDGE Magazine/House of Tomorrow; 158 (all), 159 (all), 229, 231,
232, 233, 286, 287 © Framestore/Painting Practice/House of Tomorrow; 160–161 ©
Carlos Ramos/House of Tomorrow/Applied Works; 183 (above), 290, 291 © Susie
Coulthard/House of Tomorrow; 190, 238 (above right), 307 © Billy Butcher/House
of Tomorrow; 192–193 © Jay Maidment/House of Tomorrow/Applied Works; 194,
195, 198–199, 200 (above), 201 © Jay Maidment/House of Tomorrow; 224–225,
270–271, 294–295 © House of Tomorrow/Netflix/Applied Works; 226, 234–235,
272, 276–277, 284, 285, 288–289, 296, 300, 304–305 © Jonathan Prime/House of
Tomorrow/Netflix; 237 © Maja Meschede/House of Tomorrow; 238 (above left)
© Bill Elliott/House of Tomorrow; 244, 245, 247, 250–251, 254–255 © Christos
Kalohoridis/House of Tomorrow/Netflix; 258, 259, 261, 266, 267 © Arnaldur
Halldórsson/House of Tomorrow/Netflix; cover image © Getty Images.